British Warships 1860–1906

For my parents

British Warships 1860–1906
A Photographic History

N J Dingle

Pen & Sword
MARITIME

First published in Great Britain in 2009 by
Pen & Sword Maritime
an imprint of
Pen & Sword Books Ltd
47 Church Street
Barnsley
South Yorkshire S70 2AS

ISBN 978-1-84415-980-2

A CIP catalogue record for this book is available from the British Library.

Typeset in Sabon 11/13pt by
Concept, Huddersfield

Printed and bound in Malaysia
for Imago

Pen & Sword Books Ltd incorporates the imprints of Pen & Sword Aviation,
Pen & Sword Maritime, Pen & Sword Military, Wharncliffe Local History,
Pen & Sword Select, Pen & Sword Military Classics, Leo Cooper, Remember When,
Seaforth Publishing and Frontline Publishing.

For a complete list of Pen & Sword titles please contact
PEN & SWORD BOOKS LIMITED
47 Church Street, Barnsley, South Yorkshire, S70 2AS, England
E-mail: enquiries@pen-and-sword.co.uk
Website: www.pen-and-sword.co.uk

Contents

Acknowledgements

I would like to thank Phil Sidnell, my editor at Pen & Sword Books, for offering me the chance to write this book, and then for guiding a first-time author through the process of turning it into reality. I would also like to thank Hugh Alexander and all the staff of the Image Library at the National Archives, Kew, for their invaluable help in providing the production-quality copies of the approximately two hundred photographs that comprise the heart of this book in a very short space of time. In many ways, obtaining these illustrations was the most nerve-wracking part of writing this book as it was something that was entirely new to me, but Hugh ensured that the process went as smoothly as I could possibly have hoped.

On a personal note, I would like to thank my dear friend Alastair for allowing me to borrow freely from his library, and for reading and commenting on an early draught of the text. Finally, but by no means least, thank you to my family for their enduring love and support. And to Laura, with all my love, for enduring a year of pre-occupation and busy weekends.

Introduction

The United Kingdom's National Archives, housed at Kew in London, contain a collection of photographs of Royal Navy warships dating from approximately 1860 to the end of the Second World War that were formerly held by the Naval Construction Department (NCD). Although their subjects will be familiar, these photographs do not appear to have been much used by naval historians despite the fact that they document a fascinating period of warship development. This book is structured around a selection from these photographs that cover the period from *Warrior* in 1860 to *Dreadnought* of 1906.

The photographs themselves date largely from the 1880s onwards, with a few notable exceptions, and this obviously affects the ships that are depicted. Fortunately, the RN of the mid and late nineteenth century kept older ships in service perhaps longer than was strictly warranted: while this may have boosted the number of ships nominally available for service even if they were of questionable fighting value, it does mean that ships from the 1860s and 1870s survived long enough to be photographed for the collection now housed at Kew.

Ships lost before the 1880s, for example the masted turret battleship *Captain*, are obviously not part of the archive, but perhaps more surprising is the lack of photographs of vessels that at the time enjoyed a high profile and have continued to be well known to this day – for example, *Polyphemus* is conspicuous by her absence. Because of these omissions, the photographs must be supported by text if the present book is to describe adequately the story of British warship development in the period. Fortunately, there is a great deal of pre-existing scholarship on Victorian warship development on which to draw. Oscar Parkes' *British Battleships* is rightly considered to be one of the seminal works in the area, while D.K. Brown's books are perhaps unmatched in terms of both their technical content and the author's own experience of the warship design process. At the same time, authors like John Beeler, Paul Kennedy and Andrew Lambert (under whom I was fortunate enough to study for part of my undergraduate degree) have done so much to advance our knowledge of the strategic context that surrounded the development of the warships of the period. For the details of the careers of the ships featured here in photographs, I have drawn heavily from the relevant editions of *Conway's All The World's Fighting Ships* (namely *1860–1905* and *1906–1921*).

Beyond the value of these photographs as historical records, there remains the fact that, for some of us at least, simply looking at pictures of old warships holds a pleasure all of its own. Naval history has been a long-term interest of mine, and when I was offered the opportunity to write this book, I was quick to accept as I could not resist the chance to view an archive full of relatively unseen pictures of some of the most interesting RN warships of the past two hundred years. I am in full agreement with Lt Cdr Richard Barker RNR, who wrote in his foreword to Wilfrid Pym Trotter's 1975 book, *The Royal Navy in Old Photographs*:

> For no reason I could possibly explain, I like to know that the HMS *Donegal* of the 1850s had a funnel between the foremast and mainmast, while HMS *Sans Pareil* had one between the mainmast and mizzen; that in 1867, HMS *Hector* was re-armed with two eight-inch and sixteen seven-inch muzzle-loading rifled guns; and that HMS *Inflexible*, launched in 1881, was the first ironclad to be lit by electricity and had armour twenty-four inches thick.

On reading this passage, it was reassuring to know that I wasn't alone!

Chapter 1

The Royal Navy 1815–60

The British Empire of the nineteenth century was based on maritime trade and communications. The key to Britain's position was control of the sea, for it was on this medium that her trade was carried and via which her possessions could be attacked. From this maritime basis of power flowed a number of vital interests that held true throughout the period. Firstly, Britain was concerned with the maintenance of naval supremacy to ensure the safety of her territorial possessions, especially the British Isles themselves. Secondly, it was seen as vital to protect and promote British trade – retaining her existing commerce and expanding into new areas was highly important. Finally, successive governments strove to maintain an international situation that was conducive to the profitable conduct of trade. This meant avoiding another general Continental war in which European markets would become closed to British merchants. Lord Palmerston identified this in 1832 when, as Foreign Secretary, he said that a key British interest was 'the maintenance of general peace throughout Europe'.[1] British trade with the Continent was very valuable indeed: between 1815 and 1860, Europe was still in the process of industrialisation and therefore provided huge markets for the machinery and expertise of which Britain, as the first industrialised nation, had an effective monopoly.[2] A general war could endanger these markets and so British statesmen were anxious to avoid such a calamity.

To support these interests, Britain relied on the Royal Navy. To discharge the varied roles required, the RN was composed of a range of ship types each suited to a particular role. The largest, most imposing vessels were the battleships or ships-of-the-line. These formed the battlefleet that was designed to confront and defeat similar enemy ships to secure command of the sea for Britain. Cruising ships, from frigates down through corvettes and sloops, provided the eyes of the fleet, and also performed the vital role of commerce protection by escorting convoys and hunting enemy commerce raiders, as well as harassing the enemy's own trade. Finally, small gunvessels and gunboats were needed for in-shore work in shallow waters where larger ships could not safely venture.

Contemporary British policymakers were aware of the primacy of the RN in securing Britain's vital interests. Sir James Graham, who served as First Lord of the Admiralty twice (first from 1830 to 1834 and again from 1852 to 1855), said that:

> . . . if the British Navy be not ready at all times, and in all places, to sustain our greatness, to assert our rights, and to vindicate our maritime supremacy, then, indeed, is our glory departed.[3]

The experience of the French Revolutionary and Napoleonic Wars had a huge effect on nineteenth century British strategy. Despite naval defeats such as Trafalgar, Napoleon had attempted to exploit his control of Europe's resources and naval bases to build a large navy. Although he ultimately failed, the attempt demonstrated the conditions under which a credible challenge to the RN could be mounted.

Britain was determined, therefore, to be able to counter a similar threat should it occur again. This meant preparing for another long war against a power or coalition of powers that controlled all of Europe. For most of the nineteenth century, such a threat seemed most likely to come from a combination of France and Russia. There was a precedent for this as it had happened in 1807, when France and Russia agreed to share Europe between themselves. In 1818 the Foreign Secretary, Castlereagh, described a Franco-Russian combination as 'the only one that can prove really formidable to the liberties of Europe'.[4] This was the reason for Castlereagh's declaration in 1817 of the Two Power Standard: Britain should maintain a navy 'equal to the navies of any two Powers that can be brought against us'.[5] In effect, this meant a fleet larger than the navies of France and Russia combined.

The desired post-war size of the RN was set in 1815 as 100 ships-of-the-line and 160 frigates. This establishment was chosen because it was estimated that 100,000 seamen could be raised in the first two years of war and this was the largest fleet that this number of sailors could man.[6] Only fourteen of these ships-of-the-line would be in active service

as guard- or flagships, the rest being laid-up in Ordinary until they were required.[7] The strength of the RN would therefore lie not in the forces immediately available but in those that could be mobilised in time of need – an arrangement clearly aimed at a protracted conflict in which there would be sufficient time to recruit the necessary number of men.

These ambitious force levels were never actually achieved, however. In 1827, the RN possessed seventy-four battleships, of which seventeen were in service and fifty-seven laid-up in reserve (in addition to those currently building).[8] In comparison, by 1833 France had an estimated thirty-four effective ships-of-the-line and Russia thirty-six (which were of questionable value due to their poor crew quality and lack of an ice-free port in the north) making a total of seventy.[9] The RN battlefleet may have been smaller than the proposed establishment of 1815, therefore, but it was still sufficiently large to meet the Two Power Standard of 1817. The figure of one hundred battleships stipulated in 1815 was the maximum number of ships that could be manned, but the major factor in deciding fleet size was the comparative strengths of its likely opponents. Indeed, it has been suggested that the Admiralty in 1815 deliberately over-specified its requirements, knowing that there would be 'a political tendency to the other extreme'.[10] Better to ask for one hundred battleships and receive seventy-four than to ask for seventy-four and get even fewer! Furthermore, although the fleet was numerically smaller than the fleet proposed in 1815, the larger

battleships constructed in the 1820s, especially with their uniform 32-pdr armaments after 1825, were superior in firepower to the equivalent number of 1815-vintage ships.

The RN battlefleet of 1830 was therefore better than ever in terms of the quality and quantity of ships available for service. Britain succeeded in creating a durable battlefleet with significant numerical and qualitative superiority over its rivals, and its durability was shown by the fact that many of the units built in the is period went on to serve in the Crimean War. Indeed, some went on to be converted into steam battleships and a handful survived, as hulks, until the end of the Second World War.[11]

Technological Advances 1815–60: The Introduction of Iron Construction and Steam Propulsion

The period 1815–60 witnessed the introduction of several new technologies that had a dramatic effect on the design and construction of warships. Key amongst these were the adoption of iron as the main structural material for ships' hulls and the widespread introduction of steam propulsion first to power paddle wheels and then later screw propellers. Of the two, steam propulsion became more widely accepted in this period: the RN fleet of 1815 was built of wood and powered by sail, and while the Crimean War of 1854–6 saw the first deployment of steam battleships alongside their sail-powered sisters, the RN's warships were still constructed mainly out of timber.

THE ROYAL NAVY 1815–60   3

The reasons for this will be discussed below.

The Admiralty of the period has often been accused of excessive conservatism in the face of the potentials offered by these new technologies. This was not the case. That the RN did not rush into the construction of an iron-built, steam-powered battlefleet in the 1840s can partly be attributed to the pursuit of a deliberate policy of experimentation with new technology and consequently its incremental adoption starting with the smaller ships of the fleet. Britain also had a vested interest in not altering the status quo of naval technology unless she absolutely had to, because this would wipe out the massive investment that had already been made in a wooden sailing fleet. When discussing the design and construction of *Warrior* in 1860, the Surveyor of the Navy, Sir Baldwin Walker, explicitly spelt out this policy:

> Although I have frequently stated that it is not to the interest of Great Britain – possessing as she does so large a navy – to adopt any important change in the construction of ships of war which might have the effect of rendering necessary the introduction of a new class of very costly vessels, until such a course is forced upon her by the adoption by foreign powers of formidable ships of a novel character requiring similar ships to cope with them, yet it then becomes a matter not only of expediency, but of absolute necessity . . .[12]

This was as applicable as a general comment on British naval construction policy up until the launch of *Dreadnought* in 1906 as it was to the specific situation surrounding *Warrior*. With her existing large battlefleet Britain had no interest in pioneering a naval technological revolution, but with her industrial might (or, in the period 1815–60 it might be truer to talk of industrial pre-eminence) she could afford to wait to act until the activities of other nations forced her hand and then use this power to re-establish her dominant position.

Steam Power

Practical steam-powered ships had become possible at the turn of the nineteenth century, and the end of the Napoleonic Wars saw a rapid growth of the number employed on both inland waterways and across the Irish Sea and English Channel. The Admiralty commissioned their first paddle wheel-propelled steamship, *Comet*, in 1821 to act as a river tug and tender, and by 1830 had eleven such ships in service, all operating in similar roles. Other nations built similar ships at the same time; the French navy completed its first steam ship, *Sphinx*, in 1829 and three steam warships were built in Britain for the Greeks to be used against Turkey in the late 1820s. Steam vessels demonstrated their utility on active operations as well as acting as peacetime tugs and packets – for example, the RN fleet deployed to blockade the Dutch coast in 1832 during the Belgian crisis included

two steamships, whose ability to operate in-shore without dependency on wind and tide proved extremely advantageous. As a result, increasing numbers were built for the RN throughout the 1830s and by 1837 there were twenty-nine steamships in service as well as thirty-seven mail packets (government-owned ships for transporting mail).[13]

A major development in the capability of RN steam warships occurred in 1835 when the paddle sloop *Gorgon* was laid down. She was constructed using the wooden frames of an incomplete sailing frigate (*Tigris*) and, at 1,610 tons, was therefore considerably larger than the steamships then in service. Her size allowed her to mount a heavy armament, and her direct-acting engines powered her to a top speed of about 9 kts. *Gorgon* and a number of other steamships were deployed to the Mediterranean in 1840 for the campaign against Mehemet Ali and were described as 'eminently useful' by Admiral Stopford, both for moving troops along the coast and attacking fortifications ashore. A near sister to *Gorgon*, *Cyclops*, was laid down shortly afterwards and was rated a frigate. Together, *Gorgon* and *Cyclops* provided the pattern for eighteen First Class wooden paddle sloops and six Second Class wooden paddle frigates laid down before 1845. They were also followed by five First Class wooden paddle frigates, including *Penelope* of 1843 (a unique conversion from a sailing frigate) and *Terrible* (completed in 1845 and the largest paddle warship ever built).[14]

The RN clearly appreciated the usefulness of steam-powered paddle ships, but there were a number of fundamental limitations that made the paddle unsuitable for adoption in all classes of warship. In particular, the paddle wheels and their sponsons took up a large amount of space along the sides of the ship and consequently restricted the number of guns that could be mounted on the broadside. It was also feared that paddles would interfere with boarding operations and that they were vulnerable to enemy fire. The screw propeller, on the other hand, appeared to overcome all these problems as it could be mounted underwater at the stern of the ship and so leave the broadsides available for guns. In this position the propeller and its driving machinery would be far less vulnerable to enemy fire, and the screw would also interfere far less with the sailing qualities of the ship than paddles and sponsons. This latter point was still important as the range of steamships was limited by the amount of coal that could be carried, and as a result sail was often used on long voyages.[15]

As with paddles, the first screwships were commercial rather than military. In 1838, the Admiralty conducted trials using one such ship, *Francis Smith*, and based on favourable reports decided to commission a demonstration ship, *Archimedes*, to use in further tests. Of particular concern was the comparison between the performance of screw vessels and those with paddles. *Archimedes* carried out a number of races across the English Channel against fast mail packets, and based on the outcome of these the Admiralty ordered *Rattler* to conduct further trials. These took place in 1844, where twenty-eight different propeller forms were tried, and again in 1845, where *Rattler* competed against her paddle-powered sister *Alecto*. The 1845 trials included the famous 'tug of war' won by *Rattler*, where the two ships were connected by their sterns.[16]

1844–5 saw a major increase in Anglo-French tensions and as a result a Commission on Coast Defence was set up, which recommended strengthening the defences around naval bases with both forts and mobile batteries. It was ultimately decided to construct a number of such batteries by fitting engines and screw propellers to four old 72-gun sailing battleships and the same number of 44-gun frigates. Although originally intended to operate purely close to the coast, it was soon decided to fit the ships with a full sailing rig and as such the four 'blockships', reduced to sixty guns each, became the first ocean-going steam battleships. The lead ship, *Ajax*, was completed on 23 August 1845 and was followed by *Blenheim*, *Edinburgh* and *Hogue*. *Ajax*'s conversion cost £44,500 and *Blenheim*'s £74,800, which can be compared with an estimated cost of £120,000 for constructing a similar ship from scratch.[17]

The success of the smaller screwships and the blockship conversion paved the way for ordering the first purpose-built British steam battleship in July 1849, the wooden 91-gun *Agamemnon*. By the outbreak of the Crimean War in 1854 Britain had eight screw battleships in service in addition to the four blockships. These battleships included both new constructions like *Agamemnon* and conversion of existing sailing ships like the 131-gun *Duke of Wellington*. By comparison, France laid down her first screw battleship, *Napoleon*, in 1848 and had nine such ships in service by 1854. Both powers still maintained large numbers of sailing battleships as well as a steam battlefleet, however: in 1854 Britain had seventy-eight and France thirty-six.[18]

Iron Hulls

The relatively smooth introduction of steam power in the Royal Navy can be contrasted with the protracted adoption of iron warships. As a shipbuilding material, iron has much to recommend it over wood. Exact numerical comparisons are difficult, but one modern source calculates that an iron hull could be made approximately 15–20% lighter than the corresponding wooden hull, and the internal capacity of such an iron-hulled ship could be up to 20% greater as the internal structural members could be made less bulky than the wooden versions. In addition, the iron plates that make up the skin of the hull would be riveted together at the edges (something not possible with wooden planks), and this would increase the rigidity of the iron hull and thus prevent the seams from opening in a seaway and allowing water to enter the ship. This extra rigidity of the hull allowed iron ships to introduce watertight subdivision, something that was not possible in wooden ships.[19]

The first vessels to be made entirely of iron were canal barges in the late eighteenth century, leading to the first iron ocean-going ship in 1821 when the iron paddle wheel steamship *Aaron Manby* made the crossing from London to France. Commercial iron ship construction flourished, and in 1835 the first iron warship, the 28-gun paddle sloop *Nemesis*, was laid down at Laird's in Birkenhead for the Honourable East India Company. Completed in 1840, she sailed to the Far East and survived grounding off St Ives and then a severe storm in the Indian Ocean, where the strong waves caused 7-foot cracks down both sides of her 11-foot deep hull. She went on to fight successfully in the First Opium War. At the same time, three small iron gunboats (*Albert*, *Soudan* and *Wilberforce*) were commissioned into the RN and thus became that force's first entirely iron-hulled warships.[20]

The success of *Nemesis* (both structurally and operationally) prompted the RN to order larger iron warships. The first of these, the Second Class paddle sloop *Trident* (a descendant of *Gorgon* described above), was ordered in 1843 and launched on 16 December 1845 as the first sea-going iron warship in RN service. She was followed two weeks later by the first iron paddle frigate, *Birkenhead*. The growth in size of iron-hulled ships in the RN had been rapid: *Birkenhead*'s displacement was 1,405 tons, which

can be compared with *Nemesis*'s 660 tons just five years previously. *Birkenhead* had a comparatively short life: converted into a troopship in 1851, she sank off Danger Point (in modern-day South Africa) with the estimated loss of 455 lives, but the discipline of the troops in obeying orders to remain on-board while the women and children were rowed to safety became justly celebrated.[21]

Birkenhead was followed by a number of small iron sloops and tenders until, in late 1845, four large iron screw frigates (*Megaera*, *Greenock*, *Vulcan* and *Simoom* of 2,025, 2,065, 2,474 and 2,920 tons displacement respectively) were laid down. These were not only the largest iron warships built for the RN at that time, but were also approaching the size of Brunel's *Great Britain* (laid down 1839), which displaced 3,675 tons. They were also the last iron warships constructed for the RN until the Crimean War and in the early 1850s were either converted to troopships (as with *Birkenhead*) or sold for commercial use.[22]

The four frigates fell foul of a developing belief within the Admiralty that iron ships were not suitable for war-fighting. Initial problems that had been encountered with early iron ships included their hulls rusting from the continued immersion in sea-water, the ferrous metal of the ships' structures causing compasses' deviation, and the fouling of their bottoms that could not be solved by copper sheathing due to electrolytic action between the iron of the hull and the protective copper. Solutions to

these were quickly found, however. Ensuring correct compass readings was so fundamental to the operation of ocean-going iron ships that a method for correction was developed, and regular docking for cleaning mitigated the fouling problem. Applying red lead below the waterline proved successful in preventing corrosion of the hull.[23]

What particularly concerned the Admiralty, however, was the extent to which iron hulls could resist enemy fire. In an attempt to answer this, a series of experiments was carried out at Woolwich Arsenal in 1845–6 where 32-pdr cannon were fired at a number of targets constructed to represent the sides and deck of an iron ship. These were followed by a further experiment in 1846 when the iron-hulled harbour launch *Ruby* was expended as a live-fire target for the gunnery training ship *Excellent*. Neither of the trials were particularly damning of iron construction, but neither did they produce strong evidence in support; the Woolwich trials showed that iron plate could splinter when hit and that slow-moving projectiles produced jagged holes that would be difficult to plug, while the conclusions of the *Ruby* trial were limited to identifying that ships of her class were 'unfit for war purposes', which was unsurprising as she was a small harbour launch rather than a warship. Nevertheless, the decision was taken in 1847 to convert the four large iron frigates into troopships and this marked the end of large iron warship construction until after the end of the Crimean War.[24]

The Crimean War 1854–6 and the Development of the Armoured Warship

Britain had long feared Russian expansion into the area controlled by the Ottoman Empire, and so when tensions between the two Eastern powers rose in the 1853 she moved in concert with France to support Turkey by stationing a combined fleet at Constantinople. Suitably emboldened, Turkey declared war on Russia in October 1853, but Russian successes (including the destruction of a Turkish squadron at Sinope on 30 November 1853) prompted Britain and France to intervene directly in March 1854.

The two major theatres of operations in the Crimean War were the campaign in the Crimea itself, centring around the primarily land-based efforts to destroy the naval arsenal of Sevastopol, and the primarily naval war in the Baltic. The most dramatic applications of naval power were the Allied attacks on Russian coastal fortifications in both theatres, but navies also played an important role in deciding the outcome of the war by enforcing a blockade on Russia that dramatically limited her ability to conduct international trade.

The two attacks that took place in the Baltic were the attack on Bomarsund in the Åland Islands in June–August 1854 and the destruction of Sveaborg on 8–10 August 1855. Although the fortifications at Bomarsund were not finished, contemporary British observers were worried that they could one day pose a threat as a major naval base. At the time of the attack they were made up of a main fort and three armed towers, but the intention on completion was to have a circular defensive wall linking the main fort to five towers with two further towers to the north covering the deep-water harbour of Vargatafjärd.[25] Following the successful Allied attack, the existing fortifications were raised. By contrast, Sveaborg was a fully developed centre of naval power, and the Allied bombardment succeeded in destroying most of the arsenal, the gunboat fleet, a number of magazines and several large warehouses filled with naval stores. The result was that Sveaborg was rendered useless as a naval base.[26]

The Development of the Armoured Warship

The Crimean War proved to be a major driver of a development that would shape warships for the next century: armour. It also provided the opportunity for the first use of armoured warships in battle. It was the French who pioneered the building of armoured warships, spurred by the outbreak of the war and the perceived weakness of unarmoured ships to explosive shells following the Russian destruction of the Turkish squadron at Sinope. Such ships were also seen as vital for the successful attacks of coastal fortifications where thick armour was needed to resist the massed fire of their batteries.

The French planned to build ten iron-armoured steam-propelled floating batteries in time for the 1855 campaign but lacked the industrial capabilities to build that number. The work was therefore divided between Britain and France, with each nation building five. The five British batteries were ordered on 4 October 1854, having been delayed by Sir James Graham's insistence on trialling the resistance of their armour to various shot (perhaps with memories of the iron ship problems in mind). When completed, these ships mounted fourteen or sixteen 68-pdrs, were protected by 4 inches of rolled iron armour and were capable of approximately 5 kts.[27]

The delay imposed by Graham's tests meant that the British ships were not completed in time to participate in the war, but the French batteries saw action during the attack on the fortifications at Kinburn in the Black Sea on 17 October 1855. The success of their armour in resisting Russian fire was shown by the fact that only two crewmen were killed and twenty-two wounded across all three ships, in all cases by shot entering through gunports rather than penetrating their armour. The fort surrendered after five hours of bombardment from a combination of the armoured batteries, ships-of-the-line, frigates, gunboats and mortar vessels.[28] As at Bomarsund and Sveaborg, the Allies demonstrated that ships were capable of successfully engaging and defeating coastal fortifications.

In December 1855 Britain ordered three further armoured batteries. Crucially, these later ships had iron hulls, unlike the first five that had wooden hulls covered with iron armour plates. They were therefore the first warships to combine two of the main features (namely an iron hull and armour) that would be found in *Warrior* five years later.

Preparations for the Attack on Kronstadt

The naval campaign in the Baltic resulted in the permanent destruction of a promising naval base and severe damage to an existing major fortified naval base. The Allies also demonstrated that coastal fortifications were not invulnerable at Kinburn. Perhaps even more important than these actions in determining the outcome of the war, however, was one that never occurred: the attack on Kronstadt that would open St Petersburg to attack from the sea. The prospect of a direct attack on his capital worried the Tsar greatly. To guard against this possibility, the Tsar kept as many as 200,000 troops specifically to defend St Petersburg. Furthermore, these men were equipped with modern rifles and artillery at a time when those troops sent to the Crimea armed with smooth-bore muskets and cannon were suffering at the hands of the Allies' modern weaponry.[29]

The reason that the attack on Kronstadt never took place was that the Allies lacked the forces in 1854–5 to carry out the task effectively. Prior to the outbreak of war, Britain had been more concerned with building steam-powered battleships in competition with France than the small gun- and mortar-boats needed to bombard fortifications successfully, reasoning that these light vessels could be built far more

quickly when required than ships-of-the-line.[30] Mortar vessels had proven their value in the Napoleonic Wars but only limited numbers had remained in service after 1815 and by 1854 even these had been retired (incidentally many having proven, thanks to their robust construction, to be well-suited for polar exploration).[31] Over the winter of 1855–6, therefore, the Allies began the Great Armament to furnish the necessary forces – Britain alone built some 337 vessels including 164 gunboats and 100 mortar vessels.[32] As Sevastopol had fallen in early September 1855 the only possible theatre in which they could be used with the Baltic, and the only targets there worthy of such effort were Kronstadt and St Petersburg.

One plan for such an attack, proposed by the hydrographer to the fleet in the Baltic, Captain Sullivan, called for eight armoured batteries to move through swept channels in the defensive minefields laid by the Russians and destroy the northern defences before thirty mortar vessels would be brought up to fire over the island at the naval dockyard on the other side. Thirty Allied gunboats would be employed to prevent their Russia counterparts (believed to number twenty-three) from engaging the mortar vessels and armoured batteries.[33]

More unconventionally, the seventy-nine-year-old Thomas Cochrane, 10th Earl of Dundonald – famous for the 1809 attack on the Basque Roads, his subsequent fall from grace and his role in the South American and Greek wars of independence – proposed a plan to capture Kronstadt by means of a

poisoned gas attack. He had first conceived the idea of using sulphur dioxide carried on the wind to kill or disable a fortification's garrison without needing to engage with heavy gunfire in 1811, and had presented a plan as to how it could be employed to Lord Auckland, then First Lord of the Admiralty, in September 1846. With the outbreak of war in 1854, Dundonald once again proposed his idea to the Admiralty and a committee was convened to investigate its feasibility. Taking evidence from senior military officers and Professor Michael Faraday, the committee concluded that the plan was not practical and Kronstadt was thus spared becoming the site of the first chemical weapon attack.[34]

The Importance of Naval Power in Deciding the Crimean War

The Tsar's decision to seek peace was therefore heavily influenced by the consideration that his capital, the very heart of his empire, now faced the threat of enemy attack.[35] More importantly, the Russians did not think that they could stop this attack despite building additional fortifications and gunboats.[36] Their fear of the Allies' ability to tackle coastal fortifications can be seen from the summer of 1854 onwards when the Russians abandoned and destroyed a host of smaller positions rather than have the Allies do it.[37]

In addition to direct attacks on targets ashore, the British were also attempting to impose a commercial blockade against Russia. Judging the effect this had on the war is difficult. Exact figures are hard to come by, but by way of example one source estimates that Britain controlled 44% of Russia's exports and 27.6% of her imports and in return Russia's share of Britain's exports and imports was 5.4% and 5.6% respectively.[38] Furthermore, Britain could usually find alternative sources for goods that she could no longer obtain from Russia during the war. Swedish timber replaced Russian, whilst raw wool was obtained instead from domestic and colonial sources. Similarly, the RN switched to Italian hemp supplies and India became the chief source of oil seed. This may have been a continuation of a pre-war trend rather than an indication of the success of the blockade, but it showed that Britain was not really vulnerable to an end of Russian trade.[39]

What really hurt the Russian war effort most, however, was the reduction in customs revenue that the blockade caused by restricting the amount of trade.[40] Russia's grain exports were also seriously curtailed and so she was deprived of her major source of overseas credit. The only way for Russia to finance the war, therefore, was to borrow – and for 1854 and 1855 the amount required was 500 million roubles per year, as opposed to a military budget of 220 million in 1853.[41] Her overseas credit

was poor, however, which meant that she could only borrow at high rates of interest. On 15 January 1856, the Crown Council was advised that if Russia were to keep on fighting she would go bankrupt, and the only way to avoid this was to negotiate. By 1856, therefore, Russia was facing the prospect of bankruptcy and a major assault on her capital city that she felt she was incapable of stopping with the forces available, and theses two factors enormously influenced her decision to seek peace. The RN was instrumental in creating this situation.

The Coming of *Warrior* 1856–60

At the end of the Crimean War the RN staged a naval review at Portsmouth on 23 April 1856 that featured twenty-four steam battleships, nineteen screw frigates, eighteen paddle frigates, one sailing frigate, four armoured batteries, 120 gunboats, fifty mortar vessels and four auxiliaries. Underscoring the RN's ability to make war successfully on an enemy's coast (as had been demonstrated so tellingly against Russia), a mock attack was staged against Southsea Castle.[42]

Despite their successful cooperation against Russia, post-

war Britain continued to see France as the major threat and devoted considerable resources to ensure superiority in modern wooden steam-propelled battleships. In order to achieve this, new battleships patterned on *Agamemnon* were constructed, and existing ships were either lengthened during construction to take engines or fitted with steam propulsion without extra modification. By 1858 Britain had thirty-four steam battleships to France's twenty-eight, and furthermore Britain had a higher proportion of newer, more heavily armed ships.[43] This fleet was composed of the ultimate wooden battleships. Although they may have looked very like much like their eighteenth century predecessors (save for their funnels), they were actually far more powerful vessels: the first-rate *Victoria* of 1857 displaced 6,959 tons (approximately twice as much as Nelson's *Victory*, built in 1759), had approximately double the weight of broadside and could steam at 11 kts.[44] *Victoria* and her sisters were the last of their breed, however, as a ship was coming that would mark the end of the era of the wooden-built battlefleet and the introduction of the iron one: *Warrior*.

Chapter 2

Broadsides, Central Batteries and Turrets 1860–73

In the years after the Crimean War Britain had built a commanding lead over France in wooden steam battleships. This lead can partially be attributed to France's decision after October 1855 not to lay down any more such ships, being inspired by the success of the floating armoured batteries at Kinburn and seeing in them the shape of things to come.[1] It must also be noted, however, that France also lacked sufficient spare large slipways on which to construct more battleships at the time.[2] Britain was therefore in a very strong naval position in 1860 as the RN possessed the largest, most modern steam battlefleet in the world, and in addition had developed and demonstrated the capability to attack positions ashore during the war with Russia. This combination gave the RN strong deterrent power that was used by the British government to continue to shape the international situation in a way that

was favourable to British interests.[3] This deterrence was a continuation of the traditional British policy outlined at the beginning of the previous chapter, but in the period 1860–73 it had to be maintained in the face of the rise of a French threat that wiped out the lead that Britain had accumulated in wooden steam battleships.

Gloire, *Warrior* and the Initial Ironclad Building Race 1858–61

In March 1858 France laid down *Gloire*, a steam-powered ocean-going warship that displaced 5,630 tons and carried thirty-six guns. Like the French armoured batteries of the Crimean War, her wooden hull was clad in iron armour – the use of a wooden hull was recognised as a drawback by the French but they lacked the industrial capacity to manufacture sufficient iron to construct the entire hull from that

material.[4] Recognising the advance *Gloire* offered over existing unarmoured steamships, Britain was quick to respond with an armoured ocean-going warship of her own: money was made available in July 1858 and the resulting armoured iron steamship, *Warrior*, was laid down in May 1859 and launched in December 1860, four months after *Gloire*.[5] *Warrior* did have 18-inch-thick wooden backing to her iron armour but, unlike *Gloire*, her hull structure was made of iron rather than wood.

Warrior was superior in almost every way to *Gloire*: she was larger (at 9,180 tons), faster (14 kts versus 12½ kts) and carried more guns (forty versus thirty-six, although in *Warrior* these were a mixture of calibres and rifled and non-rifled patterns, while *Gloire*'s thirty-six guns were all 6.4-inch rifled muzzle-loaders).[6] *Warrior* also incorporated watertight subdivision, which was

Sister-ship of the more famous *Warrior*, *Black Prince* was a 9,250-ton ironclad laid down in October 1859 and completed in September 1862. She underwent a number of changes of armament in her life, reflecting contemporary developments in naval gun technology: she was initially designed to carry a uniform armament of forty 68-pdr smooth-bores, but these were replaced by a mixed armament of ten 110-pdr breech-loaders, four 70-pdr breech-loaders and twenty-six 68-pdr smooth-bores. The withdrawal of heavy breech-loaders in the late 1860s, however, saw the ship rearmed again with four 8-inch and twenty-four 7-inch muzzle-loading rifles (MLRs) and four 20-pdr breech-loaders. Once at the forefront of ironclad technology, *Black Prince* had been transferred to the reserve by 1880, and in 1899 was reduced to a training ship. She was sold for scrap in 1923. (© The National Archives, United Kingdom, ADM 176/81)

impossible in *Gloire* due to the flexibility of her wooden hull. Only in armour were the two equal as both were protected by 4½ inches of iron, which in *Warrior* covered the battery amidships but not the ends while *Gloire* was armoured from stem to stern.[7] Although officially rated a frigate because of her single-deck main battery, *Warrior* was nevertheless larger than the wooden battleship *Victoria*. *Warrior* embodied the technical advances of the preceding three decades (namely iron hulls, steam propulsion and armour) and was followed, in 1861, by an identical sister, *Black Prince*.

Although an inferior warship to *Warrior*, *Gloire*'s true importance was that almost at a stroke she removed the lead Britain had gained over France in wooden steam-propelled capital ships. *Gloire* was not laid down in isolation but was part of a concerted building programme: in March 1858 France laid down five further ironclads, including two direct repeats of *Gloire*, an iron-hulled version of *Gloire* and two wooden-hulled two-decked ironclads (*Magenta* and *Solferino*). By 1862 France had ordered another ten *Gloire*-class ironclads that were all completed by 1867.[8] Britain responded with an ironclad building programme of her own: by the time *Warrior* was completed in 1861, Britain was building a further nine ironclads and armouring seven wooden steam battleships.[9] Numerically, then, Britain matched the French ironclad challenge almost immediately and demonstrated once again just how seriously she took the maintenance

of naval supremacy. Furthermore, the larger size and stronger construction of the British ironclads (with even the smallest British ships being similar in size to the largest French ironclads) meant that the British ironclad fleet was actually more powerful than France's.[10]

The British ironclad construction programme began with *Warrior* and her sister *Black Prince*. These two ships were followed closely by the sisters *Defence* and *Resistance* (laid down in 1859) and a second pair, *Hector* and *Valiant* (laid down in 1861). These two pairs of successor ships were all smaller than *Warrior* (displacing 6,070 and 6,710 tons respectively) and consequently less capable, but a major consideration in their design was that there were only two docks then in existence capable of containing vessels of *Warrior*'s size. *Hector* and *Valiant* did improve on previous ships, however, as their armour was extended to cover most of the ships' sides with only the waterline right forward and aft remaining unarmoured – this arrangement was similar to that used on contemporary French ironclads and replaced the previous British practice of only armouring the batteries that had been closed fore and aft by armoured bulkheads.[11] Their smaller size also made them cheaper to build (£252,422 and £294,000 for *Defence* and *Hector* respectively, compared with £377,292 for *Warrior*), which was attractive as the government was unwilling to spend too much on novel ironclads.[12] It was still possible (although perhaps unlikely) that they would prove to be failures and that Britain's wooden walls would

continue to be the capital ships of choice. By the time *Hector* and *Valiant* were started, however, *Gloire* had successfully put to sea and therefore these doubts had receded and all further wooden capital ship construction (bar the conversions discussed below) ended in 1861.[13]

The next ship, *Achilles* (also laid down in 1861), was the first to offer improvements over *Warrior* by rectifying obvious problems such as the lack of armour protection for all guns and steering gear.[14] To carry this extra protection her displacement was increased from previous ships to 9,829 tons, and she was given a full-length armoured belt along her entire waterline (4½ inches thick, thinning to 2½ inches at the ends) as well as 4½-inch armour over her battery.[15] Her sailing rig was altered during her life: she was completed with four masts but was reduced to a more conventional three in June 1865 and had her bowsprit restored in the following year.[16] In the first eight years of her life *Achilles* also experienced numerous changes of main armament that reflected contemporary developments and uncertainties in heavy artillery technology. In 1861 *Achilles* was listed as having all breech-loading guns but in 1863 this was changed to twenty-four 100-pdr smooth-bores. By 1865, however, she was fitted with a mixed armament of four 110-pdr breech-loaders, sixteen 100-pdr smooth-bores and six 68-pdr smooth-bores.[17]

Armstrong heavy breech-loading guns had first been introduced into RN service in 1860 but had quickly proven problematic: during the bombardment of Kagoshima in August 1863 (which was undertaken to compel the local Japanese prince to surrender the murderer of a British citizen and to pay an indemnity), British breech-loaders suffered an average of one accident for every thirteen rounds fired. Such guns were therefore withdrawn from service as main armament from 1864 onwards, although smaller pieces did remain.[18]

In their place, the RN reverted to smooth-bore weapons. Although these were seemingly a step backwards, in the mid-1860s such weapons were still capable of

piercing French armour (which tended to be built up of thinner plates) whilst homogeneous British armour was able to withstand French rifled guns. In order to pierce the thicker armour being fitted from the late 1860s onwards the British adopted rifled guns that could fire a more powerful shell further and with more accuracy than smooth-bores, although these guns were still loaded via the muzzle. Such muzzle-loading rifles (MLRs) formed the main armament of all British ironclads from 1866 onwards, both on new constructions and being retrofitted to older vessels.[19] *Warrior*, for example, received four 8-inch and

twenty-eight 7-inch MLRs in 1867 while *Achilles* was rearmed with twenty-two 7-inch MLRs and four 8-inch MLRs in 1868.[20]

The final class of three broadside ironclads laid down in 1861 (*Minotaur*, *Agincourt* and *Northumberland*) were larger than *Achilles* (at 10,690, 10,600 and 10,784 tons respectively) and were intended as a match for the French two-decked ironclads *Magenta* and *Solferino*.[21] As such, they were initially designed to mount fifty breech-loading guns (forty in their main deck battery and ten on the upper deck) behind 5½-inch thick armour (1 inch thicker than previous

Although she underwent a number of changes in rig and armament, this photograph of *Minotaur* from July 1890 gives a good indication of her general appearance for most of her life. Probably the most visible alteration was the removal in the 1870s of two of the five masts with which she had originally been fitted, leaving her with the configuration shown here. Her armament was also modified a number of times during her life: she was originally intended to have a wholly breech-loading armament but, following the withdrawal of this pattern of artillery from RN service, she was commissioned with four 9-inch MLRs, twenty-four 7-inch MLRs and eight 24-pdr smooth-bores. From 1873–5, however, she was rearmed with seventeen 9-inch MLRs and two 20-pdr breech-loaders, and then in the early 1880s two of these MLRs were replaced with two 6-inch breech-loaders. Finally, she received four 4.7-inch breech-loaders, eight 3-pdr quick-firers and two torpedo tubes in 1891–2. She became a training ship in the following year and was stationed at first Portland and then Harwich, until she was finally sold off in 1922. (© The National Archives, United Kingdom, ADM 176/453)

Like her sisters *Agincourt* and *Minotaur*, *Northumberland* originally had five masts but was reduced to a more conventional three (as seen here) during the 1870s. Also like her sisters, she underwent numerous changes in armament: her initial outfit was four 9-inch, twenty-two 8-inch and two 7-inch MLRs, but between 1875 and 1879 this was changed to seven 9-inch and twenty 8-inch MLRs. She was later given one 6-inch and one 5-inch breech-loader during the late 1880s, and then also received six 4.7-inch breech-loaders and ten 3-pdrs. Like many British ironclads, she had an extremely long life that stretched from 1868 to 1927, by the end of which she was known as the coal hulk *C68*. (© The National Archives, United Kingdom, ADM 176/486)

British ironclads). The withdrawal of breech-loaders meant, however, that *Minotaur* and *Agincourt* completed with a mixed armament of eight 24-pdr smooth-bores, twenty-four 7-inch MLRs and four 9-inch MLRs while *Northumberland* had a slightly different mix, substituting twenty-two 8-inch MLRs for twenty-two of the 7-inch MLRs and all the smooth-bores.[22]

Armour protection for *Minotaur* and *Agincourt* followed the pattern of *Hector* and *Valiant* with their sides being covered with 5½-inch plate (thinning to 4½ inches fore and aft) stretching from the upper deck to 5 feet 9 inches below their waterlines for all but their bows.[23] *Northumberland*'s less numerous guns required fewer gunports and hence allowed a shorter battery, but as these guns were heavier (some 68 tons in total) weight had to be saved by reducing the area protected by her side armour to just the length of her shorter battery – her armour scheme therefore resembled *Achilles*'s armoured belt and battery rather than her sisters' almost total covering.[24]

The decision to place the ships' main armament on a single deck was presumably taken to ensure that they all remained at an acceptable height above water in a seaway, but to mount so many main guns on a single deck required an extremely long hull and as a result they were the longest single-screw battleships ever completed (407 feet overall). They were also rather ugly vessels with five masts each, but this veritable forest of masts did not, however, make them good sailing vessels. This was primarily because their propellers could not be lifted

when not in use (unlike *Warrior*'s) and therefore created large amounts of drag. They were all reduced to three masts during their careers.[25]

The design changes necessitated by the revised armaments and experiments with suitable rig meant that all three ships took longer than other contemporary British ironclads to enter service: all three were laid down in 1861 but did not commission until 1867–8.[26] *Northumberland* had a fraught start to life: her great weight resulted in her becoming stuck whilst launching, and then while she was being freed her builders went out of business. She was also delayed for a further eight months until the Admiralty paid the final amount due for her.[27]

The final ships in Britain's response to France's initial ironclad building programme were the seven wooden ironclad conversions begun in 1859–61. It was recognised that these vessels would not be as capable or long-lasting as purpose-built iron-hulled ships, but it was felt that they would be comparable to the French wooden-hulled ironclads and (perhaps as importantly) their reconstruction could be undertaken without increasing the Naval Estimates.[28] Only four were actually completed as broadside ironclads, however, as rapid advances in ironclad design led to the remainder being finished as centre battery ships (see below). *Prince Consort*, *Caledonia*, *Ocean* and *Royal Oak* were all laid down as 91-gun second rate ships-of-the-line, but were converted during construction and completed in 1863–5 as 6,832-ton (*Royal Oak* 6,366-ton) ironclads with the same thickness of armour

(4½ inches) as the other early British broadside ironclads.[29] The sides of these four ships were all completely covered in iron armour (as in *Hector* and *Minotaur*) in order to protect their wooden hulls from explosive shells.[30] They were armed on completion with between twenty-four (*Ocean*) and thirty-six guns (*Royal Oak*) of a mixture of calibres and types, although all were rearmed with varying mixes of 7-inch and 8-inch MLRs in the late 1860s.[31]

The British reaction to the French ironclad challenge was underpinned by her industrial strength. In 1860, Britain produced 3,772,000 metric tonnes of pig-iron while France (the largest European producer behind Britain) produced 898,000 metric tonnes.[32] This meant that France was only able to produce enough iron to build the hulls of two of her initial sixteen ironclads entirely out of iron, while Britain was able to build ten larger iron-hulled ships and covert six more wooden ships in the same amount of time.[33] These iron British ships also lasted longer than the French wooden-hulled ironclads: *Warrior* is still afloat in 2009 and *Black Prince* was scrapped in 1923, while *Gloire* was scrapped in 1879 and two of her sister-ships (*Normandie* and *Invincible*) were scrapped in 1871 and 1872 respectively.[34] Indeed, it is notable that the iron-hulled early French ironclads lasted longer than their wooden-hulled sisters: *Couronne* remained afloat until 1932 and *Héroïne* was still afloat in 1901 when she had to be scuttled due to an outbreak of yellow fever.[35] In building *Gloire* France had hoped to obtain parity with Britain by rendering her established strength in wooden battleships obsolescent, but Britain's position as the world's premier industrial power allowed her to meet the challenge and surpass it.

Despite the image that this ironclad building race suggests of Britain and France locked in some sort of nineteenth century 'Cold War', relations were cordial enough that mutual fleet visits, accompanied by suitably lavish civic receptions, did occur.[36] Such visits also gave each side the opportunity to inspect the latest warships of the other at close hand. 1865 saw a number of reciprocal cross-Channel visits, starting with the French Channel Squadron visiting Plymouth in July, before the British Channel Fleet was invited to Cherbourg and Brest as part of the birthday celebrations for Napoleon III, and finally the French were invited to visit Portsmouth.

Contemporary accounts survive and the details that were noted ranged from the seemingly mundane (that all French ironclads, in contrast with the British, were equipped with a steam launch) to comparisons of the relative fighting power of state-of-the-art British and French ironclads. In particular, the British examined the two-decked *Magenta* closely. Although seemingly impressive, British observers disapprovingly noted the French ship's thinner armour, the lack of armoured bulkheads to close the ends of her batteries and the large size and close spacing of her gunports. It was also recognised that *Magenta*'s lower-deck gunports were much closer to the water than on comparable single-decked British ships and tended to be closed and

sealed when at sea, which obviously reduced the power of her broadside. The use of screws rather than bolts to secure their armour and the inclusion of a ram and an armoured conning tower were seen as points in *Magenta*'s favour, however. For their part, the French were impressed by the British warships' iron construction. Both nations appear to have been satisfied with their warships' powers *vis-à-vis* those of their opponents, however. Despite the differences described above, Dupuy de Lôme (the designer of *Gloire* and the other French ironclads) was one of those present and he was reportedly very happy with the strength of his ships.[37]

France and Britain were not the only nations to construct ironclads at this time. By March 1862 France had completed four ironclads and Britain two, while Austria had laid down five, Italy four, Russia three and Spain two. Although these numbers might suggest Britain initially fell behind her Continental rivals, even the largest of these ships, Spain's iron-hulled *Numancia* of 7,190 tons, was smaller than *Warrior* and the remainder displaced between 3,000 and 6,000 tons.[38] At the same time, the American Civil War saw the use of armoured coastal and riverine craft of which the USS *Monitor* and CSS *Virginia* were the archetypes; indeed, such craft became known generically as 'monitors'.

Central Battery Ships and Second Class Ironclads

The introduction of armoured warships stimulated the development of more powerful guns that could

penetrate these ships' protection. The obvious counter to this was to fit even thicker armour to ironclads, but due to the weight of wrought iron it would not be possible to armour a large proportion of ships' sides to a sufficient thickness as well as mount these larger, heavier guns without a drastic increase in displacement and cost.[39] The British experienced this problem with *Minotaur* and *Agincourt*: thickening their all-over armour by 1 inch and mounting heavier guns resulted in them displacing over half as much again as *Hector*, which had similar distribution of armour. *Northumberland* carried an even heavier weight of guns and thus had to sacrifice all-over armour for the belt-and-battery configuration of *Achilles* and still displaced 10% more than that ship.

Sir Edward Reed (Chief Constructor 1863–70) developed the pattern begun in *Achilles* and *Northumberland* of concentrating fewer heavier guns behind thicker armour into the central battery design. Here, a smaller number of heavier guns were mounted amidships in a smaller heavily armoured battery and the ship's waterline was protected by a belt of similar thickness, leaving the rest of the hull unarmoured.

A number of small ironclads with these central batteries were built, both converted from existing vessels (*Research*, *Enterprise* and *Favorite* of 1,900, 1,350 and 3,232 tons respectively) and purpose-built (*Pallas*, 3,794 tons, and *Penelope*, 4,470 tons), before the first central battery ironclad battleship, *Bellerophon*, was completed in 1866. *Bellerophon*'s main armament of ten 9-inch MLRs was mounted in a 6-inch thick armoured battery amidships, with a further 6-inch belt of armour along her waterline. This concentration of heavy armour and guns made *Bellerophon* shorter than *Warrior*, and at 7,551 tons over 2,000 tons lighter, but her thicker armour made her effectively invulnerable to the earlier ship's gunfire while still able to match her top speed of 14 kts. Although she only mounted five guns on each broadside, these were of a larger calibre than those mounted on previous ships and so *Bellerophon* actually had a heavier weight of broadside. Their heavier shells were also capable of penetrating the thinner armour of earlier ironclads.[40]

It is important to realise the pace at which these advances in warship design happened: *Bellerophon* was laid down only two years after the *Minotaur*-class broadside ironclads (in 1863) and, due to the delays to those ships caused by the removal of breech-loaders from service, was completed approximately two years before they entered service. *Bellerophon* was also laid down at the same time as the last two broadside ironclads (*Lord Clyde* and *Lord Warden*) – these two ships were based on the design of *Bellerophon* but modified for a wooden rather than iron hull and with 5½-inch armour along the entire length of their hull. These two vessels were the heaviest wooden ships ever constructed (7,040 tons for *Lord Warden* and 7,750 tons for *Lord Clyde*) and by 1867 mounted twenty-four 7-inch MLRs as their main armament. They had contrasting lives: *Lord Warden* finally paid off in 1885, while *Lord Clyde* was sold off ten years earlier (and only eleven years after she was completed) when her hull was found to be rotten.[41]

The last wooden battleships to enter RN service were the three conversions (*Royal Alfred*, *Zealous* and *Repulse*[42]) begun as a response to *Gloire* as broadside ironclads but completed as central battery ships similar to *Bellerophon*. Whereas the first conversions were lengthened to incorporate new steam machinery at the expense of weakening their hulls, the compact central battery design meant that *Zealous* and *Repulse* did not have to be extended. The two ships were generally similar, although *Repulse* mounted fewer heavier guns in a shorter, better-protected battery (eight 8-inch MLRs behind 6-inch armour) than *Zealous* (sixteen 7-inch MLRs behind 4½-inch armour). *Repulse*'s belt was also thicker than *Zealous*'s (6-inch amidships thinning to 4½-inch at the bow and stern, compared with 4½-inch amidships thinning to 2½-inch respectively). In addition, both ships mounted four more MLRs of the same calibre as their battery guns as bow and stern chasers to cover the arcs where the battery guns could not be brought to bear. *Zealous* was deployed to the Pacific from 1866 to 1873 and consequently spent much of her life cruising under sail – on her last commission she travelled approximately 30,000 miles while using only 1,600 tons of coal.[43] Discussing her retirement in 1875, Parkes laments:

And so passed the lonely *Zealous* – the ship which never once steamed in company with another battleship, and covered the greatest mileage with cold boilers.[44]

Royal Alfred was lengthened to allow her to carry armament and armour comparable to *Bellerophon*'s, but this came at considerable expense: *Royal Alfred* cost £282,803, compared with £356,493 for the iron *Bellerophon*.[45] In light of the benefits of durability and rigidity granted by iron construction, therefore, this small saving might have been something of a false economy.

The *Warrior*-style broadside ironclad was therefore a design that was only state-of-the-art in the RN for some five years or so, before advances in gun power led to the development of the better-protected central battery ironclad. *Bellerophon* was followed by an improved design, *Hercules*, which was laid down in 1866 and completed in 1868. *Hercules* mounted a heavier battery armament (eight 10-inch MLRs) and was protected by thicker armour with a maximum thickness of 9 inches on the belt and 8 inches on the battery (reducing to a minimum of 6 inches in both cases). Despite this increase in armament (and a consequent increase in displacement over *Bellerophon* of 1,100 tons), improvements in construction techniques meant *Hercules* cost only £20,000 more. She was kept in service until 1905, being reconstructed from 1892 with the fitting of new engines and the removal of her masts – her main armament was untouched, however, even though all new battleships by then mounted breech-loaders.[46] Her value as an effective fighting vessel was therefore minimal.

In the discussions so far we have referred only to the thickness of the armour mounted on ironclads. It must be remembered, however, that the armour was only one part of the protective scheme of these ships: all had thick wooden backing to their armour that was not structural but provided further protection.

Hercules provides a good example of this: her sides behind her 9-inch armour were 10 inches of teak, then a 1½-inch iron skin over her iron frames filled-in with a further 10 inches of teak, 20 inches more of teak and then ¾ inches of iron plate, making a grand total of 11½ inches of iron and 40 inches of teak. The rapid development in gun power and consequently protection are shown by the fact that, during trials, a

reproduction of *Hercules*'s protective scheme successfully withstood fire from a 600-pdr gun – by contrast, *Warrior*'s sides were designed to withstand 68-pdr gunfire.[47]

A further improvement in *Hercules* over *Bellerophon* was the added provision of end-on fire from her battery guns. The design of *Hercules* allowed for the four end guns in her battery to be relocated to

The manoeuvrability of steam-ships led to a widespread belief that ramming was once again a feasible tactic, and consequently many navies constructed purpose-designed ramming vessels. In the RN, the first of these was the 4,300-ton *Hotspur*, which was laid down in 1868 and completed in 1871. As it was feared that any impact would render a turret unusable, she was initially completed with a circular armoured gun-house forward with multiple ports through which a single 12-inch MLR could fire. In 1881–3, however, she was reconstructed at considerable expense and acquired the form shown in this photograph. The fixed gun-house was replaced by a conventional turret containing two 12-inch MLRs, and in addition she was given two 6-inch breech-loaders. She originally had an 8-inch-thick breastwork, but this was replaced during her reconstruction with an armoured belt and bulkheads of the same thickness. *Hotspur* was not, however, a success as a ramming vessel as she was too slow (*c.* 12½ kts) and unseaworthy, although she survived in service until 1904. (© The National Archives, United Kingdom, ADM 176/343)

fire fore and aft through a set of alternative gunports, and large recesses were provided in the sides of her hull to allow the guns firing through these ports to do so as close to dead ahead and astern as possible. This arrangement was first trialled by Reed in *Research* and *Pallas*, but was not used in the larger *Bellerophon*. The ability to fire directly ahead was thought to be particularly useful in steam-powered warships as their ability to travel in any desired direction appeared to make deliberate ramming a viable tactic once more. It was therefore seen as important that such ships should be able to shoot effectively as they bore down on their target. The importance of ramming gained further prominence in naval tactics and designs following the Battle of

Lissa on 20 July 1866, where two Italian ships were sunk by ramming, as well as the loss of a number ironclads to peacetime collisions (including the British *Audacious*-class ironclad *Vanguard*, which was struck by her sister *Iron Duke* in 1875).[48]

How viable a tactic ramming would actually have been in practice, however, has been questioned both by contemporary naval officers and later authors, although this did not stop many navies building small, purpose-designed ramming vessels (including the RN's *Hotspur* and *Rupert*, laid down in 1868 and 1870 respectively). In addition, end-on fire so close to the hull would cause damage to the firing ship from muzzle blast, moving heavy guns (those on *Hercules* weighed 10 tons

apiece) to alternative gunports whilst the ship was moving could be extremely dangerous, and the recesses in some ships generated large amounts of spray whilst underway.[49] Nevertheless, the perceived importance of end-on fire meant that the practice of incorporating extra gunports was continued in subsequent British central battery ironclads, and also adopted in the ships of several other nations.

Second Class Ironclads

Up until 1865 the French ironclad challenge was confined to European waters; her ironclads were unsuitable for cruising and fighting in the open oceans as their large gunports were sited close to the waterline and so

A 5,400-ton armoured ram, *Rupert* was a development of the type pioneered in RN service by *Hotspur*. She was begun in June 1870 and the biggest change was the replacement of the earlier ship's fixed gun-house with a conventional turret mounting two 10-inch MLRs. This photograph shows her after she was reconstructed between 1891 and 1893, during which her turret was rearmed with two 9.2-inch breech-loaders and four 6-pdr and six 3-pdr quick-firers were added. Her original foremast was removed at the same time, and her mainmast was given the fighting-top visible here. Despite these changes, *Rupert* was no more successful than *Hotspur*, perhaps because the concept of the dedicated ram was fundamentally unsound, although she was not sold off until 1907. (© The National Archives, United Kingdom, ADM 176/604)

put them at risk of foundering if they were opened in heavy seas. This focus on building a European battlefleet reflected French strategic priorities: Britain's strength lay in her naval power, which allowed her, through deterrence or intervention, to shape the international situation to her favour, and this power was rooted in her home dockyards and the ships based there-at. A powerful French fleet based in Europe was an obvious threat to these and hence had to be countered – if it were ignored, France could threaten Britain with the destruction of her centre of power. The RN's battlefleet was therefore concentrated in home waters to counter this, and colonial protection was left to lighter ships.[50]

In 1865, however, the French launched the small wooden-hulled broadside ironclad *Belliqueuse* and began work on seven *Alma*-class ships of the more up-to-date central battery configuration, all of which were designed to serve outside European waters. The three ships of the *La Galissonnière* class followed in 1868, although the construction of these ships was much delayed by the Franco–Prussian War and they were not finished until 1874–9. The British response was to match this French development with their own ships designed for overseas service, starting in 1867 with the four ships of the *Audacious* class (*Audacious*, *Invincible*, *Iron Duke* and *Vanguard*) and continuing with the two *Swiftsure*-class ironclads (*Swiftsure* and *Triumph*) laid down in 1868.[51]

Triumph was a 6,660-ton Second Class central battery ironclad laid down in 1868 and completed in 1873. She and her sister *Swiftsure* were identical to the preceding *Audacious*-class vessels in terms of armament (ten 9-inch and four 6-inch MLRs) and armour (8–6-inch belt and 6-inch battery), and also in general appearance. In particular, the two classes shared a two-decked central battery, with the upper level projecting out from the hull to give the guns mounted at its corners the ability to fire fore and aft. This feature can clearly be seen in this photograph, which shows *Triumph* after her 1882–4 refit when four 5-inch breech-loaders were added on her upper deck. She was also given eight 6-pdr and eight 3-pdr quick-firers at the same time. *Triumph* was decommissioned in 1900 and sold off 1921. (© The National Archives, United Kingdom, ADM 176/723)

All six ships were modern iron-hulled central battery ironclads featuring a two-decked central battery. The upper level of the battery projected out from the ship's sides to allow the four 9-inch MLRs mounted in its corners to fire fore and aft – an arrangement first employed by Reed in his design of the Turkish ironclad *Fatikh*.[52] They were designated as Second Class ironclads, to distinguish them from the larger British vessels intended to form the home-based battlefleet. Like *Warrior*, however, they were larger and more capable than their French equivalents. *Audacious* displaced 6,010 tons, and *Swiftsure* 6,910 tons, and all six mounted the same main armament as *Bellerophon* (ten 9-inch MLRs) protected by an 8-inch belt and 6-inch battery armour. In comparison, the largest *Alma*-class vessel (*Montcalm*) displaced 3,828 tons and carried six 7.6-inch main guns protected by a 6-inch belt and 4.7-inch battery armour.[53]

The *Swiftsure* class ships were the first large British ironclads to have wooden sheaths to their iron hulls, which could in turn be coppered – as described in the previous chapter, coppering could not be applied directly to iron hulls due to the effects of electrolysis.[54] This was an important development for an iron-hulled ship intended to operate on overseas stations in the 1870s. In home waters, ships could call on a well-established support infrastructure where they could be docked regularly for cleaning. Overseas, however, such docks were in very limited supply when these ships were built: for example,

there were no British docks in the Pacific until the dockyard at Esquimalt on Vancouver Island was completed in 1886.[55] Effective anti-fouling measures were therefore extremely important in ensuring that the ships' sailing properties were not compromised on long deployments.

In common with the other British ironclads described so far the *Audacious* and *Swiftsure* classes were powered by both steam engines and sails. The retention of sailing rig reduced their dependence on coaling stations when on foreign service by allowing them to cruise without using their engines. *Swiftsure* and *Triumph* had single propellers and so could be fitted with lifting screws to reduce drag when not using their engines (like *Warrior* and other single-screw British ironclads), but *Audacious* and her sister-ships could not be so fitted as they had two screws. Instead, they were fitted with auxiliary steam engines to turn their propellers while sailing and thus reduce drag.[56]

Audacious and her sisters were begun after the laying down of the ocean-going turret ironclads *Monarch* and *Captain* discussed below. As such, they would seem to be a step backwards in technological terms as it was the turret rather than the central battery that was to prove ultimately the preferred configuration for mounting heavy guns. However, there was an understandable reluctance on the part of the RN to continue building any more turret battleships until the comparative merits of the *Monarch* and *Captain* designs could be ascertained in service.[57]

Furthermore, overseas service clearly placed a premium on long-distance cruising range, and with the fuel-inefficient steam engines of the 1860s this could be most readily provided by sail power. Reed felt that rigging and turrets were essentially incompatible as the former inevitably compromised the strength of the latter in being able to fire through a very wide arc – and so, as sails were required on these ships, the best disposition of their guns was in a central battery as it maximised their protection and was not obstructed by masts mounted on the upper deck.[58]

It can be seen that British strategy was essentially reactive: there was no technological reason why ships of the *Audacious* type could not have been built before 1865, but upping the ante by introducing global ironclads was not in Britain's interest. Such ships were expensive, as were the dockyard facilities required to support them, and as long as no other power possessed them then smaller and cheaper sloops and gunboats could defend Britain's empire much more cheaply.[59] As with *Warrior*, Britain therefore waited for France to make the first move before using her industrial power to match and overcome the French challenge.

The two-decked battery introduced in *Audacious* was also incorporated into the next First Class ironclad, *Sultan* (laid down in 1868 and completed in 1871), which was otherwise very similar to *Hercules* – at 9,540 tons she displaced 700 tons more but her armour was of a similar thickness and her top speed was

This photograph shows the central battery ironclad *Sultan* in August 1896 upon completion of a refit following her stranding off Malta in 1889. This refit dramatically altered her appearance; most noticeably, two military masts with large fighting-tops have replaced her masts and rigging, her funnels have been raised and a bridge structure has been added. Nevertheless, the most interesting feature of her original design, her two-decked battery with the forward embrasure on the bottom deck and the overhanging top deck, can still be discerned amidships. Both of these features were designed to allow her main armament to fire fore and aft as well as on the broadside. Also visible in her bow are the original ports for two 9-inch MLR bow chasers. *Sultan* was still extant at the end of the Second World War, although she had long ceased to be a warship, and was only broken up in 1946. (© The National Archives, United Kingdom, ADM 176/676)

also around 14 kts. As with the *Audacious* class, at the time she was ordered the outcome of the *Monarch* and *Captain* trial was not known and so it was decided to construct her as a central battery design. Like *Hercules*, *Sultan* was reconstructed in 1893–6 with new engines, although her main armament was similarly untouched. This cost over £200,000 and resulted in a ship of dubious fighting power compared with the state-of-the-art ships – she was kept in reserve as a Third Class battleship before being finally retired in the early 1900s.[60]

Following the initial French challenge embodied by *Gloire* and her sisters, France's smaller industrial base compared with Britain meant that she was unable to keep pace in the building race that she had begun. The eleven British central battery ironclads laid down in the period 1863–8 took, on average, three years to build while the seven comparable French ships started in response in 1865–70 took seven and a half.[61] Furthermore, as with the *Gloire*-class ironclads, a restricted supply of iron meant that only one of these French central battery battleships (*Friedland*) and none of the ten contemporary Second Class central battery ships were built with an iron hull (with all the consequent lack of subdivision and longevity that implies).[62] By 1870 France had approximately the same number of ironclad warships as Britain, but only twelve of these were larger than 6,000 tons and so the balance of naval power was firmly in Britain's favour.[63] After 1870, with her failure in the building race and then

the cost of the Franco–Prussian War, France began to look at other ways of countering the RN's supremacy without building large armoured warships.

The Turret Battleships *Monarch* and *Captain*

In Britain the genesis of the turret can be attributed to the work of Captain Cowper Coles. Based on his experiences as a gunnery officer during the Crimean War, Coles designed and patented an armoured revolving structure containing heavy guns to be mounted on warships. The Board of Admiralty[64] were sufficiently interested to procure a single-gunned prototype in 1861 that was fitted to the armoured battery *Trusty* for a series of trials. These highlighted the advantages offered by turrets over broadside mountings, as well as revealing some drawbacks. It was found that a turret gun could be operated by a smaller gun-crew than the same weapon mounted on the broadside, and that it could achieve a higher effective rate of fire as the gun could be kept trained on the enemy at all times. Furthermore, as they could be mounted closer to the ship's centre line than broadside guns, turrets guns were less affected by the motion of the ship and so could be fired more accurately. Finally, concentrating the ship's guns in a single smaller location allowed them to be protected by thicker armour than the more widely dispersed broadside guns. On the downside, it was recognised that the rotating mechanism of the turret could be jammed by enemy fire or

mishap and thus prevent the guns being trained in the desired direction.[65]

The Admiralty were sufficiently impressed by the outcome of the *Trusty* trials to order two turret-armed low-freeboard warships in 1862. The first, *Royal Sovereign* (5,080 tons), was converted from a 121-gun wooden battleship by cutting down the number of decks and fitting three single-gun and one twin-gun turrets (all carrying 10½-inch smooth-bores, although these were replaced in 1867 with 9-inch MLRs). She was both an experiment into the practicality of turret armament in general, and also, if the conversion was a success, it was hoped that she might provide the pattern for a large number of similar conversions to make use of Britain's large reserve of now-obsolete two- and three-deck wooden battleships.[66]

The second ship, *Prince Albert* (3,687 tons), was a purpose-designed iron vessel with four 9-inch MLRs in four single-gun turrets. Comparing her with *Bellerophon* illustrates the economy provided by turrets over broadside guns: *Prince Albert* displaced half as much as *Bellerophon* and mounted only two-fifths of her main armament (four guns versus ten), but thanks to her turrets' ability to fire on either beam she could fire on one broadside with only one fewer gun than the larger ship. These turret guns were also carried at the same height above water (7 feet) as *Bellerophon*'s and so could be fought in similar weather.[67]

Both *Royal Sovereign* and *Prince Albert* were armoured with a belt and between 5½ inches and 10½ inches of armour on their turrets. As they were not intended for operation on the open oceans but instead in coastal waters near established bases, both ships relied on steam power alone and were not fitted with masts or sails – the first RN capital ships to be so propelled.[68] Given the chance to view *Royal Sovereign* at close quarters during the mutual naval visits of 1865 described above, the French were very impressed by her design and thought that she would be a match for any existing French ironclad in calm conditions.[69]

During the American Civil War Britain also took over two turret vessels being built for the Confederacy and commissioned them into the RN in 1864 as *Scorpion* and *Wivern*. These ships mounted four 9-inch MLRs in two twin turrets and were barque-rigged as well as steam-powered. Like *Royal Sovereign* and *Prince Albert* they were employed as inshore vessels because of their low freeboard, although they were better seaboats as they were fitted with forecastles and poops.[70]

These conversions and purpose-built turret ships proved that the advantages of turrets over broadside guns in theory were borne out in practice, and so the Admiralty decided to use them to mount the armament in a full-size ironclad battleship. Given that steam engines were still too inefficient to provide the range required of a British battleship, it was decided that this ship should be fully rigged and that it should have high freeboard and a

forecastle to allow it to fight on the open ocean. Reed was opposed to this mixture of masts and turrets as he judged correctly that the former would inevitably block the arcs of fire of the latter, thus compromising one of the main strengths of a turret-mounted armament. In 1868 the incoming Gladstone government had undertaken a review of the current state of the RN and plans for future ironclads and, as part of this, Reed had been invited to provide a description of his preferred design for future battleships. His submission described a vessel with a 12-inch armoured breastwork and belt, two twin turrets at either end of a central superstructure and no masts or rigging – almost exactly the form *Devastation* was to take (see below).[71]

In 1866, however, it was the Board's ideas that triumphed. The resulting ship, *Monarch*, displaced 8,322 tons, was capable of nearly 15 kts (making her the fastest battleship then in service) and carried four 12-inch MLRs in two twin turrets grouped centrally on top of what would have been her battery, had she been a central battery ship. Despite Reed's objections she was given a freeboard of 14 feet and fitted with three masts and a forecastle. As these features prevented her turrets from firing fore and aft, she mounted two 7-inch MLRs forward and another aft to enable her to fire straight ahead and to the rear. Her armour was disposed in a similar fashion to contemporary central battery ships, with a central armoured citadel and belt covering her turret bases and waterline (7 inches thick, thinning to 4½ inches

at the ends), while the turrets themselves were protected by between 8 inches and 10 inches of armour.[72]

Like Reed, Coles did not agree with the design of *Monarch* as he had his own conception of the ideal turret battleship – the key feature of which was low freeboard (c. 8–11 feet) to present a small target and stop the vessel becoming too top-heavy due to carrying her heavy turrets too high.[73] Through a campaign backed by the press, Coles persuaded the Admiralty to commission an ocean-going turret ironclad that embodied his ideas. This ship, *Captain*, was laid down in 1867 and completed in 1870, some six months after *Monarch*. Displacing 7,767 tons, she was armed with the same turrets and guns as *Monarch* and was similarly protected. The biggest difference between the two ships lay in their freeboard: *Captain* was designed with 8 feet, already less than *Monarch*, but due to weight gained during construction (including from errors made by her builders, Laird's) she actually completed with only 6 feet 7 inches. She also differed from Coles' original ideal in that she had a forecastle and poop added to her design by Laird's in light of their experience in designing turret ships for other countries. *Captain* was also given the heaviest masts and largest spars of any sailing battleship to date, presumably to maximise her performance under sail.[74]

It is instructive to compare these two turret ironclads with their central battery contemporaries. *Captain* and *Monarch* were laid down at approximately the same time as *Hercules* and were of roughly the same displacement and length (some 320 feet). *Hercules* mounted eight 10-inch MLRs in her main battery, but as these were deposed on her broadsides only half could be fired at any one target. The turret vessels carried half that number of large guns, but because their turrets could train on either beam they had the same effective broadside and required less than half the number of gun-crew (total complements were 500 for *Captain* and 575 for *Monarch*, as opposed to 638 for *Hercules*). In fact, as the turret battleships carried 12-inch guns their weight of broadside was actually greater than the central battery ship. The one advantage the central battery ship had was that it could fight with both broadsides at the same time, although how often this would be used is debatable.[75]

Reed was concerned about *Captain*'s combination of low freeboard and full rigging. This was potentially dangerous as, like all sailing ships, she was liable to heel when under sail, but her low freeboard meant that she would not have to heel over very far before water would come up over her decks and possibly cause her to capsize. Normally, sailing ships had sufficiently high freeboard that the angle at which this would happen was very unlikely to be reached before something could be done to prevent it, but *Captain*'s low height above water meant that for her this angle was much smaller. Reed's worries intensified when calculations revealed that *Captain*'s centre of

gravity was higher than originally thought, and he unsuccessfully attempted to convince the Board members of the dangers she faced unless changes were made. He even went as far as to tell her commanding officer, Captain Hugh Talbot Burgoyne, VC, that:

> I don't want to say any more against her, but I am glad that it is your fate and not mine to go to sea in her.[76]

Burgoyne was not a man to be afraid of a little peril, however. He had won the Victoria Cross as a twenty-one-year-old lieutenant in the Crimea, and spent time serving in the 'Vampire Fleet' in the Far East under the employ of the Imperial Chinese government and as a blockade runner for the Confederacy during the American Civil War before subsequently returning to the RN.[77]

Despite Reed's fears, *Captain* completed her first trial cruise successfully, including sailing in a gale, and it appeared that Coles had been vindicated. Embittered by the long-running dispute over the relative merits of *Monarch* and *Captain*, Reed resigned on 8 July 1870. Events were to prove Reed's fears had been well-founded, however: off Cape Finisterre on the night of 6 September 1870, *Captain*'s sails caused her to heel over in very strong winds and, before they could be cut away, her low decks became awash and she capsized. Only seventeen of her crew survived, and amongst those lost were Coles and Burgoyne.[78]

Turrets, Coastal Assault and the Coming of the Mastless Battleship

The arrival of steam power had a profound impact on British naval strategy. Previously, blockading enemy fleets in their home ports had formed the cornerstone, and although this might be seen to depend on the vagaries of the wind it should be remembered that these affected the fleet being blockaded as well as the blockaders: unfavourable winds might drive off the watching ships, but they could equally prevent the enemy from coming out. Steam power removed this dependence on the wind and consequently made the job of the blockader much harder: the enemy could now sortie at any time and not just when the winds were favourable. To meet this new situation the RN developed a new strategy. In addition to waiting for the enemy to come out to defeat him, the RN developed the capability to assault the enemy in his fortified harbours to destroy him before he could slip away.[79] The Crimean War convincingly demonstrated that such a strategy was feasible and that damage could be inflicted by coastal assault on an opponent sufficient to decide the outcome of the war.

The RN constructed specialist coastal assault ships to implement this strategy. Initially these were the armoured batteries, mortar vessels and gunboats of the Great Armament, but the adoption of the turret led to the introduction of purpose-designed coastal assault ironclads. The turret was well suited to the role of fighting fortifications because it concentrated the ship's firepower in one location where it could be protected by sufficiently thick armour. Furthermore the heavy weight of an armoured turret was best mounted low down where it would not affect the stability of the ship, and this lent itself well to a low freeboard that minimised the vulnerable areas of the ship. The *Captain* tragedy had shown the danger of trying to combine these features with the full rig of a sailing battleship, but it was recognised that sails were not required for the intended role of such ships; not only were masts and spars very vulnerable but they were unnecessary as the likely targets for coastal assault were

all to be found in Europe (especially France and Russia) and therefore the worldwide strategic mobility provided by sails was unnecessary.[80]

As the RN was still required to be able to act on a global rather than purely European scale, however, the mastless turret ironclad could not completely replace the traditional masted ironclad in the 1860s and 1870s. The RN battlefleet of the time therefore came to be composed of two distinct types of ship, each best suited to its particular role: the heavily armoured, shallow draught turret ships for coastal attack in Europe and the high-freeboard, sail-and-steam 'cruising' ironclads for fighting on the high seas.[81]

In the late 1860s Reed had designed a number of twin-turret coastal monitors for both the RN and colonial navies – the remains of one of these, *Cerberus*, still exists as part of a man-made breakwater at Half Moon Bay in the state of Victoria, Australia. These were followed in 1870 by the single-turreted *Glatton* and the four ships of the *Cyclops* class. These ships all had very little freeboard and were therefore intended only to operate close to the coast – they were styled 'coastal defence vessels' to mollify contemporary opinion, but this disguised the fact they were also intended to operate offensively against the enemy's coast and naval

Glatton was a 4,900-ton monitor laid down in 1868. She was completed in 1872 and was based at Portsmouth for her entire career, moving into the reserve in 1889 and finally being sold off in 1903. Although she only had a single turret (mounting two 12-inch MLRs), she resembled Reed's later twin-turret monitors in that she had low freeboard all around and a central breastwork to keep her turret, funnel and hatches at a suitable height above the water. (© The National Archives, United Kingdom, ADM 176/294)

The name-ship of a class of four 3,500-ton breastwork monitors, *Cyclops* was laid down in 1870 and completed in 1877. The photograph illustrates well the main features of her design, which was essentially a repeat of the earlier *Cerberus*: extremely low freeboard fore, aft and at the sides, with the bridge, funnel and main armament (two turrets each mounting two 10-inch MLRs) carried behind a central armoured breastwork to keep them sufficiently high above the water. In accordance with her designer Reed's views on the impracticality of combining masts, turrets and low freeboard, she dispensed with sails and relied entirely on steam propulsion for a top speed of approximately 11 kts. She was protected by an armoured belt up to 8 inches thick, while the breastwork itself was up to 9 inches thick and the turrets up to 10 inches. Along with her sisters, *Cyclops* was sold off in 1903. (© The National Archives, United Kingdom, ADM 176/176)

Gorgon was a sister-ship of *Cyclops*. She was completed in 1874, but the photograph shows her some time after 1885–9 when, like the larger *Devastation*, light plating had been added to carry the central breastwork out to her sides. The same modification was applied to the other three ships of the class. (© The National Archives, United Kingdom, ADM 176/303)

bases. Contemporary naval officers were more forthright in identifying the true role of these ships as being offensive rather than defensive.[82] To give these vessels sufficient freeboard to prevent them from being swamped, Reed designed them with armoured breastwork amidships behind which the turrets, funnels and superstructure were mounted. Low freeboard was still seen as desirable to maintain a low silhouette and to improve steadiness by allowing heavy seas to wash over the decks, and so was retained fore and aft and around the sides of this breastwork. Sails were not fitted and they relied entirely on steam propulsion.[83]

Reed carried over the general features of these breastwork monitors into the construction of the RN's first battleship-sized mastless armoured turret ships. Laid down in 1869, *Devastation* (completed in 1873) and her sister *Thunderer* (completed in 1877) were 9,330-ton vessels with four 12-inch MLRs in two twin turrets disposed one ahead and one behind the central superstructure. Their breastwork gave them 10¾ feet of freeboard amidships, decreasing to 10½ feet forward and 4 feet aft.[84] Initially low freeboard was also present around the sides of the breastwork in the same fashion as the smaller monitors. However, low freeboard was recognised as contributing to the capsizing of *Captain* and there were some concerns that *Devastation* and *Thunderer* could suffer a similar fate. It was therefore decided that the freeboard provided by the breastwork should be maintained amidships by the addition of light

Thunderer was the sister-ship of *Devastation*. This photograph shows her following her refit of the early 1890s, during which she received the same modifications as her sister. It also illustrates well the class's similarities with Reed's breastwork monitors, although the battleships' freeboard forward and amidships was maintained to the same height as the breastwork, and only reduced to the height of the main hull right aft. Like *Devastation*, *Thunderer* was moved into reserve in the early 1900s and was sold off in 1909. (© The National Archives, United Kingdom, ADM 176/711)

Devastation was the RN's first mastless ocean-going battleship and was based on the design of Reed's breastwork monitors. At over 9,000 tons, however, *Devastation* displaced nearly three times as much and was consequently much more heavily armed and armoured.

Taken in December 1893, this photograph show *Devastation* following a major refit during which she was rearmed with 10-inch breech-loaders, six 6-pdrs and eight 3-pdrs. She was also given new triple-expansion engines and new boilers that restored her

top speed of 14 kts. Perhaps because of worries about the growing strengths of foreign navies, *Devastation* was maintained in service until 1902, and was sold off in May 1908. (© The National Archives, United Kingdom, ADM 176/195B) plating extending out to the ships' sides.[85]

These additions were probably unnecessary as concerns for these ships' stability ignored the fact that, although if these ships did heel too far they would be vulnerable to submerging their deck edges and capsizing, without masts and sails they were far less likely to be pushed over far enough for this to happen. The removal of rigging also reduced the total size of the crew that the ships required (358 men each, compared with 638 for the masted *Hercules*) but the low freeboard and lack of superstructure as initially completed did reduce the space available for the crew's berths. The additional enclosed volume provided by the additional plating may not have been necessary to protect against capsizing but it did, however, provide much need extra accommodation space.[86]

Both ships were protected by an armoured belt and breastwork with a maximum thickness of 12 inches, while their turrets had 14-inch fronts and 10-inch walls.[87] In common with the central battery ironclads, this armour was backed by a significant thickness of wood to give extra protection. They relied entirely on steam power for propulsion and did not carry any sails – the first battleships in British service so to do.

Devastation and *Thunderer* were the last major ships designed for the RN by Reed. A third mastless turret ship based on Reed's *Devastation*, known as *Fury*, had been laid down in September 1870 but work on her was stopped following the loss of *Captain*. Reed's successor as Chief

Constructor, Nathaniel Barnaby, consequently embarked upon a redesign, which aimed to improve her stability by extending the armoured breastwork out to the ship's side, and also with the addition of armoured plating between the breastwork and the bow and the stern to give her a full end-to-end armoured belt. The intention was to protect the ship's freeboard in the event of enemy action – the light structure added to *Devastation* and *Thunderer* was seen as insufficient as it could be riddled by enemy fire. So comprehensive was Barnaby's redesign that the ship was renamed *Dreadnought*. Compared with *Devastation*, *Dreadnought* displaced more (10,886 tons versus 9,330 tons), carried a slightly heavier main armament (four 12½-inch MLRs in two twin turrets) and was protected by a 14-inch armoured breastwork and 14-inch armoured belt (thinning to 8 inches at the ends).[88]

The mastless turret ship did not immediately become the pattern for all subsequent British battleships, however. To some, this has been taken as evidence of the confused state of warship development in the mid-nineteenth century, especially as *Devastation* resembled the battleships of the 1880s and 1890s in general layout far more than she did the central battery and citadel turret ships of the 1870s that immediately followed her. The decision not to abandon masts and switch to a battlefleet composed entirely of the mastless turret battleships in the early 1870s is sometimes presented as evidence that the mid-nineteenth century RN was excessively technologically conservative,

preferring to stick with the familiarity of sails even when the warship of the future was upon them.

As has been argued by historians such as Beeler and Lambert, however, such an argument rests on a good deal of hindsight and overlooks the fact that there were compelling reasons for the RN to maintain a fleet of masted battleships in the 1870s. The three mastless turret battleships described above notionally had the ability to cross the Atlantic despite their lack of sails: *Devastation* and *Thunderer* carried sufficient coal to steam for 5,500 miles at 10 kts, while *Dreadnought* could travel for 7,500 miles at the same speed thanks to her more efficient compound engines. As a result they have sometimes been described as the first ocean-going turret battleships and the direct forebears of the ships of the 1880s and 1890s. This overlooks, however, the fact that their ability to operate effectively once they were overseas was circumscribed by the lack of supporting docks and coal depots *at the time that they came into service*. The mastless barbette and turret battleships of the last decade of the nineteenth century could operate overseas as by that time this worldwide supporting infrastructure was in place, but this simply did not exist in 1870. Without it, the more self-reliant masted ironclad continued to be the best capital ship for a navy that required worldwide strategic reach. Reed was explicit that the intended main theatre of operations for *Devastation* was Europe, specifically the English Channel and the Mediterranean.[89]

As a result, two final masted ironclads (*Alexandra* and *Temeraire*) were laid down for the RN in 1873 and completed between 1877 and 1880. Given their long build times and the rapid advances of the 1870s (described in the next chapter), however, they were almost obsolete by the time that they entered service.[90] *Alexandra* was a development of *Sultan* with heavier armament (two 11-inch and ten 10-inch MLRs) and thicker armour (a maximum belt thickness of 12-inch and a similar thickness on the main battery). Like *Sultan* she featured a two-decked main battery but both levels included large embrasures to permit end-on fire. As it was thought unwise to have the front guns on both levels directly on top of each other, the lower gun was placed 25 feet further forward. Like other central battery ironclads, the actual value of the end-on fire provided by these recesses was debatable, and the embrasures cut into the internal volume of the hull available for accommodation.[91]

One of the last central battery ironclads built for the RN, *Alexandra* was based on the design of the preceding *Sultan* but featured heavier armament and thicker armour. Her most distinguishing feature, clearly visible in this photograph, was her two-level battery with large cut-outs fore and aft to permit end-on fire. As can also be seen, the forward gun in the lower battery was set further forward than the corresponding weapon in the upper, giving her a distinctive step-sided appearance. These steps did, however, generate large amounts of spray when she was under-way. Originally barque-rigged in addition to her vertical compound engines and armed with two 11-inch and ten 10-inch MLRs, this photograph was taken after her 1889–91 reconstruction when her rig was removed and the four 10-inch MLRs in the upper battery were replaced with 9.2-inch breech-loaders. *Alexandra* was taken out of front-line service in 1889 and eventually sold off in 1908. (© The National Archives, United Kingdom, ADM 176/19)

Alexandra did not perform well under sail and legend has it that her masts and rigging were only ever used for drill.[92] The reason for this was due to improvements in steam engine technology: *Alexandra* was one of the first battleships in the RN to be powered by new compound engines (*Dreadnought* was another), which were more efficient than the single-expansion engines fitted to previous ships. She was therefore capable of just over 15 kts and could cross the Atlantic under steam alone – she once towed a broken-down troop transport at 12 kts, which was faster than that transport's own engines had ever propelled her.[93]

Like many technological advances, compound engines had initially been pioneered in the civilian sector and were first fitted in a number of merchant ships from 1855 onwards, where their increased efficiency and improved fuel economy were felt to outweigh the slight increase in weight. In 1860 the Admiralty fitted compound engines in the wooden frigate *Constance*, and in 1865 she raced from Plymouth to Madeira against two conventionally engined sisters (*Arethusa* and *Octavia*). The result was convincingly in favour of compound engines: *Constance* was thirty miles from Madeira when her fuel ran out, compared with 200 and 160 miles for *Arethusa* and *Octavia* respectively (although how much sailing was done by each ship along the way was not taken into account).[94]

The final central battery ironclad designed for the RN, *Temeraire*, was something of a hybrid. She had an octagonal central battery containing two 11-inch and four 10-inch MLRs, but the upper deck battery was replaced by two teardrop-shaped barbettes fore and aft each mounting one 11-inch MLR on a disappearing mounting. Being muzzle-loaders, these guns had to be rotated 180° about their trunnions from the loading to firing position whilst at the same time being raised out of their barbettes and trained on to the target – a procedure said to resemble 'an elephant getting on its legs, and turning to make a charge'.[95] This arrangement was not as weight- or space-efficient as turrets and so was not repeated: *Dreadnought*'s 32½-foot diameter turrets carried two 12½-inch guns, while *Temeraire*'s larger 33-foot diameter barbettes only protected a single 11-inch weapon. Like all other central battery ironclads *Temeraire* was propelled by both sail and steam, although uniquely she was rigged as a brig with two masts. Her large size and distinctive rig earned her the nickname 'The Great Brig', although when she was given a limited modernisation in 1899 this distinguishing feature was removed.[96]

Cruisers and Smaller Vessels 1860–73

While the development of battleships in the period 1860–73 led to an apparent confusion of designs, with masts, turrets, central batteries and steam-power appearing in numerous different combinations, the form of cruisers and smaller vessels in the same period appeared to be much more stable: given their primary roles of trade protection and Imperial defence, long range and endurance were paramount and could still best be provided by sail power rather than steam. Unlike Reed's low-freeboard turret battleships, almost all the vessels described below featured masts and rigging as well as steam propulsion. That is not to say, however, that the designs of such ships were without interest: innovative technical features were often introduced first on smaller, lower cost ships before being adopted on larger vessels. This has already been remarked upon above with reference to the compound engines that were trialled in the frigate *Constance* prior to their use in the ironclads *Devastation* and *Alexandra*.

The ranges over which cruising ships had to operate were illustrated by the worldwide cruises of the Flying Squadrons. In 1868 Gladstone's ministry reduced naval strength on foreign stations and used the savings to institute a Flying Squadron intended as a worldwide quick reaction force. For the 1869 voyage it was comprised of the frigates *Liverpool*, *Liffey*, *Bristol* (replaced during the voyage by *Phoebe*) and *Endymion* and the corvettes *Scylla* (replaced by *Charybdis*) and *Barossa* (replaced by *Pearl*) and sailed under the command of the forty-four-year-old Rear Admiral Geoffrey Phipps Hornby. In seventeen months the squadron visited Brazil, Argentina, Cape Town, Australia, New Zealand, Japan, British Columbia, Hawaii and Chile, leaving from and returning to Plymouth. Similar squadrons sailed in 1874–5 and 1880–82. The

Laid down in response to the American *Wampanoag*-class commerce-raiding frigates, *Inconstant* (pictured), *Shah* and *Raleigh* were the last large unarmoured iron frigates built for the RN. Displacing 5,700 tons, *Inconstant* mounted a powerful armament of ten 9-inch and six 7-inch MLRs and was extremely fast both under sail (13½ kts) and steam (16 kts). Her armament remained largely unchanged throughout her life, although she did receive a number of light breech-loaders in the 1870s. Like many early iron warships that managed to avoid the breaker's yard on retirement, *Inconstant* was extremely long-lived: laid down in 1866, she was hulked in 1898 but remained afloat and was not broken up until 1956. (© The National Archives, United Kingdom, ADM 176/358)

strategic value of the Flying Squadron was questioned by some naval officers, however, as although the overseas strength of the RN would be boosted wherever the Flying Squadron happened to be at any one time, it would remain weak in other areas compared with the standing strength of foreign navies.[97]

The importance of defence of trade was brought home to Britain by the events of the American Civil War. The Union's blockade of the Confederacy was a success, but in turn the Confederacy's use of commerce raiders seriously affected the Union's merchant fleet. Seven Confederate cruisers captured 201 merchant ships, out of the 261 in total that the Confederacy seized. Furthermore, even more Union merchant ships were laid up, sold or transferred to other nations rather than risk capture. Overall the size of the seagoing US merchant fleet fell from 2.4 million tons in 1860 to 1.3 million in 1870 (although factors beyond Confederate raiding contributed to this, for example the post-war focus on westward-expansion instead of building merchant ships).[98]

In 1864 the US began building a number of fast wooden steam frigates for the explicit role of commerce raiding, and given the preponderance of British shipping these were taken by Britain to be aimed at her. The four ships of the *Wampanoag* class were credited with extremely high speed (it was claimed *Wampanoag* had reached 17½ kts on trial) but did not prove successful once in service. A great deal of their displacement was taken up by

machinery at the expense of crew accommodation and coal bunkers, and their fine lines (designed for high speed) meant that they could not be armed with bow guns, a weakness in ships designed to hunt down slower quarry.[99]

Nevertheless they caused alarm in Britain, and from 1866 the RN laid down their own large fast frigates in response. As with *Warrior*, these ships (*Inconstant*, *Shah* and their half-sister *Raleigh*) were larger and more capable than the foreign vessels they were intended to counter: *Wampanoag* displaced 4,215 tons while *Inconstant* displaced 5,780 tons, *Shah* 6,250 tons and *Raleigh* 5,200 tons.[100] The British ships were also built of iron while the American vessels were wooden, with all the advantages of durability and watertight subdivision that granted, and were capable of over 16 kts. Building large unarmoured iron vessels, it will be recalled, had been abandoned in the late 1840s due to concerns about battleworthiness, and therefore Reed encased their iron hulls in a 6-inch wooden sheath. Although trials had shown that this was not terribly effective as armour, it did have the benefit that a copper anti-fouling layer could be added on top of it. Given their role as cruisers spending a great deal of time at sea, this was of particular importance.[101]

The *Inconstant*-class ships were the last large unarmoured frigates constructed for the RN. They were extremely expensive to build (*Inconstant* cost £300,000, almost as much as the £377,000 for the larger armoured *Warrior*) and required a crew of 600 (only fifty

fewer than that of *Bellerophon*).[102] Instead, the smaller and cheaper corvette took their place. Given the large size of Britain's merchant marine and her far-flung interests, more numerous smaller cruisers were seen as preferable to a few expensive vessels.

To this end, three *c.* 3,000-ton iron-hulled *Volage*-class corvettes (*Volage*, *Active* and *Rover*) were laid down in 1867–72. At £130,000 per ship they were less than half the price of *Inconstant* and were completed with six 7-inch MLRs and four 64-pdrs, compared with the ten 9-inch and six 7-inch MLRs of the larger vessel.[103] They were followed by three larger (*c.* 4,000-ton) iron-hulled corvettes of the *Bacchante* class (*Bacchante*, *Boadicea* and *Euryalus*), which had a heavier armament of fourteen 7-inch MLRs.[104] Like *Inconstant*, all these iron-hulled ships were given wooden sheaths to which a copper or zinc anti-fouling layer could safely be attached. Twenty-three smaller wooden corvettes of *Jason*, *Juno*, *Eclipse*, *Briton* and *Amethyst* classes were also laid down between 1858 and 1874, all of them propelled by both sail and steam.

Smaller sloops built up to this point had been wooden (for example, the twenty vessels of the *Cameleon*, *Rosario* and *Amazon* classes launched between 1858 and 1866). This was a deliberate cost-saving measure by the Admiralty: due to the high price of iron compared with wood it had been decided only to give ships above 3,000 tons metal hulls. The composite hull came about as a compromise. In such a hull the frames and keel were made

Boadicea was a 3,900-ton iron-hulled corvette completed in 1877. She differed in appearance from her two sisters (*Bacchante* and *Euryalus*) as she had a knee-bow and figurehead (visible in photograph) while the other two had straight stems. The class comprised the last RN ships to be built wholly of iron; they came into service at a time when steel was being adopted for larger ships, while smaller masted cruisers and gunboats were being built with first composite and then steel hulls. *Boadicea* was initially armed with fourteen 7-inch and two 6-inch MLRs, although by 1885 four of her 7-inch MLRs had been replaced by four 6-inch breech-loaders. Events during her career illustrate well the varied nature of the tasks expected of RN cruisers in the latter half of the nineteenth century. She participated in anti-piracy and anti-slavery patrols off the coast of Africa, and also landed members of her crew to form part of the Naval Brigade that fought in the Zulu and First Boer Wars of 1879 and 1881 respectively. She also participated in the punitive raid on Witu (in modern-day Kenya) in 1890 in response to the murder of a number of German merchants. *Boadicea* was broken up 1905. (© The National Archives, United Kingdom, ADM 176/89)

Thalia was a 2,240-ton wooden-hulled corvette laid down in 1866 at Woolwich Royal Dockyard, and was the last ship to be completed at that yard as it closed after she was delivered in 1870. She and her sister *Juno* were designed to serve as transports, and their lower decks were consequently given over to troop accommodation. Her initial armament of two 7-inch MLRs and four 64-pdr MLRs was repeated in the following *Eclipse* class, although *Thalia* herself was rearmed with a uniform armament of six 64-pdr MLRs in 1876. She was finally broken up in 1920. (© The National Archives, United Kingdom, ADM 176/701)

Egeria was a 940-ton *Fantome*-class sloop launched in 1874. The *Fantome* class comprised the first RN sloops to be given composite hulls, and were also the first sloops to be powered by compound engines. Their armament (two 7-inch guns and two 64-pdr MLRs) was notable as being entirely mounted on centreline pivots, after the fashion of contemporary gunvessels, rather than on a mixture of pivots and broadside mountings as in previous sloops. *Egeria* was the longest-lived of her class, probably by virtue of the fact that she was converted into a survey ship, and was only sold off in 1911. (© The National Archives, United Kingdom, ADM 176/229)

Penguin, a 1,130-ton composite-hulled sloop launched in 1876. One of five *Osprey*-class vessels, she was armed with two 7-inch and four 64-pdr MLRs. Like the preceding *Amazon* and *Fantome* class sloops, the 7-inch MLRs of the *Osprey* class were mounted on pivots on the centreline, a configuration shared with contemporary gunvessels, while the 64-pdrs were side-mounted. *Penguin* has a special significance to the author: his great-great-grandfather served in the RN during the period covered by the present book, including as a stoker aboard *Penguin* during the late 1870s when she was stationed in the Pacific. *Penguin* had a long and varied life: she was converted into a survey ship in 1890, became a harbour depot ship in 1909 and was then transferred to the Royal Australian Navy in 1913. She was finally sold off in 1924, but was still in use as a crane vessel when she was lost to a fire in 1960. (© The National Archives, United Kingdom, ADM 176/515)

The *Osprey*-class sloop *Wild Swan*, launched in 1876. *Wild Swan* was one of only two of the class to be rearmed, receiving two 6-inch and six 5-inch breech-loaders in place of all of her MLRs during the mid-1880s. This photograph shows her following her rearmament and the layout of these new guns can clearly be seen. *Wild Swan* was sold off in 1920. (© The National Archives, United Kingdom, ADM 176/776)

Garnet, a 2,100-ton composite-hulled corvette completed in 1878. She was a member of the *Emerald* class, one of the few classes of RN corvettes to be built with composite hulls before steel took over as the preferred material for warship construction. Like the other ships of the class she was originally armed with twelve 64-pdr MLRs (ten on the broadside and two on centre-line pivots) but was the only ship of the class to be rearmed with fourteen 5-inch breech-loaders (ten on the broadside and the remaining four as chase guns). *Garnet* was sold off in 1904. (© The National Archives, United Kingdom, ADM 176/288)

Tourmaline was 2,100-ton composite-hulled corvette of the *Emerald* class that was completed in 1876. She was originally armed with a uniform broadside armament of twelve 64-pdr MLRs, but in the mid-1880s was rearmed, as shown in this photograph, with four shielded 6-inch breech-loaders and eight broadside-mounted 5-inch breech-loaders. All of the six vessels of the class were plagued with extremely unreliable engines, but they were reportedly so bad on *Tourmaline* that they drove her chief engineer to a nervous breakdown and suicide. *Tourmaline* was sold off and scrapped 1920. (© The National Archives, United Kingdom, ADM 176/716)

of iron, giving the hull greater strength than one made purely of wood and allowing for effective watertight subdivision, but these were then clad in wood rather than iron. This was first used in the gunboat *Vixen* of 1864 (see below) and was introduced in larger ships with the six 940-ton *Fantome*-class and five 1,130-ton *Osprey*-class sloops laid-down in 1874–7. It was also used for the six larger 2,120-ton *Emerald*-class corvettes laid down in 1874–7. These composite hulls were rapidly eclipsed in larger cruisers such as corvettes by the use of steel as the main structural material,

although masted sloops continued to be built with composite hulls up to the late 1880s.[105]

Sloops had originally been used as cruising vessels like their larger cousin the frigate, but as this role was taken over by the corvette they came to resemble something more akin to a large gunvessel. No longer suitable for tackling enemy cruisers, sloops served as colonial police vessels and as such retained their sails. Tellingly, the sloop's frigate-style broadside-mounted armament was replaced by gunvessel-type centre-line pivot guns in the *Amazon* class, and this arrangement

continued in the sloops of the 1870s and 1880s. The armament of the *Amazon*, *Fantome* and *Osprey* classes (two 7-inch MLRs and two or four 64-pdr MLRs) was very similar to that of the contemporary *Plover*-class gunvessels (one 7-inch MLR and two 64-pdr MLRs) described in the next section, rather than that of the new, large metal-hulled corvettes from *Volage* onwards.[106]

Gunvessels and Gunboats

The terms 'gunboat' and 'gunvessel' were used to denote small shallow-draught vessels (typically sub-1,000 tons displacement) usually armed with between two and six heavy guns. Although originally oar-powered, by the 1850s British craft of these types were powered by both sail and steam in common with their larger contemporaries. Large numbers of gunboats and gunvessels were built as part of the Crimean War Great Armament, but by the mid-1860s these quickly-constructed vessels, many of which had been laid-up on completion rather than entering service, had deteriorated and so replacements were needed.[107] In the same way as with the larger sloops and corvettes, successive classes introduced improvements in hull construction technology by moving from wooden to composite hulls.

In total forty-four wooden gunvessels of the *Philomel*, *Cormorant*, *Plover* and *Frolic* classes were constructed between 1859 and 1872. The first of these, the nineteen *Philomel* vessels laid down between 1859 and 1862 displaced 570 tons and mounted a mixed armament of a single 110-pdr breech-loader, two 20-pdr breech-loaders and two 24-pdr howitzers. The nine *Cormorant*-class ships of 1860–67 were the largest of the wooden gunvessels at 877 tons and they initially mounted a similar armament to the *Philomel* class, although this was later changed to a single 7-inch MLR and two 64-pdr smooth-bores. The ships did not remain long in service and most had been broken up by the mid-1870s, although three *Cormorant*-class ships did serve as survey vessels and lasted longer. The twelve *Plover* and four *Frolic*-class ships that followed were

slightly smaller than the *Cormorant* class, at 755 and 610 tons respectively, but mounted a similar armament. The *Plover*-class ships were all out of service by 1888, but the *Frolic*-class ships seem to have lasted until the turn of the twentieth century.[108]

Like corvettes and sloops, gunvessels and gunboats were initially considered too small to warrant the expense of iron hulls. The three-ship *Vixen*-class ships (*Vixen*, *Viper* and *Waterwitch*) laid down in 1864 were notable for *Vixen* being the first composite-hulled warships in RN service (the other two being made of iron). They were an attempt to build an armoured gunboat, after the pattern of the ironclad battleship, and at 1,200 tons they were protected by 4½ inches of iron over 10 inches wood and mounted two 7-inch MLRs and two 20-pdrs. *Waterwitch* was even more novel, being double-ended and propelled by an early form of water-jet. Despite a menacing appearance, resembling 'enormous black crocodiles, with long low silhouettes and blunt snout-bows',[109] they handled extremely badly and were regarded as failures. The experiment was consequently not repeated.[110]

Although the attempt to design a viable armoured gunboat failed, the composite hull was seen as a success. The eighteen 603-ton *Beacon*-class ships of 1867–8 introduced such hulls into gunvessels, and were also notable in that each was powered by two engines salvaged from scrapped Crimean-era gunboats.[111]

Conventional gunboats showed a similar progression in technology:

the sixteen 330-ton wooden *Britomart* class of 1860–67 (armed with two guns each) were followed by nine slightly larger (430-ton) *Ariel*-class ships in 1871–3 that featured composite hulls.[112] Both introduced design features first seen on larger warships into gunboats: the *Britomart* class featured lifting screws, which improved their sailing performance, while the *Ariels* marked a further improvement with the incorporation of watertight subdivision and compound engines. Both these classes therefore had improved sailing performance, which was especially important in their role as colonial police vessels as it granted them the strategic mobility to cover Britain's widely spread global interests.[113] In conjunction with these masted 'cruising' gunboats, other vessels were constructed purely for coastal assault and defence: twenty 254-ton *Ant*-class Rendel or 'flatiron' gunboats propelled entirely by steam and armed with a single 10-inch MLR were launched in 1870–74.

In a war against another European power, gunboats and gunvessels would likely have performed the same role as their Crimean War forebears, namely close in-shore work such as blockade and land-attack. The international situation was such that they were never called upon to discharge this function against a European enemy, but given Britain's desire to expand her global trade they were used in this way elsewhere in the world. The Second Opium War of 1856–60 was fought to compel China to obey the provisions of the Treaty of Nanking of 1842 that had ended the First

Opium War. The actions at Fatshan Creek and at the mouth of the Pei Ho River showed these little craft in their element: operating close in-shore where larger warships could not venture to both engage other ships and to capture positions ashore.[114]

As well as engaging in set-piece attacks against the instruments of the Chinese state, the task of suppressing piracy in the Far East also fell to such vessels. This led to them being used to mount numerous small-scale assaults against villages and other coastal communities known to harbour pirates. By and large such actions appear to have had the desired effect: in 1860 there were twenty-four gunboats and six gunvessels on the China Station, but by 1873 these numbers had fallen to three and eleven respectively in light of the reduced threat. Small craft were also called upon to defend Britain's interests in the rest of the world. This included the suppression of the slave trade in both East and West African waters that, like the campaign against Far Eastern piracy, placed a premium on large numbers of small vessels able to operate close in-shore.[115]

One of twenty Ant-class flatiron gunboats launched between 1870 and 1874, Pike was armed with a single 10-inch MLR. Given their small size and low freeboard, both evident in this photograph, these vessels were obviously intended purely for operations close to the shore, either defending the British coast or attacking that of an enemy. As part of the general run-down of the RN's gunboat fleet from 1889 onwards, Pike was converted into a boom defence vessel in 1908 and was sold off in 1920. (© The National Archives, United Kingdom, ADM 176/527)

Chapter 3

Steel, Turrets and Torpedoes 1873–89

The RN finished the 1860s with a battlefleet almost completely composed of large iron-hulled ships that enjoyed qualitative superiority over the more homogenous but wooden-hulled ironclads of its only serious competitor, France. Other European navies, such as Russia, lagged behind the RN both in the quality and quantity of ships they possessed. The defeat of France by Prussia in 1871 only improved the situation by removing Napoleon III from power and ensured that, for the short term at least, France would have to concentrate on rebuilding her army and paying off reparations. For a period in the early- and mid-1870s, therefore, Britannia truly did rule the waves.

The traditional historical view is that this command of the seas was squandered from the mid-1870s to the mid-1880s by a succession of parsimonious governments who were more concerned with economy than naval superiority.[1] Although ships were becoming individually more expensive, the Naval Estimates were kept at around £11 million over the period.[2] The result was the rate at which capital ships were constructed for the RN slowed dramatically as the decade progressed: in 1866–8 thirteen ironclads were laid down, followed by a further eleven in the period 1868–74, but only nine were begun during 1874–80 of which five were underway by 1876.[3] The supposed pursuit of economy meant that the displacement of these vessels was constrained to reduce their cost and so compromised their protection and fighting power. At the same time, building fewer ships increased the time taken to complete each one, and so these ships often found themselves made obsolete by the rapid pace of technological change soon after they entered service.

At the same time France embarked on a major shipbuilding programme. From 1875 to 1880, France laid down thirteen sea-going battleships and a further four coastal defence battleships, more than twice the British figures in the same period.[4]

It has been suggested that these French ships were better protected by their complete thick belts than contemporary British vessels with their thick central citadels and unarmoured ends.[5] When war threatened, as it did in the Russian War Scares of 1878 and 1885, the RN had to resort to the short-term expediency of buying ships being built in British yards for other countries to supplement its strength.

This traditional view has been challenged in recent years, however, by historians such as Beeler and Lambert, who have sought to overturn the view that the RN was hamstrung by government penny-pinching.[6] They point instead to wider strategic and technological causes for the low building rates seen between 1874 and 1880. Money was certainly tight in the late 1870s as the government was financing colonial wars in Afghanistan and Africa, and the 1878 Russian War Scare additionally resulted in budget deficits of over £2 million each year between 1877 and 1880, but this was not the only reason for the reduction in warship building.[7]

Strategically, there was no need to maintain the building rate of the 1860s into the 1870s because, as noted, the RN was clearly the world's premier maritime fighting force. In the 1870s, therefore, Britain reaped a 'peace dividend' from the collapse of the French naval challenge and in this climate no government would continue to build expensive ships when there was no obvious need. Although the French building programme of 1875–80 caused some concern in Britain, it was recognised that the situation was very different from 1860. Then, France had attempted to steal a march on the RN by introducing a new type of warship, but the intention of the building programme fifteen years later was simply to replace these early ironclads that, thanks to their wooden construction, were having to be retired. In the period 1876–85 France completed seven First Class iron- and steel-hulled battleships and launched a further seven, but by 1885 eleven early ironclads had been taken out of service and a further three followed in 1890.[8]

The low British building rate in the mid- to late-1870s was also a conscious reaction to the rapidly evolving state of naval technology. Iron was being replaced by steel, the traditional British reliance on muzzle-loading artillery was being challenged and the arrival of the torpedo was claimed by some to herald the end of the large armoured warship as an effective combatant. Faced by this, the Admiralty decided

to hedge its bets by not committing itself to building large numbers of expensive warships that, for all it knew, could quickly become outdated. The RN was also at the forefront of technical innovation, being one of the first navies to adopt the torpedo.

When challenged, however, British governments did show that they were willing to spend money to preserve the RN's superiority. The continuation of the French capital-ship building programme into the early 1880s prompted the building of six *Admiral*-class battleships, the first homogenous class of British battleships since the late 1860s, and subsequently two final classes of turret-armed vessels. Concerns about the threat to British trade from French and Russian cruisers also led to the development of fast, well-protected cruisers that dispensed with the sailing rig that had hitherto been the mark of such vessels. The 1880s also marked the beginning of public concerns over the strength of the RN, and this was ultimately to lead to the Naval Defence Act of 1889.

Technical Innovation 1873–89

There were three main areas in which naval technology progressed between 1873 and 1889: the introduction of steel, improvements in naval ordnance and the invention of the torpedo.

Steel for Hulls and Armour

By 1870 iron had largely replaced wood in the construction of large British warships, but the

introduction of stronger steel offered the potential to make even lighter structures that could bear the same loads. This was obviously beneficial to warships as a lighter structure could free up weight for heavier guns and armour. Steel could also be made harder than iron and so offered the possibility of making armour thinner (and therefore lighter) than a comparable protective thickness of wrought iron.[9] Initially, however, steel proved too brittle to be used by itself as effective armour and so compound armour, where a hard steel face-plate was welded to a thick iron backing, was adopted in an attempt to combine the best qualities of both materials.

Somewhat surprisingly, France took the lead over Britain in the manufacture of high-quality steel and consequently was the first nation to construct a steel battleship. The problem for Britain was not that France produced larger quantities of steel than her: in 1875 Britain produced 719,000 metric tonnes, 150,000 tonnes more than the combined output of France and Germany and almost as much as the entire steel production of all of Europe. Instead, due to different processes used from the Continent, in the early 1870s not enough British steel was of sufficiently high enough quality to be used in warship construction, and the large British investment in existing iron production facilities slowed adoption of better manufacturing techniques.[10]

The French 9,224-ton central battery ironclad *Redoubtable*, laid down in 1873 and completed in 1878, was consequently the world's first steel battleship. She was followed by two larger sisters, *Courbet* and *Dévastation*, which were completed in 1882 and 1886 respectively. Although referred to as central battery ships, only four guns were mounted in their batteries and another four were carried in barbettes on the upper deck – subsequent French battleships would dispense with the central battery altogether and instead mount their entire main armament in barbettes. The French were therefore in a position to build up a lead over the British in steel battleships, just as they had been with iron. Financial problems and production difficulties on the part of the French and a battleship construction programme by Britain, however, ultimately meant that this challenge could not be sustained.[11]

In Britain, steel was initially used in small amounts in engine and gun manufacture as well as in non-vital areas of ironclads like *Audacious* and *Hercules*.[12] The first RN warships with steel hulls, however, were the two 3,730-ton despatch vessels (later re-rated as Second Class cruisers) *Iris* and *Mercury* laid down in 1875–6. The weight saved by the introduction of steel was used to carry sufficiently powerful machinery to provide a top speed under steam of 17 kts. They were unarmoured, instead relying on coal bunkers to both protect their machinery (2 feet of coal being thought to be equivalent to 1 inch of iron armour) and preserving

Mercury, the sister-ship of *Iris*. Taken in March 1890, this photograph shows the appearance of the two ships after their rig had been reduced and they had been rearmed in 1886–7 with a uniform outfit of thirteen 5-inch breech-loaders. *Mercury* was even faster than her sister and was capable of over 18½ kts, which made her the fastest warship in the world when she was launched in 1879. *Mercury* lasted longer than her sister: she was converted into a submarine depot ship in 1905 before being sold off in 1919. (© The National Archives, United Kingdom, ADM 176/445)

The RN's first warship with a steel hull, *Iris* was a 3,700-ton dispatch vessel (later Second Class cruiser) that was laid down in 1875 and completed in 1879. As befitted her intended role, she was given a very high top speed and proved capable, once given suitable propellers, of making nearly 18 kts. This photograph shows *Iris* early in her career when she was still rigged as a barque. *Iris* could be distinguished from her sister *Mercury* as she had a clipper bow instead of *Mercury*'s straight stem. She was sold off in 1905. (© The National Archives, United Kingdom, ADM 176/367)

buoyancy when flooded. They were fitted with sailing rig, but this was soon removed to leave them entirely steam-propelled.[13]

Improvements in Naval Ordnance

The performance of British muzzle-loading guns originally compared well with that of breech-loaders, but new developments in the 1870s made them increasingly less competitive. A major advance was slow-burning gunpowder, which kept the pressure behind a projectile for longer and therefore increased its velocity and also decreased the initial pressure in the breech. This meant that guns did not have to be as strong around the breech as had previously been the case, eliminating a major source of weakness in early breech-loaders.[14] To take advantage of this increased burn time, guns had to be longer as otherwise not all of the charge was consumed before the projectile reached the end of the barrel. There was a limit, however, to how far this could be applied to muzzle-loading weapons as the gun-crew still had to have access to the muzzle in order to be able to insert the charge and projectile. Indeed, later British MLR-armed battleships had to have loading arrangements external to their turrets (in deckhouses or recessed into the deck) as their guns could not be run fully back into their turrets.[15] This was obviously not a problem for breech-loading guns, which could be made long enough to exploit these new powders without interfering with their loading and operation.

In 1878, therefore, Armstrong started to develop large breech-loaders again, and incorporated the French innovation of an interrupted-screw breech-block that prevented the gun from firing if the breech was not fully closed. This addressed the Admiralty's main concerns over the safety of breech-loaders relative to MLRs. The bursting of one of *Thunderer*'s front guns in January 1879, which killed eleven and injured thirty-five, provided further impetus for change as the accident was caused by double-loading, which could not happen to breech-loaders. In light of the greater performance and safety of breech-loaders compared with MLRs, it was therefore decided in 1879 to fit the next class of British battleships (*Colossus* and *Edinburgh*) with breech-loading main guns.[16]

The technology of smaller-calibre weaponry also improved in this period. The rise of the small, fast torpedo boat described in the next section prompted the War Office in 1881 to invite designs for a gun capable of firing twelve 6-lb shells a minute. By 1883 both Hotchkiss and Nordenfelt had developed suitable weapons and Elswick was trialling a quick-firing 4.7-inch gun capable of ten rounds per minute. Although this weapon was of similar calibre to the existing 5-inch breech-loader, its revised breech and mounting meant that its rate-of-fire was up to six times higher. This 4.7-inch quick-firer (QF) was developed by the end of the 1880s into a 6-inch weapon with a rate-of-fire of five rounds per minute. This became the standard secondary armament to the battleships and

cruisers of the 1890s both for use against unarmoured opponents and also to attack the lightly armoured areas of major enemy warships.[17]

The Introduction of the Locomotive Torpedo

While replacing MLRs with breech-loaders was an evolution in the state-of-the-art of naval firepower, the introduction of the self-propelled or locomotive torpedo in the 1870s appeared to be revolutionary: underwater attack offered the prospect of a 'wonder weapon' capable of sinking even the most powerful ironclad with a single hit.

In the mid-nineteenth century the word 'torpedo' was used to refer to any underwater explosive weapon. Command-detonated mines had been employed by the Prussians to protect Kiel against the Danish in 1848, and the Crimean War saw the use of primitive contact mines by the Russians. In the following decade, the American Civil War saw the successful use of both fixed mines and small craft armed with spar torpedoes – the latter accounting for the Federal sloop *Housatonic* and the Confederate ironclad *Albermarle* in 1864. These spar torpedoes consisted of an explosive charge mounted on the end of a long pole and, like their cousins the towed Harvey torpedoes, often proved as dangerous to the craft armed with them as to their targets.[18]

A major attraction of the locomotive torpedo was its increased stand-off range, which had the potential to remove the danger to the firing craft. This range also increased the element of surprise and made it harder for the target to take evasive action: it was harder to spot a small submerged torpedo than it was an enemy launch, no matter how small or fast it might have been. By 1868, the first practical self-propelled torpedo had been developed in Fiume by an Austrian, Johann Luppis, and an expatriate Briton, Robert Whitehead. Luppis had developed the initial version but it required the addition of Whitehead's depth-regulator (the so-called 'Whitehead Secret') to turn it into an effective weapon.[19] Whitehead and Luppis succeeded in selling the weapon to the Austrian navy and then approached the RN to do the same. Although they were initially unsuccessful, the RN observed a demonstration at Fiume in 1869 and based on the strength of the recommendations in the resulting report agreed to purchase the Whitehead Secret in July 1871.[20] This made Britain the first country, after Austria, to adopt the torpedo – well in advance of other European nations.[21]

In so doing the RN showed considerable foresight as the torpedo was not initially the fearsome weapon that it would become in the twentieth century. The 1872 incarnation of Whitehead's weapon carried a 115-lb warhead for 400 yards at a speed of 8 kts, which was slower than the maximum speed of any of the large ironclads that such weapons were supposed to threaten. Early torpedoes therefore posed little threat to a battlefleet in good condition with room to manoeuvre, although damaged or anchored vessels were obviously far more vulnerable. Development of the

torpedo continued, however, and by 1884 Woolwich was producing a version under licence armed with a 70-lb warhead and a range of 600 yards at 24 kts. It was arguably not until the turn of the twentieth century, however, with the extra range and speed granted by the adoption of the air heater and the extra accuracy given by the invention of gyroscopic steering and depth control, that the torpedo fulfilled all of its original promise.[22]

A Torpedo Committee was established in 1873 to consider how best to exploit the new weapon and its recommendations would guide its incorporation into the RN for the rest of the century. It concluded that the locomotive torpedo was vastly superior to the spar and towed versions and so recommended their removal from service, as well as reporting on initial attempts at using nets to protect warships against the new threat. The Committee also recommended that torpedo launchers be fitted to RN vessels then in service and incorporated into the designs of those building. This recommendation was acted upon and the first use of a locomotive torpedo in anger anywhere in the world came in 1877 when the unarmoured iron frigate *Shah* fired one unsuccessfully at the rebel Peruvian ironclad *Huascar*. Finally, the Committee recommended the construction of both large and small specialist craft armed primarily with locomotive torpedoes.[23]

RN Torpedo Vessels 1874–89

The RN quickly started building these specialised torpedo craft. The

first of these, *Vesuvius*, was laid down in 1873 and completed in 1874. A small vessel of 245 tons, she was a low-freeboard craft armed with a single bow tube and given coke-burning engines, which vented underwater (although a funnel was fitted for use in peacetime) in an effort to minimise the amount of smoke she produced.[24] Given her low top speed of 9½ kts, her design suggests that the primary role envisaged for her was for stealthy attacks on enemy ships in port.[25] Indeed, she was built at a time when, as discussed in the previous chapter, the RN was clearly building other warships expressly intended for attacking heavily defended anchorages.

Stealth also dominated the design of *Vesuvius*'s successor, the famous *Polyphemus*. Laid down in 1878 and completed four years later, *Polyphemus* was a much larger vessel of 2,640 tons armed with five torpedo tubes (one bow and four broadside), eighteen reloads and a ram. She was given a low silhouette by virtue of her cigar-shaped hull, which would be largely submerged, and a small upper hull and superstructure, and was one of the first RN warships to be given a low-visibility grey paint scheme. To allow her to close rapidly with her targets she was given the (for the time) incredible top speed of 18 kts, and in case she was not successful at avoiding detection a curved 3-inch steel protective deck protected her vitals.[26]

The RN had high hopes that *Polyphemus* would displace the larger and more expensive ironclad as the preferred form of capital ship (*Polyphemus* cost £226,000), but the increasing range and rate-of-fire of naval ordnance in the decade after her launch quickly rendered her too vulnerable and so she remained a one-off. At the time of her design, however, guns capable of penetrating her armour did not have the rate-of-fire or ease of training required to engage successfully warships travelling at the speeds of which she was capable. She remains one of the most well-known Victorian warships, thanks largely to having captured the public's attention by dramatically breaking the barrier protecting Berehaven during the 1885 Manoeuvres, and is generally taken to have appeared, under the alias *Thunder Child*, in H.G. Wells' *War of the Worlds*.[27]

First Class Torpedo Boats

In accordance with the recommendations of the 1873 Torpedo Committee, smaller purpose-built craft were also constructed for the RN. Firms such as Thornycroft and Yarrow had already started building high-speed steam launches in the early 1870s and successfully sold them to foreign navies to act as towed- or spar-torpedo craft.[28] They were therefore keen to sell such vessels to the RN as well, and Thornycroft lobbied as such from 1874 onwards. This evidently paid off, as in 1876 Thornycroft was contracted to construct *Torpedo Boat No. 1 (Lightning)* that, as her name suggests, was the RN's first torpedo boat. This 87-foot 32½-ton craft was capable of 19 kts and was initially armed with two 'torpedo

frames' amidships, which were lowered into the water to discharge the weapons, but these were replaced by a single bow tube with two reloads in 1879.[29] *TB 1* was followed by an order of eleven very similar craft (*TB 2–12*) from Thornycroft in 1878–9, which completed with a single bow tube instead of *Lightning*'s two cradles, as well as seven further *Lightning*s (*TB 13–15* and *TB 17–20*) from a number of other builders by 1880. Four larger (113-foot 64-ton) craft were ordered from Thornycroft (*TB 21–22*) and Yarrow (*TB 23–24*) in 1884–6; the extra displacement and length enabled their armament to be increased to two torpedo tubes and, for the first time on British torpedo boats, two 3-pdr guns.[30]

Both France and Russia saw the torpedo boat as a cheap and effective counter to the RN's strength in large armoured warships and consequently built large numbers. In France they formed a key part of the *Jeune École* movement of the 1880s, not only as a defensive weapon but also to attack British merchant vessels and coastal installations. The Russians demonstrated how a fleet of small torpedo craft could neutralise a stronger navy during the Russo–Turkish War of 1877–8 where the powerful Turkish fleet, which included the largest central battery ironclad in the world (*Mesudiye*), was largely deterred from acting by an aggressive Russian force of small torpedo-armed steam launches supported by a number of tenders. This war saw the first successful use of the locomotive torpedo when, less than a year after *Shah*'s

unsuccessful attempt, two Russian steam launches sank the Turkish gunboat *Intikbah* during a night attack on Batum on 25–6 January 1878.[31]

When Britain was faced with the threat of war with Russia in 1885 over the latter's advances in Central Asia (particularly the Russian attack on Afghanistan at Panjdeh), the RN was faced with the threat of confronting a navy equipped with a large number of torpedo craft that had recently demonstrated the ability to use them. The RN's response was to commission larger torpedo boats of its own that were designed to protect the battlefleet from attack by Russian torpedo craft.[32] This foreshadowed the development of the torpedo boat destroyer in the 1890s, although the 1885 craft were ultimately completed with additional torpedo tubes in place of their designed heavy guns armament. Fifty-three of these 20-kt, 125-foot, 60-ton vessels (armed with one bow and two twin torpedo tubes and two twin-barrelled Nordenfelt machine-guns) were ordered between 1885 and 1887.[33] In addition, one 153-foot White boat (*TB 81*) and two 100-foot, one 105-foot and six 130-foot Yarrow craft (*TB 39-40, TB 80* and *TB 82-87*) were ordered or purchased from those building for other navies at the same time.[34] All these early torpedo craft suffered from a lack of freeboard, which greatly reduced their ability to operate in all but fine weather, and so the Yarrow 130-foot boats were the first to be fitted with a turtle-back forecastle (characteristic of later destroyers) in an attempt to improve their sea-keeping.[35]

Torpedo Boat No. 38 was a one of a large number of 125-foot torpedo boats built for the RN in response to the Russian War Scare of 1885. TB 38 was built by the firm of White and, like the 125-foot torpedo boats from other builders, she was given the armament visible here of five 14-inch torpedo tubes (one in the bow and two twin tubes on deck) and two machine-guns, although some thought was initially given to completing all the 125-foot boats with only the bow tube and two extra 3-pdr guns to enable them to be used as torpedo boat destroyers. TB 38 was still in service at the outbreak of the First World War, based at Hong Kong, and like most of the surviving 125-foot torpedo boats was used for patrol and harbour defence duties before being broken up in 1919. (© The National Archives, United Kingdom, ADM 176/728a)

Torpedo Boat No. 41 was built by Thornycroft on the pattern of the prototype 125-foot craft, Torpedo Boat No. 25. That original craft was completed with a ram bow that proved totally unsuitable and so it was replaced with a simple straight stem and her bow torpedo tube was removed. This configuration was carried over into derived boats like TB 41, and can be seen here. The Thornycroft 125-foot boats therefore had no fixed tube forward, and indeed in this photograph TB 41 does not appear to mount any torpedo tubes at all. TB 41 served in the First World War and was broken up shortly afterwards. (© The National Archives, United Kingdom, ADM 176/728b)

Torpedo Boat No. 63 was built by Yarrow and, like all 125-foot boats built by that firm, featured the ram bow visible here. This photograph therefore also gives some indication of the appearance of *TB 25* and other Thornycroft 125-foot boats before their stems were rebuilt, although it should be noted that the Yarrow design was more successful and did not have to be replaced. *TB 63* served in the First World War, being initially based at Malta before being sent to defend the Suez Canal against the Turkish advance in 1915. She was broken up once hostilities had ended. (© The National Archives, United Kingdom, ADM 176/728c)

Begun as a private venture and named *Swift*, this vessel was purchased by the RN during the 1885 Russian War Scare and redesignated *Torpedo Boat No. 81*. Some thought was given to completing her with a heavy gun armament so that she could fulfil the role of a torpedo boat destroyer (several years before the RN commissioned its first TBDs), but she was ultimately fitted with a mixed gun and torpedo armament. This photograph shows most of her weaponry to good effect: her three 14-inch torpedo tubes can easily be discerned (one fixed in the bow and two on deck), as can two of her four 3-pdr guns. *TB 81* continued to serve throughout the First World War, with the addition of depth charges and primitive acoustic-detection equipment, and was finally broken up in 1921. Looming over her in the background is the white-painted *Crocodile*, a 4,100-ton troop-transport (launched in 1867 and sold in 1894) that regularly plied between Britain and India. (© The National Archives, United Kingdom, ADM 176/729)

Yarrow-built *Torpedo Boat No. 80* was one of the first of such craft to be built for the RN with a turtle-back forecastle to improve sea-keeping, a feature later incorporated into the TBDs of the 1890s. Like many RN torpedo boats of the period she was designed to be armed either mainly with torpedoes (one fixed bow tube, four deck tubes and three 3-pdrs) or with guns (the fixed bow torpedo tube plus four 3-pdrs) depending on if she was to be used as a pure torpedo boat or as a torpedo boat destroyer. She is usually recorded as having spent most of her life with the torpedo-heavy armament, but this photograph appears to show her in her alternative configuration with only the single bow tube and four 3-pdr guns. *TB 80* served as a patrol vessel during the First World War and was broken up in 1921. (© The National Archives, United Kingdom, ADM 176/729a)

Second Class Torpedo Boats

The 1873 Torpedo Committee also recommended that small torpedo craft capable of being carried on ships' davits be developed to give large warships an organic torpedo-attack capability in addition to their own torpedo launchers. The development of these Second Class torpedo boats was also inspired by the success of similar craft in Russian hands in the 1877–8 Russo-Turkish War.[36] The sixty-four built for the RN between 1878 and 1889, as well as a further eighteen for the Colonial navies, ranged in size from 11 to 16 tons, were capable of 15–16 kts and were typically armed with one or two torpedoes and a similar number of machine-guns. The RN Second Class torpedo boats were designated *TB 1–12* and *TB 39–100* and were built almost exclusively by Thornycroft, Yarrow and White, the only exception being *TB 63*, which was built in the USA by Herreschoff and was therefore the only foreign-built RN ship of any size of the entire period.[37] Ultimately, Second Class torpedo boats were not a success because of their small size and no more were built after 1889.

Although Second Class torpedo boats were conceived initially to be carried by warships, two dedicated torpedo boat base ships were also commissioned into the RN. These were also designed to act as tenders to larger torpedo vessels, where such boats could be repaired, replenished and rearmed. The importance of this type of dedicated vessel was highlighted by Russian experience in the Black Sea in 1877–8 where nineteen 1,000–1,500-ton merchant ships were requisitioned to act as tenders for their fleet of small torpedo craft.[38] Accordingly, in 1878 the 6,400-ton merchant vessel *British Crown* was bought whilst under construction and commissioned as *Hecla*, the RN's first torpedo boat tender. She was followed in 1889 by the purpose-built 6,600-ton *Vulcan*. While *Hecla* had a light armament of five 68-pdr MLRs, *Vulcan* was given a protective armoured deck like contemporary cruisers (2–5 inches thick) and armed with eight 4.7-inch guns. The two ships served in the Mediterranean Fleet and were instrumental in developing the RN's torpedo tactics.[39]

Torpedo Cruisers and Torpedo Gunboats

The need to defend against the Russian torpedo boat fleet in 1885 had led to the building of the 125-foot First Class torpedo boats,

Following Russia's successful use of torpedo craft against Turkey in 1878, the RN purchased the 6,400-ton merchant vessel *British Crown* whilst she was still under construction and commissioned her as *Hecla*, the RN's first torpedo boat depot ship. Although this photograph is undated, it appears to show her appearance after she was rebuilt in 1912. *Hecla* was finally sold in 1926. (© The National Archives, United Kingdom, ADM 176/329)

The torpedo boat base-ship *Vulcan* in a photograph taken in July 1893 that shows her similarity to contemporary cruisers, save for the large goose-necked cranes designed for launching and recovering torpedo boats. Unlike *Hecla*, she had a relatively heavy armament of eight 4.7-inch and twelve 3-pdr guns and was protected by an armoured deck. She also carried six Second Class torpedo boats, a number of which can be seen in this photograph beneath the cranes. As well as being designed to rearm torpedo craft, her speed (*c.* 20 kts), protection and armament suggest that she would have had an offensive role in the event of war, carrying her torpedo boats into positions from which they could launch their own attacks on the enemy. In later years she was used as a submarine depot ship, and was converted into a training ship in 1931. She was finally broken up in 1955. (© The National Archives, United Kingdom, ADM 176/761)

but at the same time the RN was constructing a number of small cruisers intended not only for anti-torpedo boat protection but also as offensive torpedo craft in their own right. The first of these torpedo cruisers were *Scout* and *Fearless*, laid down in 1884 and completed in 1885 and 1887 respectively. These 1,580-ton ships were capable of 17 kts, were protected by a thin splinter-proof deck and were armed with three torpedo launchers, four 5-inch breech-loaders and eight 3-pdr quick-firers. Two similar vessels (*Surprise* and *Alacrity*) were completed as armed dispatch vessels.[40]

Scout and *Fearless* were followed by eight larger *Archer*-class torpedo cruisers of nearly 2,000 tons, constructed between 1885 and 1891 as part of the Northbrook Programme. The extra displacement was necessary to incorporate a heavier gun armament of six 6-inch breech-loaders, but this extra top-weight made them unsteady and consequently poor gun platforms. Ultimately, the torpedo cruisers proved not to be a success as they were too slow to be effective in their intended role and all were reclassified as Third Class cruisers shortly after completion. Even then they were a dead-end in design terms, with subsequent Third Class cruisers being derived from the *Medea*-class cruisers (described below) rather than these vessels.[41]

Also conceived to protect the fleet from torpedo attack were the

Fearless, one of two 1,580-ton *Scout*-class cruisers laid down in 1884. Intended for fleet torpedo work (both defensive and offensive), these ships were too slow for their designed role and were instead reclassified as Third Class cruisers. *Fearless*'s torpedo armament can be seen in this photograph: she had a single fixed bow tube and two trainable launchers that could fire through ports (visible beneath her forecastle and poop) on either side of the ship. In addition, she carried four 5-inch breech-loaders (two per side in shielded mountings), which were replaced by 4.7-inch quick-firers during the 1890s, and eight 3-pdr quick-firers. The RN persisted with the concept of the torpedo cruiser with the *Archer* class, for which the design of the *Scout* class formed the basis despite their lack of success in the role. *Fearless* was sold off in 1905. (© The National Archives, United Kingdom, ADM 176/258)

The 1,650-ton *Surprise*, photographed at Portsmouth in August 1886 some two months after she was completed. Based on the *Scout*-class torpedo cruisers, *Surprise* and her sister *Alacrity* were despatch vessels intended mainly for the high-speed transport of messages and personnel. They were also armed with four 5-inch breech-loaders for their alternative wartime role as scouts, although *Surprise*'s weapons are not apparent in this photograph. *Surprise* survived until 1919, taking her sister's name in 1913 when *Alacrity* was sold off. (© The National Archives, United Kingdom, ADM 176/682)

Serpent was an *Archer*-class torpedo cruiser laid down in 1885 and completed in 1888. She was armed with six 6-inch breech-loaders, of which the three port mountings are clearly visible in this photograph, and three 14-inch above-water torpedo tubes. This photograph shows *Serpent* essentially as she was when completed, as less than two years after she entered service she was wrecked off the coast of north-west Spain with the loss of all but three of her crew. (© The National Archives, United Kingdom, ADM 176/631)

Porpoise, a 1,950-ton *Archer*-class torpedo cruiser. Taken in February 1903, this photograph shows *Porpoise*'s appearance following the removal of her rig and sails and their replacement with pole masts. Her bow 14-inch torpedo tube and the caps for the launchers mounted beneath the forecastle and poop are particularly visible in this photograph, as are her port-side 6-inch breech-loaders. It can be appreciated just how close to the water the guns amidships were, and consequently how hard they must have been to fight in heavy weather. Like all surviving members of the class, *Porpoise* was sold off in 1905. (© The National Archives, United Kingdom, ADM 176/534)

torpedo gunboats (TGBs). The first of these, *Rattlesnake*, was laid down in 1885 and completed in 1887. At 550 tons she resembled a scaled-down *Scout* and in common with the larger ship had a protective deck, the only TGB to be so fitted. She was also notable as being the first RN warship fitted with lighter, more fuel-efficient triple-expansion machinery in place of the older compound engines. She was capable of 19½ knots and was armed with four torpedo tubes, one 5-inch gun and six 3-pdrs.[42] Three similar *Grasshopper*-class vessels were constructed at the same time, and thirteen larger *Sharpshooter*-class TGBs of 735 tons were then built in 1888–91 that mounted an extra torpedo tube and two 4.7-inch guns in place of the earlier ships' single 5-inch guns. The *Sharpshooter*-class ships were designed for 21 kts but most only reached 19 kts until problems with their boilers were rectified, and they were therefore criticised for being slower than the torpedo boats they were intended to catch.[43]

An early photograph of *Rattlesnake*, the RN's first torpedo gunboat (TGB). A 550-ton vessel laid down in 1885 and completed in 1887, she differed from later TGBs in that she had a thin armoured deck. This photograph provides a good view of her bow-mounted 14-inch torpedo tube (one of a total of four) and her single 5-inch gun. *Rattlesnake* was designed for a speed of 19 kts and apparently could make this speed well into later life, unlike later TGBs. (© The National Archives, United Kingdom, ADM 176/569)

Sandfly was one of three *Grasshopper*-class TGBs built as a follow-on to *Rattlesnake*. While the photograph of *Rattlesnake* shows detail of the bows, this photograph provides a better view of the layout of the rest of the ship: the cap for the rear torpedo tube can be seen in her stern, as can the cap of the starboard-side tube just below the bridge. Also visible are two shielded 3-pdr quick-firers, out of a total armament of six. The *Grasshopper* class were not as successful as *Rattlesnake*, however, particularly with regards to their ability to continue to make their designed speed as they aged, and all three were withdrawn from service by 1905. (© The National Archives, United Kingdom, ADM 176/611)

This photograph from March 1903 shows *Gossamer*, a 735-ton torpedo gunboat of the *Sharpshooter* class laid down in January 1889 and completed in September 1891. The class were armed with five 14-inch torpedo tubes, of which the fixed bow tube and the starboard-side twin launchers are visible in this photograph. The *Sharpshooter*-class ships were the first TGBs to be given quick-firing guns (two 4.7-inch weapons) in place of the preceding class's standard breech-loaders, and they were also armed with four 3-pdr guns. *Gossamer* herself was one of four *Sharpshooter*-class ships converted into minesweepers in 1908–09, and as such survived until 1920 while the remaining vessels of the class were mostly broken up in the early 1900s. (© The National Archives, United Kingdom, ADM 176/304)

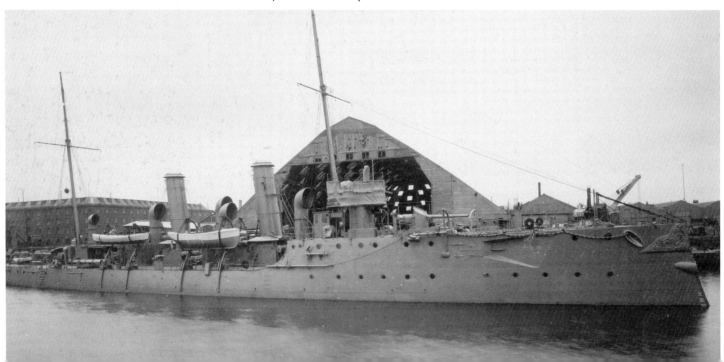

Two further classes of TGBs were constructed (the eleven 810-ton *Alarm* class of 1891–94 and the five 1,070-ton *Halcyon*-class ships of 1893–5), which were generally similar in armament and performance to the *Sharpshooter* class and therefore suffered by comparison to the nominally faster torpedo boat destroyers coming into service at the same time. The criticisms of TGB performance ignored the fact that they possessed greater freeboard than the smaller torpedo boats that they were intended to catch and were so less likely to be slowed down by heavy weather, suggesting that the difference in speeds would probably not have been as important as was made out at the time. The first effective destroyers (the *River* class of 1902) were similar in size to the TGBs and still suffered from inadequate freeboard that limited their performance in rough weather.[44]

Salamander, a *Sharpshooter*-class torpedo gunboat. The photograph illustrates to good effect the raised forecastle characteristic of the TGBs, which gave them dramatically superior sea-keeping to that of other contemporary RN torpedo craft. Also visible is the bow 14-inch torpedo tube (whose cap appears to be open) and the embrasure for the port-side 3-pdr gun, as well as the forward 4.7-inch quick-firer in front of the bridge. *Salamander* entered service in 1891 and was sold off in 1906. (© The National Archives, United Kingdom, ADM 176/609)

Citadel Battleships 1874–8

Following the trend set in the 1860s, gun calibres continued to increase in the 1870s with the development of some truly monstrous weapons. The Italian battleship *Duilio*, for example, was initially designed with four 12½-inch MLRs in two twin turrets, but these were changed to 15-inch weapons and she eventually completed with 17.7-inch guns weighing 100 tons apiece.[45] Neither high-sided central battery ironclads nor Reed's low-freeboard breastwork turret ships, both of which featured complete waterline armoured belts, could be armoured to a sufficient thickness to resist such weapons without a drastic increase in displacement.

Barnaby's solution, therefore, was to develop the citadel turret ship. As with the central battery scheme, the aim was to concentrate the ship's vitals (armament and machinery) into as small an area as possible so that sufficiently thick armour could be provided. To this end, whereas Reed's turret ships had their turrets at either end of a central superstructure to allow clear arcs fore and aft, Barnaby's vessels were characterised by turrets grouped amidships in a thickly armoured citadel. It would not be possible, however, to protect the ship's entire waterline with a sufficiently thick belt to resist contemporary heavy guns. Instead, outside of the citadel the ends of the ship would be protected by a waterline armoured deck and subdivision to preserve buoyancy, but otherwise would be unarmoured.

The first British ship to partially implement this scheme was the 5,670-ton *Shannon* laid down in 1873. Officially titled a 'broadside armour-belted cruising ship with the status of a second-class battleship'[46] she was not a success, being too slow to be an effective cruiser and too lightly armed and armoured to be an effective battleship, and only spent three of her twenty-one years in service actually on active duty. She was fitted with a 9-inch belt running from her stern to within 60 feet of her bows, and forward of this there was a 3-inch armoured deck from the bottom edge of the belt to the top of her ram. The area surrounding the armoured deck was closely subdivided to limit flooding in the event of damage. Unlike *Audacious*, which was similarly designed for overseas service, one of her main weaknesses was that her six broadside 9-inch MLRs were not protected by armour, although two 10-inch MLRs mounted on the forecastle were. To improve her sailing efficiency she was propelled by a single lifting screw, but this arrangement precluded protecting her stern in the same fashion as her bows.[47]

Shannon's shortcomings were recognised and she was followed by two larger vessels, *Northampton* and *Nelson* (both laid down 1874), which attempted to rectify them. The protective scheme of *Shannon* was replicated in these ships, but the adoption of twin screws allowed their sterns to be protected in the same fashion (armoured deck and subdivision) as their bows. Their extra 2,000 tons of displacement also allowed larger machinery, and

hence a higher top speed, and a heavier armament of four 10-inch and eight 9-inch MLRs. Their large size also made them expensive (over £400,000 each). As with *Inconstant* this meant they could not be built in sufficient quantities to be effective trade protection cruisers, whilst at the same time they were not capable of acting as battleships against similar foreign vessels.[48] As a consequence they were not repeated.

Inflexible

The first British battleship to be fully constructed in the style developed by Barnaby was *Inflexible*, laid down in 1874 and completed in 1881. Displacing 11,880 tons and costing £812,485, she was the largest and most expensive battleship yet built for the RN and featured a host of new features including internal electric lighting. Her main armament was four 16-inch 80-ton MLRs in two twin turrets, each of which fired, once every two to four minutes, a 1,684-lb shell capable of penetrating 23 inches of iron. In addition to these she carried only six 20-pdrs. Her turrets were situated in a heavily armoured citadel amidships, and were staggered so that both turrets would be capable of firing fore and after past the superstructure and also across the deck on both broadsides. The risks of blast damage to the ship's decks and superstructure if such firing was undertaken were great, however.[49]

Inflexible's citadel armour was designed to withstand shells of the same calibre as her main guns with 11 inches of teak sandwiched between two 12-inch plates (the inner reducing to 8 inches and 4 inches above and below the waterline respectively), while the turrets were 18 inches of teak with a 9-inch outer and 7-inch inner layer of iron. The outer turret plates were made of compound armour; the first time that it had been used on a British battleship. A 3-inch

armoured deck below the waterline and close subdivision with cork walls protected the ends of the ship, although the central citadel was designed to stay afloat even if these ends were flooded. Above, an unarmoured hull and superstructure were added to provide the necessary accommodation space.[50]

Although some (including Reed) questioned her protective scheme, a commission set up in 1877 to

investigate her stability with her ends flooded found that it was acceptable. The survival of the two similarly arranged, if smaller, Chinese ironclads *Ting Yuan* and *Chen Yuan* at the Battle of the Yalu Sea on 17 September 1894 also provided some belated vindication.[51] Similarly, in 1908 the later British citadel battleship *Edinburgh* (described below) was expended as a gunnery target and, despite hits from

The first RN battleship to be built according to Barnaby's citadel style, *Inflexible* also embodied the 1870s' trend of ever-larger naval artillery with four 16-inch MLRs in two twin turrets. She was also protected by an unprecedented maximum thickness of 24 inches of armour. *Inflexible* was initially given masts and rigging for peacetime sailing, but this photograph shows her appearance after these were removed and replaced with military masts in 1885. The photograph also gives an indication of the layout of her main armament: her port-side turret can be seen here, and there was a corresponding turret further aft on the other side. The thin superstructure was intended to allow her guns to fire fore and aft, and provisions were also made for cross-deck fire from both turrets. *Inflexible* was sold off in 1903. (© The National Archives, United Kingdom, ADM 176/362)

A development of the unsuccessful armoured cruiser *Shannon*, *Northampton* was one of the first RN warships (along with *Nelson*) to feature Barnaby's protective system of a heavily-armoured central citadel and ends protected by an armoured deck and subdivision. Intended for overseas service, *Northampton* accordingly served as the flagship of the North America and West Indies Station until 1886, and was then refitted and reduced to the reserve until being taken over as a training ship in 1894 and finally sold off in 1905. She was not much changed during her life, with perhaps the biggest alteration coming during her 1886 refit when she was given a fighting-top on her mizzen-mast (visible in this photograph) and had two torpedo tubes and a number of 3-pdr and 6-pdr quick-firing guns added. This photograph also shows the layout of her main battery to good advantage: the 10-inch MLRs fired through corner ports fore and aft, of which the forward starboard port is particularly obvious here, and in between these three of the four starboard 9-inch MLRs can be seen pointing towards the camera. (© The National Archives, United Kingdom, ADM 176/485)

Like *Northampton*, *Nelson* spent the initial part of her career overseas (from her launch in 1881 until 1889 she was stationed in Australia) before returning home to be refitted. During this refit, which lasted until 1891, she was more extensively modified than her sister and had military masts with fighting-tops on both the fore- and mizzen-masts fitted in place of her original barque rig. She also received four 4.7-inch, six 6-pdr and fourteen 3-pdr quick-firers as well as two torpedo tubes. This photograph therefore shows her appearance after the completion of this refit. She did not enter reserve until 1901, and was finally sold in 1910. (© The National Archives, United Kingdom, ADM 176/468)

guns far more powerful than those that she was designed to withstand, her ends retained sufficient buoyancy to keep her afloat.[52] Although very few warships from the mid-nineteenth century survive to the modern day, those interested in experiencing first-hand a Barnaby-style battleship can visit a one-to-one scale replica of *Ting Yuan* that was recently completed at Weihai in China.[53]

Essentially a low-freeboard turret ship (although the addition of extra unarmoured structure fore and aft served to disguise this), *Inflexible* was, like *Devastation*, intended to operate primarily in European waters and was well suited to the RN's strategy of coastal assault.[54] Unlike the earlier breastwork turret ships, however, she was completed with a brig rig intended for use in peacetime only, but this was removed altogether and replaced with military masts in 1885.[55] After *Inflexible*, no further battleships with sails were laid down for the RN. The 1860s-era solution of building a separate force of masted central battery ironclads was abandoned as such ships could no longer be sufficiently protected against modern heavy guns. Instead, the RN began to build a battlefleet composed of turret ships aimed squarely at operations in European waters for which the extra range provided by sails was not required. At the same time, steadily improving steam propulsive technology and the gradual build-up of overseas coaling stations and dockyards began to make sails less necessary even on cruising warships.

Ajax and Agamemnon

The next class of battleships constructed for the RN, *Ajax* and *Agamemnon*, were laid down in 1876 and completed in 1883. Each displaced 8,510 tons and resembled a smaller version of *Inflexible*, the reduction in displacement resulting in a saving of over £300,000 per ship. Their reduced size, however, compromised their effectiveness as warships and they were not popular in service. In particular, the reduction in size of their central citadel meant that it lacked the buoyancy required to keep the ship afloat in the event that both unarmoured ends were flooded.[56]

Their reduced displacement also meant they could not carry the same scale of armament and protection as *Inflexible*. Their guns were a mixture of old and new: their four main guns were 12½-inch MLRs, the last time that muzzle-loading weapons were fitted to an RN battleship, but they were also the first British battleships to be fitted with a secondary armament (in this case, two 6-inch breech-loaders and six 6-pdr quick-firers). Their citadel armour was a sandwich of 10 inches of teak between 10-inch outer and 8-inch inner iron plates, while the armoured deck was 3 inches thick. Their two turrets were protected by 16-inch faces and 14-inch walls of compound armour.[57]

Unlike *Inflexible* they were designed and completed without sails and rigging, although two military masts were provided. Their hull form was such that their rudders were found to be ineffective and as a result they handled very badly

indeed, and although this was somewhat rectified by extending their sterns in 1886 it did nothing for their reputation in the fleet.[58]

The Russian War Scare 1878

In 1878 it seemed as if Britain would once again be at war with Russia. The cause of the crisis was, as in 1853, the Russian threat to Turkey. The major concern for Britain again was that Russia would gain access through the Dardanelles, allowing a fleet in the Black Sea access to the Eastern Mediterranean, or even go as far as to take over large parts of the Ottoman Empire – either of which was seen as a major threat to British trade and to her communications with India.

In 1875 risings had occurred in Bosnia-Herzegovina against Turkish rule and these were not quickly suppressed, prompting further rebellion in Bulgaria. This Bulgarian rising of April to May 1876 was brutally repressed by the Ottoman Empire, leading Gladstone to publish his famous pamphlet 'Bulgarian Horrors and the Question of the East'. Countries including Austria and Russia called on Turkey to institute internal reforms to address the rebels' complaints but Turkey refused, and tensions further increased at the end of June 1876 when Serbia and Montenegro declared war on Turkey.[59]

The following year, further calls for reform were issued by the Great Powers in the London Protocol and were similarly rejected by Turkey, and so Russia declared war on Turkey on 24 April 1877. By 10 December 1877 Plevna had fallen and Russia was advancing on Constantinople, prompting Britain to dispatch an RN squadron up the Dardanelles to deter an attack on the Turkish capital. On 3 March 1878 the war concluded with Russia's imposition of the Treaty of San Stefano. This treaty threatened numerous British interests, particularly by creating a unified Bulgaria (which was thought to be a potential Russian client-state) and by granting Russia gains in Asia Minor, and raised the possibility of Russia and Turkey coming to an agreement between themselves about access through the Straits. On 21 March 1878 Britain therefore demanded that Russia submit the whole treaty for scrutiny by all the Great Powers, and when no response was received by 27 March she began to put in hand precautions for the event of war (including calling out the Reserve and moving troops from India to Malta). Britain also secured an agreement with Turkey to occupy Cyprus as a base in the Eastern Mediterranean to counter-balance Russian gains.[60]

As part of the response to this crisis, four ironclads being built for foreign powers in British yards were purchased for RN service at a combined cost of nearly £2,000,000. These ships were obsolete designs

This photograph shows *Neptune* (ex-*Independencia*) in 1886 following the removal of her rigging and mainmast, and the addition of fighting-tops to the fore- and mizzen-masts. This perhaps makes her similarity with *Devastation* more apparent, as her central superstructure and turrets are more visible, even though her additional forecastle and poop are perhaps more pronounced. *Neptune*'s purchase and conversion for RN service were expensive and time-consuming and she was not regarded as a success, especially as the more up-to-date barbette battleships with breech-loading armaments were entering service alongside her. For this reason she had a relatively short career: completed in 1881, she was placed in reserve in 1893 and sold off in 1903. (© The National Archives, United Kingdom, ADM 176/470)

when compared with the purpose-built RN ships commissioning at the same time and the conversion process was time-consuming and expensive, meaning that the actually value of these extra vessels to the RN was minimal. Common shortcomings were a lack of protection against the current generation of naval ordnance and insufficiently heavy weapons to penetrate the thicker armour then coming into service on contemporary foreign ships.

The masted turret ironclad then building for Brazil as *Independencia* was purchased for the RN as *Neptune*. Laid down in 1873, she

superficially resembled *Monarch* in having her main armament (four 12-inch MLRs) concentrated in two twin turrets, high freeboard for her entire length and three masts. The inspiration for her design was *Devastation*, but Brazilian requirements for full sailing rig and a forecastle and poop (and consequently high freeboard) disguised this, and also compromised her effectiveness by obscuring the firing arcs of her turrets. She provides a stark example of the false economy offered by purchasing and converting foreign warships as a short-term expedient: in total she cost £689,172, which compares

very unfavourably with the £361,438 cost of the similarly sized and more capable *Devastation*. By the time she finally entered service in 1881 she was generally considered obsolete, and she was consigned to the reserve in 1893. Probably her most spectacular feat was her departure from Portsmouth on 23 October 1903 following her decommissioning when, under tow, she collided with *Victory* and *Hero*, almost sinking Nelson's flagship, and very nearly hit a number of other ships.[61]

Superb was a central battery ironclad originally laid down for Turkey but purchased for Britain

Superb (ex-*Hamidieh*) was a central-battery ironclad purchased for the RN during the 1878 Russian War Scare. This photograph shows her after her 1887–91 refit, during which her masts and rigging were replaced with the military masts visible here, and she was also fitted with modern triple-expansion engines. The layout of her battery, with four 10-inch MLRs on each broadside and one at each corner capable of firing ahead or astern through embrasures, can, however, still be discerned. These guns were supplemented during her refit by twelve 6-inch, six 6-pdr and ten 3-pdr quick-firers. She remained in service for a further thirteen years, finally being sold off in 1906. (© The National Archives, United Kingdom, ADM 176/680)

at a cost of over £530,000 in February 1878. She was very similar to *Mesudiye*, which had also been built for Turkey in Britain, and like her resembled an enlarged *Hercules* because her battery was on a single deck with recesses fore and aft for end-on fire. Upon completion in 1880 *Superb* was the most heavily armed and best protected central battery ship in RN service, but this could not disguise the fact that central battery ironclads were by then obsolete: her sixteen 10-inch MLRs were smaller than the guns of contemporary turret ships and her belt and battery armour (with maximum thicknesses of 12 inches over 8–12 inches of teak) was only half the thickness of *Inflexible*'s citadel.[62]

The final two ships purchased were two 4,870-ton ironclad rams also being built for Turkey. Renamed *Belleisle* and *Orion*, they featured an octagonal centre battery mounting four 12-inch MLRs and were protected by a 12-inch belt (thinning to 7 inches forward and 6 inches aft) backed by a significant thickness of wood. Costing approximately £280,000 each, they were initially classified as Second Class battleships but this rating was not borne out by their shallow draught and limited range and they were eventually reclassified as coast defence ships.[63]

Ultimately, the crisis was averted. Russia had no desire for war with Britain and agreed to submit to international arbitration. On 13 June 1878 the Congress of Berlin was convened to attempt to resolve the issues that had led to the events of 1876. There, Britain succeeded in preventing the establishment of a united independent Bulgaria, which was one of the provisions of the Treaty of San Stefano that had most threatened her interests in the East Mediterranean.[64]

The Final Citadel Battleships

As a result of the Russian War Scare, the Carnarvon Committee was established in 1879 to investigate the RN's preparedness. It concluded that the RN was too small to successfully discharge its functions if war did come, and recommended a large warship construction programme to be financed by increased taxation.[65] The Gladstone administration would not countenance such a rise, however, and a concerted building programme did not materialise until the Northbrook Programme of 1884 (discussed below).[66] The committee also recommended the establishment of worldwide network of fortified coaling stations and dockyards and this was gradually adopted. This would eventually bear fruit and by the 1890s make a wholly steam-powered RN practical.[67]

Two further battleships were laid down in 1879 and completed in 1886–7. Named *Colossus* and *Edinburgh*, they appeared to be slightly larger versions (9,420 tons displacement) of *Agamemnon* and *Ajax*, but this disguised their importance in the development of the British battleship as they embodied all of the technological developments discussed at the start of this chapter: their hulls were made of steel, their main armaments were breech-loading 12-inch guns, and they were protected by compound armour. In addition, they carried five 6-inch breech-loaders and four 6-pdr quick-firing guns. At 16 kts they were also faster than previous battleships (*Agamemnon* was only capable of 13 kts) while retaining the same thickness of armour (18 inches on the citadel sides, 16 inches on turret faces and 14 inches on turret walls, all backed by significant amounts of teak) as the earlier ships. Unlike the previous class, however, both citadel and turret armour was compound and so they were better protected than the earlier ships for the same thickness of armour. They cost approximately £650,000 per ship, more than *Agamemnon* but less than *Inflexible*.[68]

Colossus and *Edinburgh* were, however, the last of the citadel battleships and subsequent classes adopted different armour and armament layouts. So long were the building times of these five citadel ships of the 1870s that newer vessels were designed and laid down before the first citadel battleship, *Inflexible*, entered service. The final citadel battleship, *Edinburgh*, was completed in 1887, only two years before the *Royal Sovereign* class (arguably the first true British ocean-going steam battleships) were started. As such, the citadel ships were almost obsolete by the time they entered service. The development of these ships that supplanted the citadel battleship will now be examined.

The 9,400-ton citadel battleship *Colossus* is seen here at about the time of her completion in 1886. This photograph illustrates well the general layout of the five citadel battleships constructed for the RN in the 1870s and 1880s. In all of these ships the main armament was mounted in two turrets carried amidships in a heavily armoured citadel. The turrets were staggered to port and starboard to achieve a degree of fire fore and aft past the superstructure, and could also fire across the deck to give a four-gun broadside. In both cases, however, there was a risk of the blast from the guns damaging the ship's own structure. Although the barbette-armed pre-dreadnoughts became the preferred type of capital ship shortly after *Colossus* entered service, she served for fifteen years before being placed in reserve in 1901 and was finally sold off in 1908. (© The National Archives, United Kingdom, ADM 176/144)

Edinburgh was the sister-ship of *Colossus*. Despite their cumbersome appearance, these two ships were notable as the first British battleships to have steel hulls and breech-loading main guns. Like her sister, *Edinburgh*'s active service life was short: she was placed in reserve in 1897 and in 1908 was expended as an experimental target. This proved belated validation of her protective scheme, which kept her afloat despite hits from numerous heavy shells. (© The National Archives, United Kingdom, ADM 176/226)

Barbette Battleships of the *Admiral* Class

The French had adopted the fixed armoured barbette in preference to the rotating armoured turret in their battleships from the 11,000-ton *Amiral Duperré* (laid down in 1875, completed in 1883) onwards. French battleships looked markedly different from their British contemporaries: the five British citadel battleships of the 1870s retained low freeboard as a consequence of their coastal attack roots, while the French battleships had high-sided hulls with pronounced tumblehome and shallow armour belts all along the waterline. This high freeboard meant the French ships' armament was carried high above the waterline, which precluded the use of heavy turrets and favoured the adoption of the lighter barbette.[69]

In 1879 Britain felt compelled to build a further battleship after the two *Colossus*-class vessels in order to keep pace with French construction. At the same time, however, given the technological uncertainty then prevalent, there was a competing pressure to avoid spending too much on large armoured warships whose future viability was uncertain.[70] This insistence on economy constrained the displacement of the resulting ships and explains many of the design compromises that were made.

The model for the new battleship (for which the name *Collingwood* was chosen) was the 7,500-ton French *Terrible*-class barbette coastal defence battleships laid down in 1877–8. Like the RN's low-freeboard turret battleships, these French ships were also designed to fight in European waters and so were seen as a major potential opponent. *Collingwood* was therefore conceived to fight the *Terrible* class battleships and this switch from a primary anti-fortification role to a primary anti-ship role meant that

The 9,500-ton barbette battleship *Collingwood* was laid down in 1880 and completed in 1887. The photograph shows the extra height above water granted to the 12-inch guns by the use of barbettes, which can be compared with the photographs of earlier turret battleships. The ship's main weakness, that of low freeboard which reduced her speed in heavy seas, can also be seen. Visible in the sides of the superstructure are the ports for the three port-side 6-inch breech-loaders. *Collingwood* was moved to reserve in 1903 and finally sold off in 1909. The only major change to her during her career was the replacement in 1896 of her 6-inch guns with quick-firers of the same calibre. (© The National Archives, United Kingdom, ADM 176/141)

heavily-armoured gun positions capable of withstanding close-range fire from the shore were no longer as important. Instead, it was seen as important that her guns be mounted sufficiently high out of the water that they could be fought in heavy weather and so barbettes were preferred. Switching to barbettes had the added advantage, given the desire to limit the displacement and hence cost, that they required less armour and so the guns could be mounted on a smaller ship.[71] The decision to reintroduce breech-loading main armaments into the RN also made the adoption of barbettes in *Collingwood* feasible – experience with *Temeraire*'s barbettes having shown that they would not scale well to contain larger or more numerous muzzle-loading weapons.

Despite the desire to build something in 1879, the benefits of barbettes versus turrets were not clear-cut and debate over the design of *Collingwood* lasted nearly a year. It was not until 15 March 1880 that the final version was settled upon.[72] She was laid down four months later and completed in 1887. *Collingwood* displaced 9,500 tons and cost just under £637,000, making her virtually the same size as *Colossus* but a little over £20,000 cheaper. The increase of 2,000 tons over the French *Terrible*-class battleships was almost entirely due to the requirement for a top speed of 16 kts, over a knot higher than the French ships, which necessitated heavier machinery and a longer hull.[73]

Collingwood mounted a main armament of four 12-inch breech-loaders in two twin barbettes (one at each end of a central superstructure),

six 6-inch breech-loaders in a secondary battery along the upper deck, and an anti-torpedo boat armament of twelve 6-pdrs and eight 3-pdrs. The barbettes were protected by 11½-inch sloping compound armour sides (thinning to 10 inches at the rear) over 13 inches of teak, while the ammunition trunk leading up to them was between 10 and 12 inches thick. *Collingwood*'s hull protection was a development of the type pioneered in *Inflexible* in that vertical armour was confined to the centre of the ship with the ends protected by an armoured deck and close subdivision. To save weight, however, the full-height central citadel of the earlier ship was reduced to a 7½-foot high 18-inch thick compound armour belt with 16-inch bulkheads at the ends and covered with a 3-inch armoured deck, while the armoured deck covering the ends was 2½ inches thick.[74] Although superior to the *Terrible* class, the insistence on economy meant that *Collingwood* was 2,220 tons lighter than the French *Amiral Baudin*-class barbette battleships laid down in 1879 and, although she was one knot faster and mounted a comparable armament, the reduced displacement meant her armour had to be thinner and less extensive than the French vessels.[75]

Judging the success of *Collingwood* is difficult. With her armament of two twin guns mounted at either end of the superstructure she appears to point the way to the standard pre-dreadnoughts of the 1890s far more than the turret ships that preceded her. This disguised the fact, however, that the insistence on

economy meant that *Collingwood*'s design was not obviously tailored towards either an open-ocean or a coastal attack role, but instead incorporated features of both, which inevitably compromised her effectiveness in both.[76] In particular, although the adoption of barbettes allowed her guns to be carried higher than those of the turret ships (22 feet above the waterline), and hence better able to be fought in a seaway, she retained the low freeboard of the turret ships, which made her very wet and limited her speed when steaming into heavy seas.[77] At the same time, for operating against coastal fortifications where her low freeboard would not be a handicap, her barbettes with their lack of armour protection for the guns were far more vulnerable than the weapons of the turret battleships. Although the citadel battleships have been denigrated as 'sullen and misshapen misfits' (to quote Parkes),[78] they were actually optimised to fulfil a specific role (namely, coastal assault) while the design of *Collingwood* was guided more by prevailing technological uncertainty and the consequent desire to minimise expenditure.[79]

Despite this, *Collingwood* provided the pattern for the next five battleships constructed for the RN, and the six ships became known collectively as the *Admiral* class. In 1880 France ordered four more battleships, and the new British Liberal ministry were aware that if nothing were done to match them the RN's superiority over the French fleet would have all but disappeared. Given this apparent imperative, however, it was not a foregone conclusion that the resulting ships would be repeats of *Collingwood* (which had after all only just been laid down and whose success or otherwise could not yet be discerned) and nine months were spent considering a range of different designs.[80]

As with *Collingwood* the way ahead was not clear: France had begun experimenting with all-steel armour on her battleships, while Italy had just launched the enormous *Italia* (although she was still five years away from completion) that dispensed with vertical armour altogether in favour of an all-over

armoured deck.[81] In the end it was decided to repeat *Collingwood*, not because she was seen as superior to the foreign vessels then building but because she offered the cheapest way of keeping pace with France – and hence reduced the risk that large amounts of money would be wasted if naval technology continued to evolve rapidly and left the new vessels quickly obsolete.[82] Increasing the homogeneity of the RN's battlefleet was also seen as a benefit, as the largest number of vessels in a single class since the four *Audacious*-class ships of the late 1860s had been two.[83]

The first two follow-on ships, *Rodney* and *Howe*, were laid down in early 1882 and completed in 1888–9, the long building time being primarily due to delays in the production of their main guns. These guns were the major difference between these ships and *Collingwood*: in place of the 12-inch weapons of the previous ship they mounted larger 13½-inch pieces, and their displacement consequently increased by 800 tons to 10,300 tons overall.[84]

The next two, *Camperdown* and *Anson*, were laid down in 1882–3 and also completed in 1889, again due to delays to their guns. As well as

Camperdown, one of the second batch of *Admiral*-class battleships. Essentially a repeat of *Collingwood*, the biggest change was the replacement of the former's 12-inch guns with the same number of larger 13½-inch guns. Like her sister *Anson* (but unlike *Howe* and *Rodney*) she also had thickened barbettes and a longer belt, and was consequently made slightly longer and wider than the earlier ships to prevent her from floating deeper. This photograph provides an excellent view of the ship's rear barbette, with the guns carried on top without the benefit of any additional protection when run out (as shown here). Also visible is her secondary armament of 6-inch guns along the side of her superstructure (six guns in total), with the 12-pdr anti-torpedo boat guns mounted on the deck above them. The class's low freeboard is also particularly evident. Completed in 1889, *Camperdown* is chiefly remembered for her part in the sinking of *Victoria* in 1893. She was converted into a depot ship in 1908 and sold off in 1911. (© The National Archives, United Kingdom, ADM 176/118)

13½-inch main guns, their armour was improved by lengthening the belt from 140 to 150 feet and increasing the thickness of the barbette armour to 14 inches on the sides and 12 inches on the rear. This further increased their displacement to 10,600 tons, and so to ensure that they did not float any lower in the water than the previous ships (which already had problems with their belts being submerged) they were lengthened by 5 feet and given 6 inches' extra beam. The four ships cost an average of just over £661,000 each, slightly more than *Collingwood* but still over £150,000 cheaper than *Inflexible* (which had finally entered service in the year before these ships were started).[85]

The sixth and final ship of the *Admiral* class, *Benbow*, was laid down towards the end of 1882 and completed in June 1888. She was identical to *Camperdown* and *Anson* in terms of her dimensions and displacement, with the main differences being confined to her armament. In an attempt to avoid the delays plaguing the early ships, readily-available 16¼-inch guns were substituted for the 13½-inch weapons, with one of these larger

Benbow, the final *Admiral*-class battleship. Completion of previous ships of the class had been held up by delays in manufacturing their 13½-inch guns, and so in *Benbow* it was decided to replace these weapons with two 16¼-inch breech-loaders. Although each barbette could only accommodate one of these monstrous weapons in place of the two 13½-inch guns, the substitution actually freed up sufficient weight to strengthen her secondary armament with four extra 6-inch breech-loaders (for a total of ten). Both the 16¼-inch guns are clearly visible here, along with the 6-inch guns ranged along her superstructure. *Benbow* entered service in 1888, serving in the Mediterranean for three years and as a guardship for ten, and was sold off in 1909. (© The National Archives, United Kingdom, ADM 176/73)

weapons mounted in each barbette. This also saved enough weight for the secondary armament to be expanded to ten 6-inch weapons. At £764,022 she was the most expensive of the *Admiral* class ships, although she was the only one to be built in a private dockyard.[86]

The Battleships of the Northbrook Programme

Towards the end of the 1880s the strength of the RN relative to the other European navies became an issue that excited public opinion. Franco–British relations had deteriorated due to the unilateral British occupation of Egypt following the bombardment of Alexandria in 1882.[87] In 1884 Britain was faced by the (albeit remote) possibility of facing a Franco–German combination that together would possess more battleships than the RN and nearly as many cruisers.[88] At the same time there appeared in the *Pall Mall Gazette* a series of articles entitled 'The Truth About The Navy' that purported to describe its weaknesses in men and materiel compared with the European powers. Modern historians have questioned the truth of these articles,[89] but as a means of stirring up public opinion to force the government to increase naval spending they proved very successful. On 10 November 1884, Lord Northbrook (the First Lord of the Admiralty) announced that £3,100,000 would be spent over five years to build two new battleships, seven armoured cruisers, six torpedo cruisers and fourteen torpedo boats.[90] This became known as the Northbrook Programme.

The design of the new battleships marked a return to the low-freeboard turret ship that had apparently been superseded by the *Admiral* class. The abandonment of the barbette in favour of turrets was probably due to public and professional opinion that the former was inadequately protected compared with the latter – indeed, this was a general criticism levelled at the overall design of the *Admiral* class by many, including Reed. At the same time, personnel changes at the Admiralty had removed from the Board those who favoured the barbette and replaced them with advocates of the turret.[91]

A number of different layouts for the new battleships were considered, including a version of the *Admiral* class with the barbettes replaced with turrets, but the final design resembled a scaled-up version of the 6,000-ton armoured rams *Conqueror* and *Hero* laid down in 1879 and 1884.[92] Being rams, these ships had their main armament of two 12-inch guns concentrated in a single forward turret, the intention presumably being that they would spend the majority of their time in battle steaming directly towards the enemy. This armament disposition, however, was not particularly well-suited to a battleship as they would be required to operate under more general tactical conditions and put them at risk of losing all their offensive power to a single hit.[93]

The two battleships were named *Sans Pareil* and *Victoria* and were laid down within two days of each other in April 1885. Both completed in 1890–91, with *Victoria* costing nearly £850,000 including her armament. They displaced 10,470 tons and mounted the same 16¼-inch guns as *Benbow* (probably for the same reason that they were readily available) in a single twin-gun turret forward of the superstructure. To cover the rear of the ship, where the turret guns could not be brought to bear, a single unarmoured 10-inch gun was mounted aft, and the long superstructure provided room to mount a powerful secondary battery of twelve 6-inch guns, supplemented by twelve 6-pdr and nine 3-pdr quick-firers.[94]

The layout of the armour of these ships followed that of the *Admiral* class but was generally thicker, being composed of an 8½-foot deep 152-foot long belt of 18-inch thick compound armour with 16-inch bulkheads at either end. This was covered by a 3-inch armoured deck, and the ends were protected by a deck of the same thickness. The turret armour was 17 inches thick, and an 18-inch thick redoubt protected its base down to the level of the armoured belt. The weight of this arrangement meant that the turret guns could only be placed 15 feet above the waterline (compared with 22 feet in the *Admiral* class) and this low height, combined with them being concentrated forward, meant that they were prone to being rendered unworkable when steaming into a heavy sea.[95]

The greatest innovation introduced in these two ships was the use of triple-expansion engines for the first time in a British battleship.

Conqueror was a purpose-designed 6,200-ton ram laid down in 1879 and completed in 1886. Her design was based on that of the earlier *Rupert*, but *Conqueror*'s increased displacement allowed for heavier armament (two 12-inch and four 6-inch breech-loaders) and thicker armour. Despite these improvements, however, her low freeboard limited her speed in bad weather and she was no more successful in her intended role than earlier purpose-designed rams. *Conqueror* was sold off in 1907, having spent most of her life as a coastal-defence vessel. (© The National Archives, United Kingdom, ADM 176/152)

A bow-on view of the turret battleship *Sans Pareil*. This class had all their main armament (two 16¼-inch breech-loaders) concentrated in a single turret, and this is clearly visible here. The photograph also shows the class's low freeboard, something that they shared with many other RN turret battleships. Unlike her sister *Victoria*, *Sans Pareil* had an uneventful career: she served in the Mediterranean from 1892 to 1895, and afterwards became rapidly eclipsed by the barbette pre-dreadnoughts and was stationed as the guardship at Sheerness until 1904. She was finally sold off and broken up in 1907. (© The National Archives, United Kingdom, ADM 176/614)

This photograph illustrates the stern of the ill-fated *Victoria*. With their main armament concentrated forward, *Victoria* and *Sans Pareil* were each given a single shield-mounted 10-inch breech-loader to the rear of their superstructures to cover the arcs in which their turret guns could not be brought to bear. This weapon can be seen in this photograph, along with the 6-inch breech-loaders (one straddled by a pair of crewmen) that were mounted in her superstructure. On the deck above these are a number of 6-pdr quick-firers. (© The National Archives, United Kingdom, ADM 176/752)

These had first been trialled in the torpedo gunboat *Rattlesnake* in 1885 and, being a success, were fitted in both *Sans Pareil* and *Victoria*. Triple-expansion engines had the benefit of being lighter and more fuel-efficient than compound engines, as shown in the re-engining of *Thunderer* with triple-expansion engines in 1889–90. Her old machinery weighed 1,080 tons and required 1,350 tons of coal to steam 4,500 nm at 10 kts, but her new triple-expansion engines weighed 800 tons and required only 950 tons of coal to steam the same distance at the same speed.[96] Reducing the weight of machinery for the same performance obviously allowed more weight to be allocated to other functions, such as armour or firepower.

Victoria is best remembered as the flagship of Vice-Admiral Sir George Tryon. 'A man of outsize physique and character',[97] Tryon belonged to the same breed of Victorian naval innovators as Scott and Fisher, and his particular passion was freeing the RN from the shackles of centralised fleet command. The complexity of naval signalling had increased seemingly inexorably since the Napoleonic Wars until, in 1886, the draft of the RN's new Signal Book was over five hundred pages long and contained sufficient flags to allow the commanding admiral to instruct the movements of his subordinates in minute detail.[98] Tryon feared that such a system of command would be unworkable in battle, where signal flags could be obscured or cut-down by enemy fire, and wanted instead to rely on the initiative of ships' captains to act as

they saw fit in accordance with their admiral's overall plans. On becoming commander of the Mediterranean Fleet in 1891, Tryon issued three memoranda setting out his ideas; put simply, if the flagship were to hoist the signal 'TA' the subsequent movements of the fleet would be regulated by only eight single-flag general instructions rather than the specific Signal Book versions. In one trial, this TA system allowed the fleet to be manoeuvred through thirteen turns and formation changes using ten flags, rather than the 202 that would have been required if the Signal Book had been used.[99]

Events would, however, bring Tryon's experiments to a dramatic end. On 22 June 1893 the Mediterranean Fleet was coming in to anchor off Tripoli in the Lebanon. It was disposed in two parallel columns 1,200 yards apart and steaming at 8 kts when Tryon, flying his flag in *Victoria* at the head of the 1st Division, ordered the two columns to turn inwards. Quite what Tryon intended by this order has been debated ever since, but the result was that *Camperdown*, leading the 2nd Division, struck *Victoria* with her ram and tore a hole in her side, which was 28 feet high, 12 feet wide and 9 feet deep. With some of her hatches and doors left open, flooding spread through the ship and *Victoria* capsized in less than fifteen minutes, killing 358 of those onboard including Tryon.[100]

Tryon's death discredited his ideas, even though it was the Signal Book and not the TA system that was in use at the time of the collision, and the RN reverted to a rigid system of

centralised command that was to prove a major handicap during the First World War.[101] In 2004 divers located the sunken *Victoria*. Unique amongst all known extant shipwrecks, she does not lie on the ocean floor but instead projects vertically up out of it at a right-angle, with her ram bow and forward turret driven into the soft clay of the seabed.[102]

Nile and *Trafalgar*

In 1885 Barnaby resigned as Director of Naval Construction (DNC) due to ill health and William White was nominated as his successor. Employed by Armstrong since 1882, White had previously worked for the Admiralty under both Reed and Barnaby; he had, for example, supervised the redesign of *Fury* into *Dreadnought* at Pembroke Dockyard and had also overseen the building of *Inflexible* at Portsmouth.[103] At the same time, the Board had sanctioned a new class of turret battleships to be built to a design of Barnaby's featuring two separate citadels, one protecting the base of each turret. Compared with the single citadels previously used, this further concentrated armour over the ships vitals, reducing the need for large amounts of vertical armour along the sides and thus allowing a greater thickness to be mounted where most required.[104]

Before White had taken up the post of DNC, however, the First Naval Lord, Admiral Sir Arthur Hood, ordered that this design be recast in the conventional mould of the *Admiral* class with a single citadel enclosing both turrets.

Barnaby and White wrote a joint memorandum to Hood asking for him to reconsider and for a new Committee on Design to be established to investigate the naval design issues of the day, such as the comparative merits of turrets and barbettes and of vertical and horizontal armour. They were unsuccessful, however, and Hood's preferred single-citadel design became the basis for the battleships *Nile* and *Trafalgar*.[105]

These two ships were laid down in 1886 and completed in 1890–91. In form they marked a reversion to the fore-and-aft armament disposition of the *Admiral* class, with guns mounted at either end of a central citadel, although they still retained the low freeboard that characterised British turret and barbette battleships of the period. At 12,590

tons each, *Nile* and *Trafalgar* were the largest battleships yet constructed for the RN. Clearly aimed at rectifying the perceived major weakness in the *Admiral* class ships and *Sans Pareil*, the extra displacement was almost entirely given over to provision of extra protection. At 230 feet, the compound-armour belt was 68 feet longer than the armoured citadel of *Sans Pareil* and, with a maximum thickness of 20 inches, was 2 inches thicker (although it did thin to 16–14 inches at the ends). The belt was also closed by 16-inch bulkheads. Above the belt, *Nile* and *Trafalgar* had an additional 192-foot long citadel of 18–16-inch armour enclosing the turret bases, which was covered by a 3-inch deck, and a deck of the same thickness covered the ends outside of the belt. Their extra

displacement and protection came at a cost, however, as they were more expensive than previous ships: *Nile* cost £885,718 and *Trafalgar* £859,070.[106]

The main armament of these ships was four 13½-inch breech-loaders carried in two twin turrets that were protected with 18 inches of armour. They were the first British battleships to mount a secondary armament of quick-firing guns (initially six 4.7-inch, later increased to 6-inch weapons) and in addition carried numerous smaller weapons (eight 6-pdrs and nine 3-pdrs) to defend against torpedo craft. The secondary armament was protected by a steel screen 4 inches thick.[107]

They were fitted with triple-expansion machinery of the same power as the lighter *Sans Pareil*, which made these two ships about

The 12,590-ton turret battleship *Trafalgar*, photographed in May 1890 some two months after she was completed. As such, her original low funnels (raised by 17 feet in 1891) and 4.7-inch quick-firing secondary guns (replaced with 6-inch weapons in 1896) are still visible. She also has the black hull and white superstructure characteristic of the late-Victorian RN. *Trafalgar* was the lead ship of the RN's final class of low-freeboard turret battleships but, like her sistership *Nile*, her active career was cut short by the introduction of the barbette-armed pre-dreadnought, and she was reduced to reserve status at the end of 1890s before becoming a training ship in 1907. She was sold off in 1911. (© The National Archives, United Kingdom, ADM 176/717)

one knot slower (for a top speed of 16¾ kts under forced draught). As with all low freeboard battleships (in *Nile* and *Trafalgar*, freeboard was 11¾ feet, with guns carried 3½ feet above that) their top speed was severely limited in heavy weather and they tended to be very wet. As a result, they spent most of their careers in the Mediterranean where such conditions were less likely to be encountered.[108]

At the time of their construction *Nile* and *Trafalgar* appeared to be the last word in ironclad battleship design. On announcing their inclusion in the Naval Estimates of 1886, the Parliamentary and Financial Secretary to the Admiralty, John Tomlinson Hibbert, prophesied:

I may safely say that these two large ironclads will probably be the last ironclads of this type that will ever be built in this or any country.[109]

Hibbert was thinking of the threat posed by the torpedo, which appeared to be on the brink of rendering large armoured warships extinct, and in this he, like many other

The 12,590-ton turret battleship *Nile*, photographed in 1905 when her Victorian colours of black, white and buff had been replaced by drab grey. By this point her secondary armament had also been upgraded to six 6-inch quick-firers, of which the three starboard weapons are visible here. The photograph also gives a good view of the class's low freeboard, which put their guns close to the water and limited their speed in rough conditions. Unlike *Trafalgar*, *Nile* was completed with tall funnels. Both ships of the class were completed at about the same time as the *Royal Sovereign* class and were quickly eclipsed by the pre-dreadnoughts of the 1890s. They were therefore placed in reserve by the turn of the twentieth century, and *Nile* was sold off and broken up in 1912. (© The National Archives, United Kingdom, ADM 176/482)

contemporary observers, was wrong. Inadvertently, however, he correctly identified these two ships as marking the end of the low-freeboard turret battleships – with one exception, subsequent British battleships would evolve along a different path.

Cruisers 1874–89

Battleship design in the period 1874–89 was dominated by the conflicting desires to provide armour of sufficient thickness to resist the latest ordnance along with guns capable of penetrating the armour of foreign warships, at a time when rapid technological change made the government and Admiralty unwilling to invest huge amounts in large warships that could rapidly become obsolete. Cruiser design in the same period was similarly beset by competing tactical, strategic and technological demands.

In the 1860s the primary large warship designed for overseas stations was the Second Class ironclad, typified by the vessels of the *Audacious* and *Swiftsure* classes. Essentially scaled-down First Class vessels, their role was to counter similar foreign vessels designed to serve abroad, such as the French *Alma*, or the small ironclads

The 2,400-ton corvette *Comus* was completed in 1878 and was the lead ship of a class of nine. The class was notable as comprising the first cruisers below 3,000 tons in displacement to be given metal hulls, and had iron or steel frames covered with steel plate. They were also the first corvettes to be fitted with an armoured deck, which covered their machinery and magazines amidships, and also made use of coal bunkers to protect their buoyancy if damaged. The ships of the class were given a range of armaments, and *Comus* was unique amongst them in having four 6-inch breech-loaders and eight 64-pdr MLRs. *Comus* was sold off in 1904. (© The National Archives, United Kingdom, ADM 176/150)

belonging to extra-European navies such as Peru's *Huascar*. *Shannon* marked a continuation of this trend into the 1870s. At the same time, faster unarmoured vessels like the *Inconstant*-class frigates and *Volage*-class corvettes were built for trade protection duties. As both types would have to operate far from supporting bases they were fitted with full sailing rig and given sheathed hulls.[110]

In the 1870s, however, the situation was beginning to change.

The overseas threat to Britain would be vested not in small battleships but cruisers targeted at her trade. Two Russian cruisers completed in 1875 and 1877 indicated the shape of things to come. These 5,000-ton ships, *General Admiral* and *Gerzog Edinburgski*, were about as fast as the British Second Class ironclads but better armoured (with a 5–6 inches complete waterline belt) than the *Inconstant* and *Volage* classes. Future British trade protection vessels would therefore

have to combine long endurance and high top speed with a good measure of armoured protection and firepower in order to counter the proliferation of such enemy craft.[111]

This changed threat condemned *Shannon*, *Nelson* and *Northampton* to obsolescence very soon after they were completed. It also spelt the end of the large masted cruiser as the primary trade-protection type. Nine *Comus*-class steel-hulled corvettes were built in 1876–81, following the successful use of that material in *Iris*

Curacoa was a *Comus*-class steel-hulled corvette completed in 1878. *Curacoa* was initially completed with two 7-inch and twelve 64-pdr MLRs, but like many RN vessels in the 1880s was rearmed with breech-loading guns. This photograph shows her after she had been rearmed with four 6-inch and eight 5-inch breech-loaders: the 6-inch guns were mounted in shields, with the 5-inch guns ranged along the broadside between them. The *Comus* class were successful corvettes, but they came into service as the era of the masted cruiser was drawing to a close and *Curacoa*, like many of her sisters, was sold off in 1904. (© The National Archives, United Kingdom, ADM 176/172)

and *Mercury*. At 2,380 tons these were smaller, slower (*c.* 13 kts) and more lightly armed than *Iris*, but they were also cheaper (£190,000 each, compared with £225,000). They were also the first cruisers smaller than 3,000 tons to be given metal hulls. The protection afforded by coal bunkers used in *Iris* was also exploited in these ships, supplemented by a 1½-inch steel protective deck covering the machinery and magazines. This combination of bunkers and armoured deck became the model for the protection of all subsequent smaller protected cruisers.[112] The seven ships of the 1,420-ton *Satellite*-class composite-hulled sloops were also uprated to corvettes in 1884, and in the same year the two *Calypso*-class corvettes entered service. Generally similar to the *Comus* class, these were the final class of masted corvettes.[113]

The masted cruiser survived with the continued building of smaller sloops, typically around 1,000 tons in displacement. Twenty-one masted sloops which were of the

Calliope was a 2,770-ton steel-hulled corvette completed in 1884. Forming a class with her sister-ship *Calypso*, the two ships were developed from the preceding *Comus* class and incorporated a similar protective deck over their machinery. Unlikely the earlier ships, however, they were completed with a main armament of breech-loading guns (four 6-inch and twelve 5-inch) instead of muzzle-loading weapons. The layout of the class's armament is shown to good advantage in this photograph: the 6-inch guns were carried in sponsons, with six 5-inch guns mounted on the broadside between them. As masted cruisers *Calliope* and *Calypso* were intended for overseas service, and it was while discharging this duty that *Calliope* found herself at Apia on the island of Samoa in March 1889 alongside six merchantmen and three American and three German warships. A tropical cyclone struck the island on 15 March and wrecked all the merchants, all three German ships and two of the American vessels. *Calliope* was the only vessel able to steam out of the harbour during the storm and thus survived; even then, the winds and waves were so fierce that she was barely able to make any headway against them despite running her engines at full power. *Calliope* became a training ship on the Tyne in 1907 and remained there until she was sold off in 1951, but her name is preserved in that of the current RNVR shore establishment in Gateshead. (© The National Archives, United Kingdom, ADM 176/112)

Pylades was a member of the *Satellite* class of composite-hulled cruisers, which were initially rated as sloops but reclassified as corvettes in 1884. At 1,420-tons displacement they were therefore the RN's smallest masted corvettes. They were also the only composite-hulled cruisers to be given an armoured deck to protect their machinery and magazines. Laid down in 1883, *Pylades* was the final ship of the class to be completed, entering service in 1886, and no further RN ships were rated as corvettes until the Second World War. She had an armament of fourteen 5-inch breech-loaders and this remained unchanged throughout her career, which lasted until she was sold off in 1906. Five guns on the broadside, and the forward embrasure on the starboard side, are visible in this photograph. (© The National Archives, United Kingdom, ADM 176/551)

composite-hulled *Doterel*, *Dolphin*, *Mariner* and *Nymphe* classes were constructed from 1879 to 1889.[114] The *Dolphin* class ships were the first sloops to be given breech-loading guns (two 6-inch and 5-inch), and the continued similarity between the sloop and the gunvessel can be seen by the fact that the contemporary *Albacore*-class gunvessels (described more fully below) had two 5-inch and two 4-inch breech-loaders. Indeed, the *Mariner* class ships were originally rated as gunvessels before they were redesignated as sloops in 1884.[115] Steel was not used for the hull of sloops until the two *Beagle*-class vessels (*Beagle* and *Basilisk*) of 1888–9. Displacing 1,170 tons, these ships introduced a 1-inch protective deck into sloops

Wanderer was a 925-ton composite-hulled sloop launched in 1883. She and her sister *Dolphin* were the first sloops to be given modern breech-loaders instead of muzzle-loading guns, mounting two 6-inch and two 5-inch weapons and three machine-guns. Particularly visible in the photograph is the port-side embrasure for the forward 6-inch gun that, in common with contemporary gunvessels and gunboats, was mounted on a centre-line pivot and could be fired through such ports on either side of the ship. *Wanderer* was sold off in 1907. (© The National Archives, United Kingdom, ADM 176/764)

Sister-ship of *Wanderer*, *Dolphin* became an accommodation ship for submarines at Gosport in 1907 and gave her name to the RN's submarine base (later training school), which was maintained until its closure in 1998. This photograph provides a good view of the forward and aft embrasures for the centre line mounted 6-inch guns, as well as the gun-port for the starboard-side 5-inch weapon. (© The National Archives, United Kingdom, ADM 176/204)

Acorn was a composite-hulled 970-ton *Mariner*-class sloop launched in 1884. Illustrating the growing convergence between the two classes of vessel as the nineteenth century progressed, this class were originally rated as gunvessels but were reclassified as sloops prior to the completion of the final ships of the class. *Acorn* was armed with eight 5-inch breech-loaders, of which the four starboard guns are visible in this photograph (two in tall shields and two in broadside mountings). *Acorn* was the first of the class to be removed from service, being sold off in 1899 and broken up in 1904. (© The National Archives, United Kingdom, ADM 176/3)

Icarus was a 970-ton *Mariner*-class composite-hulled sloop. This photograph provides an alternative view from that of *Acorn*, showing the forepart of the ship and the forward armament to good effect. The broadside 5-inch guns are not as prominent as in the previous photograph, however. As with many RN masted cruisers, *Icarus* was sold off in 1903. (© The National Archives, United Kingdom, ADM 176/349)

Melita, a 970-ton *Mariner*-class composite-hulled sloop. She was notable as one of the very few Victorian-era RN ships not to be built in a home dockyard, being instead built at the dockyard on Malta. Given the yard's inexperience, it is perhaps unsurprising that she took longer and cost more than her sisters: six years and £60,000, as opposed to an average of approximately two and a half years and £50,000 for each of the other five *Mariner* class. *Melita* was taken out of front-line service in the 1900s and, like a number of other *Mariner*-class vessels, was converted into a salvage ship in 1917. She was finally sold off in 1920. (© The National Archives, United Kingdom, ADM 176/443)

The 1,140-ton sloop *Nymphe* was completed in February 1899. *Nymphe* was the lead ship of a class of four vessels that proved to be the final composite-hulled sloops to be built for the RN. They were the first RN sloops, however, to feature triple-expansion engines and to have two (rather than a single) screws. This photograph shows her essentially as built, with three masts and her armament of eight 5-inch breech-loaders all mounted in shields on the upper deck. (© The National Archives, United Kingdom, ADM 176/488(b))

Nymphe as she appeared in December 1904. Her yards and sails have been removed to leave only a single bare pole-mast forward, reducing the elegance of her appearance considerably. *Nymphe* survived as gunnery tender until the outbreak of the First World War, when she was somewhat surprisingly recalled to active service alongside a number of other obsolete warships to form a scratch coastal bombardment squadron, and in this role she saw action off the Belgian coast in 1915. *Nymphe* was finally sold off in 1920. (© The National Archives, United Kingdom, ADM 176/488(a))

Basilisk was a 1,170-ton sloop completed in 1889. Alongside her sister *Beagle*, this class was a steel-hulled development of the composite-hulled *Nymphe* class, and included an armoured deck (1–1½ inches thick) designed to protect their machinery. They retained the earlier class's armament of eight 5-inch breech-loaders, however, all of which were mounted in shields. These weapons are particularly visible in this photograph, with two positioned ahead of the fore-mast, two on the poop deck and the remaining four mounted amidships (two to a side). Their armament and protection was thus comparable to the similarly sized *Barracouta*-class Third Class cruisers, but these sloops were only capable of 14½ kts at best while the wholly steam-propelled *Barracouta* class could manage a maximum of 16½ kts using forced draught. Both *Basilisk* and *Beagle* were sold off in 1905. (© The National Archives, United Kingdom, ADM 176/64)

and were armed with eight 5-inch breech-loaders, the same armament as had been fitted to the *Nymphe* class.[116]

From the late 1880s onwards masted sloops and gunboats were supplemented in the colonial defence role by small steam-propelled Third Class cruisers. The five *Medea*-class ships built in 1887–9 were reduced versions (sub-3,000 tons) of the *Mersey* Second Class cruisers (described below) that were fitted with a lighter armament of six 6-inch breech-loaders but retained the same full-length 1-inch protective deck with 2-inch slopes.[117] They were followed by four smaller 1,580-ton *Barracouta*-class vessels constructed in 1888–90 that benefited from the adoption of triple-expansion machinery to free up sufficient weight to allow for a protective deck of the same thickness as in the *Medea* class. They were armed with six 4.7-inch and four 3-pdr quick-firers.

Two similar but faster *Barham*-class cruisers (capable of 19½ kts) were built for service with the main battlefleet, while five *Pearl*-class vessels were constructed at the same time exclusively for use in Australian waters. The *Pearl*-class vessels were slightly reduced versions of the *Medea* class (at 2,575 tons) with the same level of protection but a modified armament of eight 4.7-inch quick-firers and triple-expansion machinery.[118]

Melpomene of the *Medea* class. The angle of this photograph provides a view of the layout of the widely spaced forward 6-inch guns of the class, as well as providing a close-up of bow-mounted scrollwork and the forward torpedo tube. Like, *Melpomene* was one member of the class that was sheathed, and was sold off in 1905. (© The National Archives, United Kingdom, ADM 176/444)

Marathon, a *Medea*-class cruiser completed in 1889. Smaller than the preceding *Mersey*-class Second Class cruisers, the *Medea* class were found to be generally unsatisfactory in terms of both sea-keeping and internal volume, and were accordingly reclassified as Third Class cruisers. The disposition of the class's armament is well shown in this photograph, however: three 6-inch breech-loaders (later quick-firers) on each side for a total of six, supplemented by a total of nine 6-pdr quick-firers. *Marathon* was one of three of the class sheathed for overseas service and had a sixteen-year service life before she was sold off in 1906. (© The National Archives, United Kingdom, ADM 176/433)

Blanche, a 1,580-ton Third Class cruiser of the *Barracouta* class, that entered service in 1890. Although seemingly inconsequential, the *Barracouta*-class ships were notable for introducing a number of 'firsts' into small British cruisers: they were the first RN vessels of their size to have triple-expansion engines, the first to have a full-length armoured deck and the first to have an armament of quick-firing guns. As can be seen from this photograph, the class's 4.7-inch quick-firers were disposed in the same way as the 6-inch guns in the preceding *Archer* class, with two on the forecastle, two on the poop and one on each beam amidships. What is not so clear is that the class had two funnels mounted side-by-side, but as can be seen these were carried so close together they resembled a single funnel in practice. (© The National Archives, United Kingdom, ADM 176/85)

Blonde was a sister-ship of *Blanche*. Taken from a slightly different angle than the previous photograph, the twin funnels can almost be distinguished. The class's low freeboard is also particularly evident. The class were intended for overseas service, alongside the RN's masted cruisers and gunboats, and all were sold off in 1905 with Fisher's drastic reorganisation of the RN to meet the German threat in European waters. (© The National Archives, United Kingdom, ADM 176/87)

The 1,830-ton Third Class cruiser *Barham*. Completed in 1890–91, *Barham* and her sister *Bellona* were developed from the preceding *Barracouta* class, but with the power of their machinery doubled to give higher speed (16½ kts at normal draught, increasing to 19½ kts with forced draught). In service, however, the use of forced draught quickly proved to be extremely hard on their boilers and they were accordingly limited to 16 kts until they were reboilered in 1898–99. *Conway's* states that on reboilering *Barham* and *Bellona* were reduced from three masts to two but, given the date on this photograph, *Barham* had either not been reboilered by October 1899, or else one of her masts was in fact removed at a later date. *Barham* and *Bellona* mounted the same armament (six 4.7-inch and four 3-pdr quick-firers and two 14-inch torpedo tubes) and armour (a sloped armoured deck 1–2 inches thick) as the *Barracouta* class. *Barham* herself remained in service until 1913 before being sold off. (© The National Archives, United Kingdom, ADM 176/60)

Tauranga (ex-*Phoenix*) was one of the initial batch of five *Pearl*-class Third Class cruisers laid down in 1888. Her name reflected the fact that she and her sisters were paid for by Australia and were to be stationed exclusively in the Antipodes. The *Pearl*-class cruisers were based on the preceding *Medea*, but with the earlier ship's armament of 6-inch breech-loaders replaced with eight 4.7-inch quick-firers. The weapons on the upper deck fore and aft are visible, as are the positions for the guns amidships. *Tauranga* was sold off in 1906. (© The National Archives, United Kingdom, ADM 176/696)

Imperieuse and *Warspite*

In the late 1870s and early 1880s, building a single vessel combining the speed of an unarmoured commerce raider with the armour and gun-power of a Second Class ironclad was technologically no more feasible than it had been in the late 1860s. This was as true for France as it was for Britain. By 1878 France had completed a number of fast but unarmoured cruisers, culminating in *Duquesne* and *Tourville* capable of nearly 17 kts, but at the same time was building four 6,000-ton Second Class ironclads of the *Bayard* and *Vauban* classes. Meanwhile, Russia had followed the armoured commerce-raiding *General Admiral* class by laying down the improved *Vladimir* *Monomakh* and *Dmitri Donskoi* in 1880–81 (both completed by 1885).[119]

In Britain, at the same time as *Collingwood* was conceived as a counter to the French battleship building programme, it was decided to build two 8,500-ton armoured cruising ships to counter the French Second Class vessels. These vessels were required to have a top speed of 16 kts to permit them to catch commerce raiders – which was higher than all the Russian ships except *Dmitri Donskoi*, suggesting these were the vessels at which the new British ships were aimed. Indeed, the Russians seem to have been so impressed with the British vessels that they commissioned a virtual copy, *Admiral Nakhimov*.[120]

The two new British ships, *Imperieuse* and *Warspite*, were laid down in 1881 and completed in 1886 and 1888 respectively. They had the distinction of being the last large British armoured warships designed with both sail and steam propulsion, although the rig was removed from *Imperieuse* shortly after completion and never fitted to *Warspite*. This was made possible by the improved efficiency of steam engines and the continued development of a network of overseas support facilities for steam ships. They were sheathed to reduce fouling and carried sufficient coal to steam for 6,500 nm at 10 kts, both necessary in ships designed as overseas cruisers.[121]

Their four 9.2-inch breech-loading guns were mounted in single-gun

This photograph shows *Imperieuse*, one of two large (8,500-ton) armoured cruisers laid down alongside the *Admiral* class battleships, with the brig-rig with which she initially completed. She was found to sail extremely badly, however, and her masts, yards and sails were quickly removed and in their place she was given a single military mast with a fighting top. The angle of this photograph makes it very hard to distinguish much of her layout, but the sponson for her port-side 9.2-inch gun and the port and embrasure for one of her 6-inch weapons can be discerned. The class's distinctive semi-circular tumblehome, intended to give the beam 9.2-inch guns clearer arcs of fire fore and aft, can also be seen. In total, *Imperieuse* was armed with four 9.2-inch and up to ten 6-inch breech-loaders (of which only eight were actually carried for much of her career). She was intended for overseas service, and consequently served on both the China and Pacific stations during in 1890s both being relegated to the reserve. She was then converted into a destroyer depot ship in 1905 and was finally disposed of in 1913. (© The National Archives, United Kingdom, ADM 176/355)

Unlike her sister *Imperieuse*, *Warspite* was completed with the single mast and no sails or rigging. This photograph provides a better view of the class's layout, with the four 9.2-inch guns mounted in single barbettes one forward, one aft and one on each beam. Her 6-inch guns, however, are not visible here. Like her sister, *Warspite* spent a large proportion of her career overseas (primarily in the Pacific), although she also had a period as guard-ship at Queenstown (modern-day Cobh in the Irish Republic), before moving to reserve at the turn of the twentieth century. She was sold off in 1905. (© The National Archives, United Kingdom, ADM 176/766)

barbettes disposed in a lozenge fashion with one forward, one aft and one on each beam, which was the layout also favoured in contemporary French First and Second Class ironclads. Supplementing these was a secondary armament of ten 6-inch breech-loaders. Their armour was disposed as in *Collingwood*, with a 140-foot waterline belt of 10-inch compound armour over 10 inches of teak amidships and closely subdivided ends protected by a 4-inch armoured deck. Both ships were overweight when they completed and their belts tended to be completely submerged – a problem they shared with the larger *Admiral* class.[122]

Second Class Cruisers

At 8,500 tons and costing approximately £540,000 each, *Imperieuse* and *Warspite* were too large and expensive to be built in the quantities required for trade protection vessels. The solution adopted was to replicate the *Inconstant*/*Volage* force mix of the 1870s by building a larger number of smaller, cheaper vessels to supplement the two large armoured cruisers. These craft came to be designated Second Class cruisers, as opposed to the larger First Class types.

To this end, four *Leander*-class cruisers were laid down in 1880–81 and completed in 1885–7. They combined the general features of *Iris* and *Mercury* with an improved version of the flat armoured deck introduced in the *Comus*-class masted corvettes to protect their machinery. In the *Leander*-class cruisers, the 1½-inch deck sloped down at the sides to protect against waterline penetration, an arrangement adopted in many subsequent cruisers both large and small. They were slightly larger than *Mercury* and mounted a heavier armament of ten 6-inch breech-loaders, but had less powerful machinery that gave them a slightly lower top speed of 16½ kts.[123]

The *Leander*-class cruisers were followed by four *Mersey*-class cruisers built between 1883 and 1889. They were slightly smaller than

Amphion was a 4,300-ton Leander-class Second Class cruiser completed in 1887. The Leander class were developed from Mercury, with the addition of a 1½-inch-thick armoured deck covering their machinery and a modified main armament of ten 6-inch breech-loaders. All of the 6-inch guns were mounted on the main deck, with the front and rear guns in sponsons to allow them to fire ahead and astern – these are visible in the photograph below the bridge and between the main- and mizzen-masts. The remaining 6-inch guns were carried in broadside mountings. The Leander class were the forerunners of almost all cruisers (First, Second and Third Class) in the late-Victorian RN that relied on an armoured deck for their main source of protection. (© The National Archives, United Kingdom, ADM 176/24)

Arethusa was a sister-ship of Amphion. This photograph shows the location of the broadside-mounted 6-inch guns to better advantage than that of Amphion, and also depicts the appearance of the class after their funnels were raised by 6 feet to improve the airflow to their boilers. In this photograph Arethusa has the full barque-rig, including bowsprit, with which all of the Leander class were completed and which was only removed from the class towards the end of the 1890s. Like her sister Amphion, Arethusa was sold off in the early 1900s. (© The National Archives, United Kingdom, ADM 176/39)

Mersey, a 4,050-ton Second Class cruiser completed in 1887. The lead ship of her class, *Mersey* was the prototype for most subsequent late-Victorian RN cruisers of all sizes. Although derived from *Leander*, she introduced a full-length armoured deck and was propelled entirely by steam. The photograph shows her appearance as completed with a low funnel, before it was raised in height during the mid-1890s. It also shows the two starboard-side sponsons for two of her 6-inch breech-loaders. *Mersey* was sold off in 1905. (© The National Archives, United Kingdom, ADM 176/448)

their predecessors (4,050 tons instead of 4,300 tons) but were faster (18 kts), more heavily armed (two 8-inch and ten 6-inch guns) and better protected (2–3-inch armoured deck and a 9-inch conning tower). Furthermore, unlike the *Leander*-class cruisers their protective deck ran the entire length of the ship and they dispensed entirely with sails. In comparison with *Imperieuse*, these ships cost £210,000 each.[124] The *Leander* class became the model for all future British Second Class cruisers.

First Class Armoured and Protected Cruisers

Foreign navies also built cruisers that dispensed with vertical armour in favour of thick horizontal protection. France started her first protected cruiser, the 4,561-ton *Sfax*, in 1882 and by 1887 had laid down another thirteen protected cruisers. Given the prominence of the *Jeune École* in French strategic thinking, the stated purpose of these ships, like the five

Russian cruisers described above, was to attack British trade.[125] The British response to these foreign vessels was to construct their own large armoured cruisers, beginning with the seven *Orlando*-class ships included in the Northbrook Programme of 1884.

The *Orlando*-class ships were conceived as enlarged versions (*c.* 5,600 tons displacement) of the *Mersey* class, with the earlier ships' protective deck replaced with a 10-inch armoured belt and a heavier

The 5,600-ton *Orlando*-class armoured cruiser *Immortalité*, completed in July 1889. This photograph provides a good view of the class's armament: two single 9.2-inch guns fore and aft and ten 6-inch breech-loaders (five per side) in single shielded mounts amidships. The 3-pdr and 6-pdr quick-firer positions on the main deck below the 6-inch guns can also be seen. The photograph shows *Immortalité* as originally completed; in 1895, like the other ships of the class, her funnels were heightened to improve draught to her boilers and the 9.2-inch and 6-inch guns were replaced by more modern marks (quick-firers in the case of the 6-inch guns). *Immortalité* joined the Channel Fleet on completion, before transferring to the China Station in 1895. She was then moved to reserve and sold off in 1907. (© The National Archives, United Kingdom, ADM 176/353)

armament of two 9.2-inch and ten 6-inch breech-loaders.[126] They were smaller and hence cheaper (c. £300,000 each) than the earlier *Imperieuse*-class ships and thus could be built in larger numbers. The provision of an armoured belt seems to have been a continuation of the desire, evident in British armoured cruisers from *Shannon* to *Warspite*, for such ships to be capable of fighting not only commerce raiding cruisers but also Second Class ironclads. George Rendel, at the time a Civil Lord of the Admiralty, felt that it:

> ... brought [the ship] up to something like the rank of a second class ironclad in point of protection at the water line while preserving much of the special qualities of the unarmoured cruiser.[127]

As with a number of British ships of the period, however, the *Orlando*-class ships gained weight during construction and when fully loaded the top of their belts would have been 6 inches under water. The adoption of more efficient triple-expansion engines, however, meant that they could carry less coal and still make their designed endurance (8,000 nm at 10 kts), and this reduced the depth at which they

The *Orlando*-class armoured cruiser *Undaunted*, as completed with short funnels. *Undaunted* was the fastest of the class during their trials and made nearly 19½ kts, almost one knot faster than her slowest sister. The *Orlando* class were protected by a waterline armoured belt, as in previous vessels such as *Shannon*, but subsequent large RN cruisers adopted the protective deck pioneered in smaller cruisers. *Undaunted* initially served in the Mediterranean, before going out to China alongside her sister *Immortalité* in 1895. She was placed in reserve at the turn of the century as newer, larger armoured cruisers entered service and was sold off in 1907. (© The National Archives, United Kingdom, ADM 176/736)

floated so that the top of their belts became level with the waterline.[128]

The British response to the French and Russian cruisers continued with the two ships of the *Blake* class (*Blake* and *Blenheim*) laid down in 1888 and completed in 1892 and 1894 respectively. These were the first large cruisers designed by White for the RN, although the *Medea*-class ships were his first RN cruisers of any sort. The biggest change from previous armoured cruisers was the removal of all vertical armour in favour of a full-length armoured

deck 3 inches thick on the flat and 6 inches on the slopes. At 9,150 tons they were also dramatically larger and, although their armament of two 9.2-inch breech-loaders and ten 6-inch quick-firers did not appear notably heavier than the *Orlando*-class ships, the replacement of the earlier ships' 6-inch breech-loaders with quick-firers meant the volume of fire the two new ships could produce was notably higher. The *Orlando*-class ships had all their 6-inch guns behind shields on the upper deck, but *Blake* and *Blenheim*

incorporated lessons from trials with the old ironclad *Resistance* and had four of their 6-inch guns in 6-inch thick armoured casemates on the main deck, the first RN warships to be completed with this feature and one which was to become standard on later ships.[129]

Instead of mounting extra armament, the extra displacement and the weight saved by suppression of the armoured belt were used to increase coal storage and engine power. This gave the *Blake*-class ships an unprecedented radius of

The 9,150-ton First Class cruiser *Blake* pictured at Chatham in the 1890s. Along with her sister *Blenheim,* she introduced the full-length protective deck in place of the armoured belt to large British cruisers – a feature that had previously been confined to smaller vessels.

This photograph also illustrates well the armament layout of these two ships, which set the pattern for subsequent British battleships and cruisers: the two heavy 9.2-inch guns are mounted singly fore and aft, while the 6-inch quick-firing guns are in a combination of

shielded mounts on the upper-deck and armoured casemates on the main deck. (© The National Archives, United Kingdom, ADM 176/84 (a))

action of 10,000 nm at 10 kts and allowed them to reach 20 kts under normal conditions, rising to 22 kts if forced draught was used. Such size came at increased cost, however: *Blake* cost £440,701, compared with approximately £300,000 for an *Orlando*-class ship.[130]

Overall, *Blake* and *Blenheim* were the first protected cruisers in the RN with the endurance required to act as true trade protection vessels and as such set the pattern for all British First Class cruisers of the next decade. At the same time, the other traditional role of the British armoured cruiser, fighting foreign battleships overseas, was taken over by purpose-designed Second Class battleships (which will be discussed in the next chapters).[131]

Gunvessels and Gunboats

The period 1874–89 proved to be the swansong of gunboat and gunvessel construction. Up until this time, the primary overseas threats to British interests (especially trade) had come in the form of low-level activities such as piracy and recalcitrant local rulers. The small gunboats and gunvessels were the ideal craft to combat these threats as they possessed sufficient firepower to overcome all likely opposition whilst remaining cheap enough to be built and manned in the large numbers required. The rise of French and Russian steam commerce-raiding cruiser, however, was a threat that the gunboat could not match as the

This second photograph of *Blake* shows her appearance in the early 1900s, probably after her 1907 conversion into a destroyer depot ship. Her classic Victorian livery of black, white and buff has been replaced with a sober grey, and the exuberant scrollwork on her bow has been removed. Her 9.2-inch guns and 6-inch main-deck casemates have also been removed, leaving only a number of guns mounted in the former 6-inch locations on the upper deck. *Blake* served in this configuration during the First World War, supporting the TBDs of the Grand Fleet, before being sold off in 1922. (© The National Archives, United Kingdom, ADM 176/84 (b))

foreign vessels were both faster and better armed and armoured. As a consequence, the RN was compelled to build its own force of steam cruisers (as described above), and the gunboat found itself marginalised. Just prior to the momentous Naval Defence Act of 1889 described in the next chapter, all surviving craft were re-designated as either First or Second Class ships depending on whether they had breech- or muzzle-loading armaments.[132]

Before 1889 only eleven additional composite-hulled masted gunboats were constructed in addition to those described in the previous chapter: the two *Arab* class ships of 1874, the four *Condor* class ships of 1876–7, the two *Linnet* class ships of 1870–80 and the three *Algerine* class ships of 1880. The main change in the 620-ton *Arab* was a main armament of two calibres (consisting of one 7-inch MLR and two 64-pdr MLRs)

instead of the three calibres of earlier vessels. This was maintained in the three subsequent classes, which also displayed a slight rise in displacement (to 780 tons, 756 tons and 835 tons respectively).[133]

The final gunvessels were the two *Curlew*-class ships (*Curlew* and *Landrail*) built between 1885–7. Although they had a similar displacement to the earlier vessels (950 tons), they represented an

Griffon was a *Condor*-class composite-hulled gunvessel of 780 tons. Her general appearance is indicative of that of many of the classes of masted gunvessels that served in the RN from the wooden-hulled *Philomel* class of the early 1860s to the composite-hulled

Algerine class of 1880. Her initial armament of one 7-inch MLR and two 64-pdr MLRs was also broadly typical of vessels of her type, and like many gunvessels she was rearmed with two 5-inch breech-loaders in place of the MLR in the mid-1880s. *Griffon* was launched in 1876

and remained in service until 1891. The name-ship of the class (*Condor*) was Lord Charles Beresford's ship at the bombardment of Alexandria in 1882. (© The National Archives, United Kingdom, ADM 176/309)

Rambler, an 835-ton *Algerine*-class gunvessel launched in 1884. Essentially repeats of the *Condor* class, the three *Algerine*-class ships were the final composite-hulled gunvessels built for the RN. Two of the class (*Algerine* and *Ranger*) commissioned as standard gunvessels with an initial armament of one 7-inch and two 64-pdr MLRs (the 7-inch MLR being later replaced with two 5-inch breech-loaders), but *Rambler* was completed as a survey vessel and in this photograph no armament is visible. *Rambler* was sold in 1907. (© The National Archives, United Kingdom, ADM 176/564)

Landrail (pictured here) and *Curlew* were gunvessels laid down in 1885. As can be seen, they lacked the sailing rig of earlier vessels and were in effect diminutive Third Class cruisers. They were also the only gunvessels to have steel hulls and to be given torpedo launchers. The gun armament of the class was one 6-inch breech-loader on the forecastle and three 5-inch breech-loaders (one on each beam and one on the poop), all of which can be seen in this photograph. The majority of *Landrail*'s service was on overseas stations, and she met her end in 1906 as a target ship. (© The National Archives, United Kingdom, ADM 176/401)

attempt to bring the concept of the gunvessel up-to-date by constructing the hull of steel and removing the sailing rig. They were given an armament of guns (one 6-inch and three 5-inch breech-loaders) and torpedoes. They were regarded as failures, however, as they lacked the speed and size to act as fleet torpedo craft (they could managed 14½ kts, compared with the 19 kts of contemporary torpedo gunboats) and at the same time were too expensive to be used for the same overseas duties as earlier gunvessels, compounded by the fact that they lacked sails and their

unsheathed steel hulls would quickly foul without regular docking.[134]

The period similarly saw the end of new gunboat construction. The composite-hulled 430-ton *Ariel*-class vessels described in the previous chapter were followed by twelve generally similar *Forester*-class ships (built in 1874–7) and eleven likewise-similar *Banterer*-class ships (built in 1880–82). The three 560-ton *Albacore*-class vessels of 1883 were the first gunboats to be given breech-loading main guns (two 5-inch and two 4-inch) and were followed in 1886 by four

Bramble-class vessels. These 715-ton composite-hulled ships were armed with six 4-inch quick-firers and were capable of 13 kts under steam propulsion; the two remaining classes of masted gunboat, the six *Pigmy* class of 1888 and the nine *Redbreast* class of 1889, were slightly enlarged derivatives.[135]

Only three further classes of the flatiron gunboats were constructed. The four *Gadfly* class of 1879 and the pair of slightly larger *Bouncer*-class vessels of 1881 were similar in displacement (*c.* 250 tons) and armament (one 10-inch MLR) to the *Ant*-class ships described in the

Foxhound was a 455-ton *Forester*-class composite-hulled gunboat launched in 1877. The class were initially armed with two 64-pdr MLRs and two 20-pdr breech-loaders, but in some vessels these were replaced with 5-inch and 4-inch breech-loaders respectively at around the time of the Naval Defence Act. At the same time, other members of the class were removed from service and sold off. *Foxhound*, however, had an unusually long life: converted into a coal hauler in the 1890s, she was sold into private hands in the 1920s and remained in use as a storeship on the Thames until she was finally broken up in 1975. (© The National Archives, United Kingdom, ADM 176/279)

Cockchafer, a 465-ton *Banterer*-class composite-hulled gunboat launched in 1881. Developed from the first composite-hulled gunboats, the *Ariel* class, the *Banterer* class mounted the standard armament of RN gunboats of the 1870s and early 1880s of two 64-pdr MLRs and two 20-pdr breech-loaders. In this photograph the forward gunport and starboard broadside gun can clearly be seen. *Cockchafer* was sold off in 1905. (© The National Archives, United Kingdom, ADM 176/140)

Watchful, a 560-ton *Albacore*-class composite-hulled gunboat launched in 1883. Although very similar in appearance to the preceding *Banterer*-class vessels, the *Albacore* class differed by being the first gunboats to be given breech-loading guns (two 5-inch and two 4-inch guns per ship) following the type's acceptance back into RN service in the 1880s. These weapons were still disposed in the same way as the muzzle-loading weapons of previous classes, however: the firing port on the port-side forward is particularly visible in this photograph. The *Albacore*-class ships were the last gunboats in which these arrangements were used, however, as subsequent classes (the *Bramble* class onwards) mounted their guns in shields on the upper deck. *Watchful* was sold in 1907. (© The National Archives, United Kingdom, ADM 176/769)

Rattler, an 810-ton composite-hulled *Bramble*-class gunboat from 1886. The *Bramble* class were the first RN gunboats to be armed with quick-firing guns, and instead of the traditional centre-line pivot mount (as used in previous gunboat classes) these were carried behind shields on both broadsides (as in contemporary sloops). This new style of mountings is visible in this photograph. *Rattler* was the longest-lived of her class, surviving in harbour service until she was sold off in 1924. (© The National Archives, United Kingdom, ADM 176/568)

A photograph of *Wasp*, an 810-ton *Bramble*-class composite-hulled gunboat, that shows her starboard-side 4-inch quick-firers to good effect. This photograph is particularly noteworthy as *Wasp* was particularly short-lived: launched in September 1886, she was lost with all hands in October 1887 *en route* from Singapore to Shanghai via Hong Kong. With no survivors the exact cause of her loss was unknown, but it seems likely that she was overwhelmed by a typhoon. The RN strenuously denied charges that her loss could be attributed to crew shortages or faulty construction; White even wrote a letter to *The Times* in September 1890 to defend her soundness. She was one of two RN gunboats named *Wasp* to be lost in the 1880s as the previous vessel of that name, a *Banterer*-class gunboat launched in 1880, had been wrecked off the coast of Ireland in 1884. (© The National Archives, United Kingdom, ADM 176/768)

The *Pigmy*-class 755-ton composite-hulled gunboat *Pigeon* was launched in 1888 and sold off in 1906. This photograph shows the layout of her 4-inch quick-firer armament, which was the same as in the preceding *Bramble*-class gunboats: two on the forecastle, two amidships and two on the poop. (© The National Archives, United Kingdom, ADM 176/525)

The *Pigmy*-class 755-ton composite-hulled gunboat *Partridge* was launched in 1888 and sold off in 1912. The two 4-inch quick-firers on her poop are particularly visible. (© The National Archives, United Kingdom, ADM 176/507)

Goldfinch was an 800-ton composite-hulled *Redbreast*-class gunboat launched in 1889. The *Redbreast*-class ships were begun just prior to the Naval Defence Act and as such were the final composite-hulled masted gunboats to be built for the RN. *Goldfinch* had the standard armament fitted to the final gunboat classes of the late 1880s of six 4-inch quick-firers, and their layout, with two on the forecastle, two amidships and two on the poop, can clearly be discerned in this photograph. She was converted into a survey ship in 1902, and sold off and broken up in 1907. (© The National Archives, United Kingdom, ADM 176/300)

Pictured here in July 1904, *Thrush* was an 805-ton *Redbreast*-class composite-hulled gunboat. Her yards and sails have been removed and her armament appears to have been slightly reduced from her original outfit, with the two forecastle-mounted 4-inch quick-firers apparently removed along with the 3-pdr normally found in the embrasure forward. *Thrush* was converted to a salvage ship in 1916 and was wrecked off the coast of Northern Ireland in April 1917. (© The National Archives, United Kingdom, ADM 176/710)

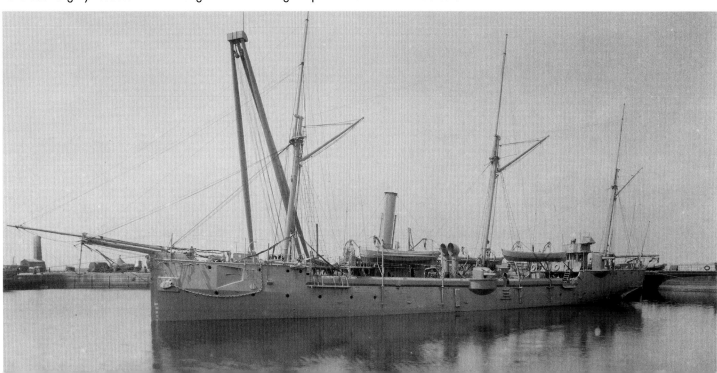

This photograph shows the flatiron gunboat *Bouncer*, which was launched in 1881. The two *Bouncer* class were slightly larger than the preceding *Ant* and *Gadfly* classes (265-tons, compared with 254-tons), but were identically armed (with one 10-inch MLR) and similarly capable of only 8½ kts. *Bouncer* here appears to be armed with a pair of light guns aft, in addition to her MLR forward. She was sold off in 1905. (© The National Archives, United Kingdom, ADM 176/93)

A most unusual-looking vessel, the 380-ton *Medina* was the name-ship of a unique class of flatiron gunboats that featured three masts, a poop and a forecastle. She was armed with three 64-pdr MLRs, one of which was fixed to fire forwards and can be seen in this photograph dated October 1897. *Medina* was launched in August 1876 and sold off in 1904.

(© The National Archives, United Kingdom, ADM 176/438)

previous chapter. Only the eleven 386-ton *Medina*-class vessels constructed between 1876 and 1877 were different as, unlike other flatiron gunboats, they were given three masts and a poop and forecastle.[136]

Ultimately, only one more class of gunboats was completed before 1906: the four mastless 710-ton steel-hulled *Bramble*-class ships of 1898–9. These carried two 4-inch quick-firers and four 12-pdrs and, being designed to serve in West Africa and China, were sheathed.[137] By the end of the 1900s most of the masted gunvessels and gunboats had been broken up or sold off, many as part of Fisher's ruthless modernisation of the service after he became First Sea Lord in 1904.

Thistle, a *Bramble*-class gunboat launched in 1898. The four *Bramble*-class gunboats launched at the turn of the twentieth century marked the final evolution of the Victorian gunboat, and differed from all previous classes in that they had a steel hull and, as can be seen here, no yards or sails. *Thistle*'s main armament of two 4-inch quick-firers, which was supplemented by four 12-pdrs, is also clearly visible in this photograph. Despite their more modern appearance, the *Bramble* class performed the same role on distant stations as did their sail-and-steam predecessors, both before and after the First World War. *Thistle* herself was not sold off until 1926, at the same time as her sister *Dwarf.*(© The National Archives, United Kingdom, ADM 176/705)

In the late 1880s Britain became worried about Portuguese expansion in East Africa, particularly along the Zambezi River, and so two small gunboats, *Mosquito* and *Herald*, were built for the specific purpose of operating on that river. They were constructed in sections to allow them to be easily transported overseas and then assembled in-theatre. This photograph is of particular interest as it shows an RN vessel of the period on deployment abroad, rather than tied up alongside in one of the Royal Dockyards. Explanatory text on the reverse of the original reads: 'HMS *Mosquito*, being "patched" in the creek, outside the British Concession. This place is tidal, the rise and fall being 10'–0". Taken at low water. Some guns unshipped.' (© The National Archives, United Kingdom, ADM 176/459)

Chapter 4

The Ships of the Naval Defence Act 1889

The doubts about the strength of the RN that had formed in the British public's consciousness in the mid-1880s had not been dispelled by 1889. The Northbrook Programme had been too small to satisfy critics, and a further war scare with Russia in 1885 seemed again (as in 1878) to highlight numerous weaknesses in ship strength and preparedness that had not been addressed. Another war scare in 1888, this time with France, once again made the matter of the RN's strength a subject of public debate. What is more, the international situation seemed to be swinging further against Britain as there were indications that France and Russia were moving towards an alliance (eventually signed in 1892), in which their combined navies would possess nearly as many battleships as the RN.[1]

A Franco–Russian combination of equal naval strength to the RN would counterbalance the RN's deterrent power and hence considerably constrain Britain's freedom of diplomatic action. In order to avert this, and to answer the domestic critics, a major shipbuilding programme would be required. By 1889 the technical and financial conditions were in place to make such a programme feasible and allow the rapid construction of large numbers of warships.

On the technical side, the second half of the 1880s saw the re-equipping and reorganisation of the Royal Dockyards. One of White's earliest actions on becoming DNC was to separate the shipbuilding functions of the Dockyards from the fleet-support activities, placing the former under a Chief Constructor for each Dockyard who reported to a newly established Director of Dockyards. Furthermore, in 1882 the Admiralty regained control of the production of the warship guns and ammunition from the War Office, which it had lost following the Crimean War with the abolition of the RN's own Bureau of Ordnance, by the transfer of the costs for these to the Navy Estimates. This was followed in 1886 by the creation of a Naval Ordnance Department, which was initially headed by the gunnery expert Captain (later Admiral) John Fisher. This was an important step as the delays in the delivery of guns had lengthened the completion time of a number of vessels in the late 1870s and early 1880s. The result of these reforms was that the Dockyards were now able to build warships more quickly and hence more cheaply – one of the major reasons for *Inflexible*'s extremely high cost was the numerous delays experienced during her construction.[2]

Britain's financial situation had also improved in the late 1880s. In the 1870s the government had taken out a number of loans to cover the cost of numerous colonial wars and the Russian War Scare of 1878, and up until 1885 had had to find money in the budget to pay off these debts. Little extra debt was incurred after 1885, however, and in the last years of the 1880s the government actually found itself in possession of budget surpluses (*c.* £2½ million in 1887–8 and again in 1888–9, rising to over £3 million in 1889–90). Also, the cost of servicing the National Debt was reduced thanks to a conversion scheme introduced in 1888 by the Chancellor of the Exchequer, George Goschen, which replaced all existing 3%-interest government-issued bonds with a new bond with a rate of 2¾% (reducing to 2½% from 1903 onwards). This helped to reduce the annual cost from £28,999,806 in 1890–91 to £27,402,132 in 1891–92, and further reductions were achieved throughout the 1890s until, by 1900–01, it stood at £20,788,292. All of these factors meant that by 1889 it was entirely feasible to finance a major expansion of the RN in response to the Franco–Russian threat without the need for loans or higher taxes, both of which would have been extremely unpopular.[3]

The RN's senior officers maintained publicly that its strength was sufficient: indeed, in June 1888 the First Naval Lord, Admiral Sir Arthur Hood, reported as much to a Commons Select Committee. Internally, however, it was recognised that there was a pressing need to build more warships. In June 1887 White had pointed out that by 1892 seventy-two obsolete vessels would have to be retired and replaced by the same number of modern ships. Furthermore, when asked by the government in July 1888 to estimate how many ships would be needed should war with France occur, the Naval Lords reported confidentially that the RN required an additional ten battleships, thirty-seven cruisers and eighteen TGBs, and proposed a

five-year building programme to deliver them. Accordingly, the First Lord of the Admiralty, Lord George Hamilton, recommended to the Cabinet on 1 December 1888 that this plan be adopted.[4]

While the RN and the government considered the issue, public concerns about the strength of the RN continued to grow. The 1888 Manoeuvres brought Vice-Admiral Tryon to the public's attention for the first time when, as the commander of B Fleet (playing the part of the enemy), he escaped from the blockading A Fleet under the cover of darkness and proceeded to ravage the coastal towns and shipping of Britain. His successes were widely reported in the press at the time, stoking further the public's concerns about the readiness of the RN for war, and the report into the manoeuvres (known as 'The Report of the Three Admirals' after its authors) that was delivered to Parliament in February 1889 was further critical about the RN's preparedness for war with one, let alone two, enemy powers.[5]

Faced with public and professional concerns over the state of the RN, the Cabinet accepted the Naval Lords' and Hamilton's recommendations. The government accordingly introduced the Naval Defence Bill to Parliament in March 1889, which provided for £21½ million over five years to construct ten battleships, forty-two cruisers and eighteen TGBs – five more cruisers than originally requested.[6]

Some £11½ million would be spent to build six battleships, twenty cruisers and twelve TGBs in the

Royal Dockyards, with a further £4¾ million being provided over the same period to complete those pre-1889 ships that were still building. The way in which these amounts were apportioned was designed to ensure that these ships were all completed within five years: the total amount of £16¼ million would be paid in five equal annual instalments of £3¼ million, with the unusual provision that any money unspent at the end of the year could be carried forward into future years rather than being returned to the Treasury. Likewise, if more than the allowance and any carried-over monies were spent in one year then borrowing could be used to fund the payment of future instalments in advance to make up the shortfall. With funding guaranteed for the whole five years, therefore, there would be less chance that construction would have to be suspended once underway for lack of funds, something that would not only lengthen the total time taken to complete the programme but also result in it costing more over-all.[7]

The balance of £10 million would be spent on building four battleships, twenty-two cruisers and six TGBs in private yards. Although these were to be constructed to the same five-year timescale as their Royal Dockyard-built sisters, and the companies building them paid accordingly, funding would be provided over a seven-year period. Some borrowing was therefore required to cover the deficit in early years until the sixth and seventh instalments were made available.[8]

Overall the Naval Defence Bill would increase the annual amount spent on warship construction by just over £2 million. Goschen's National Debt conversion would save the government £1.38 million each year from April 1889 onwards, however, and so the dramatic increase in the RN's strength could therefore be financed almost entirely by revenue and required little extra debt being incurred (and crucially no increase in taxation). This made it politically far more palatable than it would otherwise have been.[9]

Guiding the scale of the building programme was the desire to maintain the traditional Two Power Standard over Britain's naval rivals. On 7 March 1889 Hamilton reiterated this to the House of Commons when he stated:

> Our establishment should be on such a scale that it should at least be equal to the naval strength of any two other countries.[10]

Hamilton added a new twist to this, however, by saying that it should be measured only in warships 'of the newest type and most approved design', which should be larger and more capable than contemporary foreign warships.[11] He also hoped that such a large construction programme would dissuade Britain's rivals from attempting to compete, which would in the long run allow a reduction in British defence spending:

> [The completed programme will be] adequate not only to our immediate, but also to our future wants ... [it is] one which I do not think all the Dockyards of Europe would complete in the time we propose; and if there are any nations abroad

who do wish to compete with us in naval armaments, the mere enunciation of this scheme will show to them the utter futility of their desire.[12]

Given the public support for increased naval strength and the practicality of financing it without recourse to dramatically increased borrowing or taxation, there was scant opposition to the Bill and it was passed, becoming the Naval Defence Act, on 31 May 1889.

The vessels constructed under the Naval Defence Act were:

- 7 *Royal Sovereign* First Class battleships,
- 1 *Hood* First Class turret battleship,
- 2 *Centurion* Second Class battleships,
- 9 *Edgar* First Class cruisers,
- 21 *Apollo* Second Class cruisers,
- 8 *Astraea* Second Class cruisers,
- 4 *Pearl* Third Class cruisers,
- 18 TGBs.

Royal Sovereign First Class Battleships

The genesis of these ships came in August 1888 when, perhaps following the identification in the previous month of the need for ten new battleships, White was asked by the Board to design an improved *Trafalgar*. He accordingly prepared a number of alternative designs with turrets or barbettes, but he was personally convinced that barbettes were the only acceptable choice as only they would allow the ships to be given sufficient freeboard to allow them to operate effectively on the

open ocean. Turrets were simply too heavy to be carried high enough out of the water without a huge increase in displacement and cost. White correctly identified that the major weakness of British battleships of the previous decade relative to foreign designs was their lack of freeboard, which in bad weather limited their speed and prevented them from using their guns effectively. He was consequently determined that the new ships would not replicate this fault.[13]

The late 1880s marked the coming together of several strategic, technological and financial developments that would finally make the ocean-going steam battleship a practical proposition. Strategically, Britain now possessed a sufficiently developed network of overseas docks and coaling stations to support operations by large armoured steam vessels away from Europe. Technologically, triple-expansion engines were now fuel-efficient enough to give large warships an acceptable radius of action, and reliable enough to make extended operations feasible. At the same time, improved metallurgy (such as the introduction of nickel steel) made it possible to protect a ship against enemy fire with thinner (and therefore lighter) armour plates, leaving displacement free for other elements such as freeboard. Finally, sufficient finances were now available for the government to pay for battleships large enough to incorporate the required guns, armour and machinery into a hull with sufficient freeboard without having to sacrifice one or more of these elements.[14]

Although theoretically an excellent idea, in practice compound armour proved to have a major weakness in that the weld between the steel face and iron back was prone to failure when struck by a projectile. Efforts were therefore made to develop tougher steel armour that could dispense with the need for an iron back. One approach, pioneered by Schneider in France, was to add nickel to steel to make it less brittle. An American, Hayward Augustus Harvey, further improved upon this in the early 1890s by developing a process for hardening the face of a nickel steel plate (by increasing its carbon content through cementing and then heating and rapidly cooling it) and the use of annealing to toughen its back.[15] Both processes were mature in time for use (albeit on a limited scale) in ships built under the Naval Defence Act.

White's preferred battleship design, with high freeboard and the armament in two separate barbettes (one fore and one aft), was adopted on 16 November 1888 as the basis for seven of the Naval Defence Act's First Class battleships. At the insistence of the First Naval Lord, Admiral Sir Arthur Hood, however, the eighth ship was to be completed with turrets in place of barbettes, even though this would necessitate lowering her freeboard by one deck to keep her top-weight to a safe level.[16] This ship, appropriately named *Hood*, is considered separately below.

The *Royal Sovereign*-class battleship *Resolution*, photographed in January 1894 shortly after she had entered service. The *Royal Sovereign* class mounted their main armament in barbettes rather than turrets, as can be appreciated from this photograph, and the consequent reduction in top-weight allowed for an extra deck to be carried. This increased their freeboard and therefore made them better able to maintain speed and use their guns in heavy weather, compared with the earlier low-freeboard turret ships. This profile view shows the class's general appearance well, and the arrangement of their secondary guns (based on the layout first tried in contemporary First Class cruisers) can be distinguished. The lack of protection for the breeches of the main 13½-inch guns when they were run-out can also be appreciated. By the outbreak of the First World War the class was obsolete and most, including *Resolution*, had been sold off for scrap. (© The National Archives, United Kingdom, ADM 176/582)

The seven *Royal Sovereign*-class ships[17] were laid down between 1889 and 1891 and, in accordance with the five-year timetable stipulated by the Naval Defence Act, were all completed between 1892 and 1894. It says something for the urgency obviously felt at the time, as well as White's dockyard reforms and the importance of secure finance and a settled design, that the lead ship, *Royal Sovereign*, took less than three years to build – at the beginning of the 1880s, the *Admiral*-class ships had taken approximately six years each and even *Nile*, the final pre-Naval Defence Act battleship, took just over five. To achieve the required high freeboard of 18 feet, the *Royal Sovereign*-class ships were given an extra full-length deck that increased their displacement to an unprecedented 14,150 tons, 1,500 tons more than *Nile*. They were consequently the most expensive British battleships yet: at an average of £944,000 each, they cost over £60,000 more than *Nile*.[18] Again, it is indicative of the climate of political support for naval expenditure that such an increase was accepted.

Royal Sovereign's armour layout combined the features of the previous classes of British battleships (most notably the *Admiral* and *Trafalgar* classes) and was still mainly composed of compound plates, but it was generally more extensive. At 18 inches amidships (reducing to 16 inches and 14 inches at either end), the armoured belt was of a similar thickness to the previous ships, but it was deeper (at 8½ feet, compared with 7½ feet in the *Admiral*-class ships) and

protected a greater proportion of the ship's length (252 feet out of 380 feet overall). Closing the ends of the belt, as in the earlier ships, were two armoured transverse bulkheads (16 inches thick forward and 14 inches thick aft) and the horizontal protection was also similar to *Trafalgar*'s: a 3-inch armoured deck over the main belt, and a 2½-inch deck over both ends outside.[19]

Royal Sovereign also featured extra protection in the form of an upper belt stretching from the top of the main belt (some 3½ feet above the waterline) to the main deck. This was required to protect her more extensive sides (a consequence of the class's higher freeboard) from being riddled by enemy quick-firing guns and allowing water to enter the ship above the armoured deck. This belt was made of 4-inch nickel steel in four ships of the class, but this was changed to 4-inch Harvey steel in the remaining three.[20]

The upper belt was criticised by some observers for being too thin, and they instead felt that it should have been made to be the same thickness as the main belt. To have done this, however, would have added 500 tons of armour to the ship and required a further increase in displacement to carry this extra weight. Trials with the old ironclad *Resistance* in the late 1880s had also shown that the thin belt was sufficient to detonate HE (high explosive) shells before they could penetrate further into the ship, and in *Royal Sovereign* this protection was supplemented by closely subdivided coal bunkers situated behind the upper belt to preserve buoyancy if

the sides were holed. White therefore felt that the thin upper belt was sufficient, although he did say that he would have used extra displacement if it had been available to mount thicker armour.[21]

Royal Sovereign's two barbettes were disposed in what was to become the standard for all subsequent British battleships up to *Dreadnought*: one forward and one aft. They were pear-shaped in plan and constructed of 16–17-inch compound armour, thinning to 11 inches for the portions behind the 4-inch upper belt. Unlike in the *Admiral* class, these barbettes extended down as far as the 3-inch protective deck over the main belt and were therefore far less vulnerable to enemy shells bursting underneath them and putting their guns out of action. Each barbette mounted two 13½-inch guns, giving the ship the same main armament as the *Admiral*-class ships and *Trafalgar*, but although these were breech-loaders they were required to be loaded in a single position both in terms of training and elevation.[22] Thanks to *Royal Sovereign*'s higher freeboard, however, her guns were 23 feet above the water (as opposed to 14 feet in *Trafalgar*) and consequently far less likely to be rendered unusable in bad weather.[23]

The *Royal Sovereign*-class vessels were also the first British battleships to mount some of their secondary armament in casemates. Of the ten 6-inch quick-firers, six were placed on the upper deck behind shields and the remaining four were mounted in 6-inch armoured casemates on the main deck. This distribution was the same as in the First Class cruiser

Blake and was similarly designed to spread the guns out as far as possible to prevent a single hit from disabling multiple weapons. A number of problems were experienced with this arrangement, however: the casemates were too close to the waterline and could flood in heavy seas, while the shielded guns were too lightly armoured. Despite this, similar arrangements were adopted in many subsequent British battleships, although the vulnerability of the upper-deck guns in the *Royal Sovereign* class was addressed by installing 5-inch Krupp steel casemates for them in 1902–04. The *Royal Sovereign* class also mounted an anti-torpedo boat armament of sixteen 6-pdr and twelve 3-pdr quick-firers.[24]

Triple-expansion engines drove all seven ships of the class at between 17¼ and 18¼ kts under forced draught on trials, and they could carry a maximum of 1,490 tons of coal, which gave them a radius of action of 2,780 nm at 14 kts, or 4,720 nm at 10 kts.[25] Their high freeboard allowed them to maintain speed in heavy weather when earlier low-freeboard battleships could not, and many writers have commented on how well-liked they were when in service.[26] Their general configuration set the pattern for all British battleships up to *Dreadnought* in 1906, in direct contrast to the variety of designs evident over the previous twenty years – Parkes has waxed lyrical about the *Royal Sovereign* class:

For the first time since the *Devastation* set a new standard for unsightliness, a British battleship presented a proud, pleasing, and symmetrical profile which was unmatched by any other warship afloat, initiating a new era of Vulcanic beauty, after two decades of sullen and misshapen misfits.[27]

Like many ships of the period, the *Royal Sovereign* class proved to be vulnerable to underwater attack as there was insufficient experience in designing protective schemes to resist torpedoes and mines – the first large armoured warship sunk by a torpedo was the Brazilian turret battleship *Aquidaban* in 1894. Contemporary British underwater protection, fitted in all battleships from the *Royal Sovereign* to the *King Edward VII*-class ships of 1905, was designed to resist shells through a mixture of watertight subdivision and coal bunkers. These arrangements were not tested against torpedoes until 1904, when *Belleisle* (described in a previous chapter) was expended in a series of gunnery and torpedo trials, and were found to be ineffective.[28]

In the *Royal Sovereign* class this vulnerability was compounded by a central ammunition passage running between the two barbettes, which divided the engine and boiler rooms into two separate spaces port and starboard. No provisions were made for counter-flooding and so asymmetric flooding put the ships in danger of taking on a severe list or even capsizing – indeed, when the similar British-built Japanese battleship *Yashima* was mined during the Russo–Japanese War that

is exactly what happened. The ammunition passage was also dangerous as it could cause an explosion in one barbette to spread to the other, something that caused the loss of the German armoured cruiser *Blücher* at Dogger Bank and the British *Defence* at Jutland during the First World War. The danger of these features were only exposed by the experience of war in the early twentieth century, however, and so were continued in British battleships of the 1890s from *Royal Sovereign* onwards.[29]

Hood Turret Battleship

Hood was the eighth First Class battleship of the Naval Defence Act and was completed with turrets in place of barbettes for the reasons described above. Losing one deck to keep her top-weight down meant that her freeboard was reduced to 11¼ feet and this put her guns only 17 feet above the water, 5 feet lower than the other *Royal Sovereign*-class ships. As a result, in heavy seas she could not steam as fast nor fight her guns as well as her sisters and therefore provided a direct indication of the inferiority of the turret battleship compared with those with barbettes. Consequently, she was the last turret ship built for the RN. In all other respects she was nearly identical to her sisters, save that her upper-deck 6-inch guns were not remounted in casemates in the 1900s as she lacked sufficient stability. In 1914 *Hood* was scuttled as a block-ship in Portland harbour's southern entrance, and her wreck can still be seen there today.[30]

Hood was the eighth member of the *Royal Sovereign* class, and the only one to carry her main armament in turrets in place of barbettes. The extra top-weight thus incurred meant that her height was reduced by one deck fore and aft to compensate, which can easily be seen compared with the photograph of *Resolution*, and this reduced freeboard put her guns much closer to the waterline. As such, she was far less successful than the other *Royal Sovereign*-class ships and the debate between turrets and barbettes was firmly decided in favour of the latter. Visible behind *Hood* in this photograph are the funnel and upperworks of an *Agamemnon*-class citadel battleship. (© The National Archives, United Kingdom, ADM 176/340)

Centurion Second Class Battleships

Supplementing the *Royal Sovereign*-class vessels were two Second Class battleships designed for service in China and the Pacific to counter large Russian cruisers such as *Admiral Nakhimov* and *Pamiat Azova*. As these Russian ships were armed with 8-inch and 6-inch guns and capable of 17 kts, the two British ships required comparable speed (to enable them to stay with the Russian ships) and heavier guns (to be able to defeat them). The resulting ships, *Centurion* and *Barfleur*, displaced 10,500 tons and cost an average of almost £537,000 each, which made them almost the same size and cost as the First Class *Admiral*-class ships of less that a decade before. As these ships were specifically designed for overseas service they were sheathed with wood and then coppered. Their top speed was 17 kts, rising to 18½ kts if forced draught was used.[31]

In general terms these two ships resembled scaled-down *Royal Sovereign*-class ships with lighter armour and smaller guns. The 200-foot main belt was 12-inch compound armour, thinning to 9 inches at the ends, and was 7½ feet deep with 5 feet below the water. At both ends of the belt were 8-inch bulkheads that enclosed the circular barbettes, which were themselves 9-inch thick above the belt and 5 inches behind. Horizontal protection amidships was provided by a 2-inch armoured deck over the main belt, while the ends beyond the belt were protected by a 2½-inch deck. Like *Royal Sovereign*, the two Second Class ships had an upper belt of 4-inch Harvey steel covering the ships' sides between the main belt and the main-deck casemates.[32]

Centurion and *Barfleur*'s main armament was four 10-inch guns in two twin barbettes. Unlike previous British barbette ships these guns were covered by open-backed 6-inch armoured gun-houses on top of the barbettes that rotated with the guns – an arrangement that came to be known as a turret, although it was not the same as the fully armoured rotating structure that the word was originally used to describe. Improved loading arrangements compared with the 13½-inch mountings in *Royal Sovereign* meant that these weapons could be loaded at all angles of training.

A wintery photograph of the Second Class battleship *Barfleur*, which was completed in June 1894. This shows *Barfleur* in the form in which she and her sister *Centurion* entered service, with their secondary armament of ten 4.7-inch quick-firers mounted in both shields on the upper deck and casemates on the main deck (as in the larger *Royal Sovereign* class). Also like the larger First Class battleships, their main armament of four 10-inch guns was mounted in two twin barbettes, one forward and one aft. Unlike the *Royal Sovereign* class, however, these guns were further protected by an armoured gun-house on top of the barbette, and this feature was incorporated into subsequent First Class battleships. What cannot really be seen from this angle is that the gun-houses on *Barfleur* were open at the back, while in later ships (from *Renown* onwards) the gun-houses were fully enclosed. As a Second Class battleship, a great deal of *Barfleur*'s active service life was spent on overseas stations (primarily China and the Mediterranean), but from the early 1900s she moved into reserve and was based in home waters until she was sold off in 1910. (© The National Archives, United Kingdom, ADM 176/59)

Centurion, *Barfleur*'s sister-ship, photographed in November 1903. Both ships were reconstructed in the early 1900s, and this photograph shows *Centurion*'s appearance once this had been completed. The biggest change was the replacement of their 4.7-inch secondary guns with 6-inch weapons mounted in new armoured casemates, which brought their secondary armament up to the same level as that of contemporary RN First Class battleships. *Centurion* was initially based on the China Station, but was brought back to Britain following the conclusion of the Anglo–Japanese alliance and was sold off in 1910. (© The National Archives, United Kingdom, ADM 176/125)

The secondary armament was also lighter than that of the *Royal Sovereign* class, being made up of ten 4.7-inch quick-firers, although it was similarly disposed in six shielded guns on the upper deck and four in 4-inch armoured casemates on the main deck. In addition, eight 6-pdr and twelve 3-pdr quick-firers were carried to protect against torpedo boats. Between 1901 and 1904,

however, both ships were reconstructed with the substitution of ten 6-inch guns for the 4.7-inch guns. These new, heavier weapons were better protected than the guns they replaced as they were mounted in 5-inch armoured casemates. To keep the overall weight gain to a minimum, a great number of existing fittings, including the foremast and after bridge, were removed.[33]

Edgar First Class Cruisers

Although design work on the *Edgar*-class cruisers was started after the *Blake* class (described in the previous chapter), the design periods of the two classes overlapped considerably and as a result some features initially designed for the *Edgar* class were retrofitted into *Blake* and *Blenheim*, while lessons from those two ships

The 7,700-ton *Edgar*-class First Class cruiser *Gibraltar*. Completed in 1894, *Gibraltar*'s layout reflected that of the majority of the class: her main armament was two single 9.2-inch guns, one forward and one aft, and ten 6-inch quick-firers, six in shields on the upper deck and four in main deck casemates. In addition, she mounted twelve 6-pdr and five 3-pdr quick-firers to defend against torpedo craft. Of particular note in this photograph are the main-deck casemates, whose proximity to the waterline can be appreciated. *Gibraltar* saw service in the First World War, first on patrol duties enforcing the commercial blockade of Germany and then as a depot ship, and was sold off in 1923. (© The National Archives, United Kingdom, ADM 176/290)

were also incorporated into the *Edgar* class. As nine *Edgar*-class cruisers were to be built, rather than just two *Blake*-class ships, the overriding concern was to make the *Edgar* class more affordable. Consequently, their designed maximum speed and endurance were lowered (to 20 kts and 10,000 nm at 10 kts respectively[34]) and this allowed their displacement to be reduced to 7,350 tons. This was estimated to reduce their cost to £275,000 each, compared with £440,000 for *Blake*.[35]

The 6,600-ton torpedo boat depot ship *Vulcan* was chosen as the starting point for *Edgar*'s design, rather than a *Blake* scaled down by some 2,000 tons. Apart from removing the specialist torpedo boat support equipment, changes were also made to the protection and armament: *Vulcan*'s 5-inch armoured deck, slightly thinner than the 6-inch deck in *Blake*, was maintained in the new cruisers. A curved 2-inch armoured deck was also fitted to protect *Edgar*'s ends in place of *Vulcan*'s 1–2-inch flat deck. Consideration was given to fitting *Edgar* with a 3-inch armoured belt but, as this would have increased her displacement by 650 tons and required a complete redesign in return for a limited increase in protection, it was not adopted.[36]

Edgar's armament was also increased from *Vulcan*'s to match that of *Blake* (two 9.2-inch breech-loaders and ten 6-inch quick-firers). Like *Blake*, *Royal Sovereign* and *Centurion*, the 6-inch guns were disposed in six shielded mounts on the upper deck and four 6-inch-armoured casemates on the main deck – although this arrangement first went to sea in *Blake*, it was actually first designed for *Edgar* and then worked into the earlier cruisers

Like her sister-ship *Crescent*, *Royal Arthur* (pictured here) differed from the other *Edgar*-class cruisers in having a raised forecastle to improve her sea-keeping and carrying two 6-inch quick-firers forward in place of the single 9.2-inch gun. Her armament was otherwise unchanged: a single 9.2-inch aft and five 6-inch quick-firers on each side (three in shields on the upper deck and two in casemates on the main deck). Note how close to the water her main-deck casemates are – a weakness evident in many other RN ships of the period. *Royal Arthur* was completed in 1893, and saw active service in the First World War before being converted into a submarine depot ship in 1915 and sold off in 1921. (© The National Archives, United Kingdom, ADM 176/599)

whilst they were building. *Edgar*'s anti-torpedo boat guns were increased, however, from the sixteen 3-pdr quick-firers of *Blake* to twelve 6-pdr and five 3-pdr quick-firers.[37]

Two of the class (*Crescent* and *Royal Arthur*) substituted two additional 6-inch quick-firing guns for the forward 9.2-inch weapon, and were also given a raised forecastle to improve their sea-keeping. This forecastle was seen as a success and incorporated by White in the designs of all his subsequent cruisers. Even with this addition, however, *Crescent* suffered heavy damage to her bridge when operating north of Scotland to enforce the blockade of Germany in the First World War. Overall, the *Edgar* class compared favourably with the larger *Blake* class, being

cheaper and having generally the same performance (albeit a couple of knots slower) and armament with only slightly reduced protection.[38]

Apollo Second Class Cruisers

The preceding class of Second Class cruisers (the *Medeas*) were generally regarded as being too small, and indeed were later reclassified as Third Class cruisers, and so to remedy this the displacement of the Second Class cruisers of the Naval Defence Act was increased to 3,400 tons. This extra displacement was used to mount a heavier all-quick-firer armament of two 6-inch and six 4.7-inch guns, as well as eight 6-pdrs and one 3-pdr – the two 6-inch guns were mounted one forward and one aft with three 4.7-inch guns on the

upper deck on each side. A second improvement was the use of more economical triple-expansion engines in place of *Medea*'s vertical compound engines. *Apollo*'s armour protection was generally the same as *Medea*'s, however, with a 1-inch protective deck thickening to 2 inches on the slopes.[39]

Five of the class were sunk as blockships at Ostend and Zeebrugge as part of the St George's Day raid on those two ports in 1918.[40] A further ship of the class, *Scylla*, is chiefly remembered as the vessel in which Captain Percy Scott demonstrated the benefit of his gunnery innovations in May 1899 by scoring fifty-six hits from seventy rounds fired during target practice – an average of 80% accuracy, compared with the usual 20–40%.[41]

Intrepid, a 3,600-ton *Apollo*-class Second Class cruiser completed in 1894. Although they were larger derivatives of the *Medea* class, the *Apollo* class still failed to rectify the earlier class's lack of freeboard. The main improvement over the previous class was the incorporation of an all-quick-firer armament: two single 6-inch quick-firers were mounted on the centre line fore and aft, and six 4.7-inch quick-firers were carried amidships. *Intrepid*'s 6-inch mounts can clearly be seen in this photograph, but the hinged bulwarks in front of her 4.7-inch guns are still in place and therefore obscure the view of these weapons – the lack of prominent sponsons for these weapons was another criticism of this class as it limited their firepower dead ahead and astern. *Intrepid* was converted into a minelayer, along with six of her sisters, in the late 1900s and was finally expended as a blockship during the Zeebrugge raid on St George's Day 1918. (© The National Archives, United Kingdom, ADM 176/365)

Naiad, a 3,600-ton Apollo-class Second Class cruiser completed in 1893. Like Intrepid, Naiad was converted into a minelayer in the late 1900s. This photograph shows her after her conversion with large ports and rails installed in her stern for the deployment of mines. In common with many RN ships of the 1900s, she has also had the shields removed from her upper deck guns following experience from the Russo–Japanese War that suggested that they offered little protection to gun-crews and could in fact be a source of splinters if hit. Naiad survived the First World War and was sold off in 1922. (© The National Archives, United Kingdom, ADM 176/466)

Astraea Second Class Cruisers

Although larger than the *Medea* class, the *Apollo*-class cruisers were still criticised for poor sea-keeping (due to their low freeboard and turtle-back forecastle) and for the disposition of their armament. Eight Second Class cruisers of the Naval Defence Act were therefore built as the larger (4,360-ton) *Astraea* class, where the increased displacement was used to add an extra full-length deck that increased their freeboard amidships and hence improved their seaworthiness. *Astraea*'s main armament was also slightly increased over that of *Apollo*, to two 6-inch and eight 4.7-inch quick-firers, and the end 4.7-inch guns on both sides were mounted in sponsons to enable them to fire directly ahead and astern – the lack of a similar feature had been a major source of criticism of the *Apollo*-class cruisers. Performance and armour protection were otherwise similar to that of *Apollo*.[42]

Pearl Third Class Cruisers

The four *Pearl*-class Third Class cruisers were virtual repeats of the five earlier vessels built for Australian service described in the

The *Astraea*-class Second Class cruiser *Cambrian*. In this photograph, the improved seaworthiness granted by the *Astraea*'s extra deck compared with the preceding *Apollo* class can be well appreciated. Also visible are the sponsons on which the end 4.7-inch guns on each side were mounted, which allowed them to be used to support the end-on fire of the single 6-inch guns mounted fore and aft. This feature was introduced into RN Second Class cruisers by this class, and was continued in subsequent classes up to and including the *Challenger* class. *Cambrian* was converted into a training ship in 1916 and sold off in 1923. (© The National Archives, United Kingdom, ADM 176/115)

Philomel was one of four *Pearl*-class Third Class cruisers ordered under the Naval Defence Act. Displacing 2,575-tons, her main armament of eight 4.7-inch guns was laid out, as can be seen in this photograph, with two forward, two aft and two on each beam amidships. Also visible are the 3-pdrs (mounted amidships around the 4.7-inch guns and in an embrasure at the bow) and the fixed 14-inch bow torpedo tube, while the port for her port-side torpedo launcher can also be seen. *Philomel* occupies a special position in the history of the Royal New Zealand Navy as she was that service's first warship, transferred from the RN to the newly formed New Zealand Naval Forces in 1914. She became an accommodation ship in 1921, and was scuttled in 1949. (© The National Archives, United Kingdom, ADM 176/521)

previous chapter. These 2,575-ton cruisers were armed with eight 4.7-inch and eight 3-pdr quick-firers, protected by a sloped armoured deck (1 inch on the flat, 2 inches on the slopes) and propelled by triple-expansion engines to a maximum speed of 19 kts. The main improvement in the Naval Defence Act ships was to increase their normal-draught speed by ½ kt, although their maximum (forced-draught) speed was unchanged.[43]

TGBs of the Naval Defence Act

Many books refer to the TGBs built under the Naval Defence Act as the *Sharpshooter* class. However, the thirteen *Sharpshooter*-class ships had all been laid down by January 1889 (i.e. before the Naval Defence Act was passed) and so the TGBs of the Naval Dedence Act were actually the eleven 810-ton *Alarm* class and five 1,070-ton *Halcyon* class laid down between 1889 and 1893.[44] These classes were derivatives of the *Sharpshooter* class and all seem to be referred to collectively as a single class of TGBs by contemporaries, although the larger *Halcyon* class (with poops added in addition to the raised forecastles of the earlier TGBs) were sometimes identified as a class in their own right.[45]

Both classes were generally similar in performance (c. 18 kts) and gun armament (two 4.7-inch quick-firers), but the *Halcyon* class replaced the five 14-inch torpedo tubes of the earlier vessels with the same number of larger 18-inch tubes.[46] As discussed in the previous chapter, these TGBs entered service at the same time as the first torpedo boat destroyers (TBDs) and suffered by comparison with the smaller vessels' supposedly higher speed. TGB construction was therefore abandoned in favour of TBDs, although it was not until the *River* class of 1902 that TBDs could match the seaworthiness of the earlier TGBs.[47]

Circe, an 810-ton *Alarm*-class TGB that entered service in May 1893. Although slightly larger than the preceding *Sharpshooter* class, they were identical in terms of armament – *Circe*'s forward 4.7-inch quick-firer and port-side twin 14-inch torpedo tubes can be discerned in this photograph. Along with a number of her sisters, *Circe* was converted into a minesweeper between 1908 and 1909, and in this configuration saw service in the First World War. She was sold off in 1920. (© The National Archives, United Kingdom, ADM 176/133)

The Naval Defence Act Considered

Overall, the Naval Defence Act was a successful shipbuilding programme that doubled the number of effective battleships and cruisers in the RN. There were disputes between the Admiralty and the Treasury and Parliament over the accounting methods used and the carrying-forward of unspent funds, but these were resolved. Some ships also cost more than initially planned due to an unforeseen increase in the cost of labour and materials, which was caused by a contemporaneous increase in the numbers of merchant vessel being built, and also the design changes to the *Centurion*-class ships and Second Class cruisers. Both these problems were rectified by a Supplementary Act in 1893 that provided £1.35 million to fund an extra year of building and resolved the accounting problems.[48]

Nevertheless, the continuous funding of the Naval Defence Act and the dockyard reforms of the late 1880s meant that most of the programme was finished to schedule: by April 1894 all but five of the Second Class cruisers and four of the TGBs had been commissioned, and these outstanding ships were all completed within the next financial year. These two factors also meant that on average the Naval Defence Act ships only cost an average of 3% more than planned, which was a dramatic improvement on the 20–30% rises experienced on some warships between 1875 and 1885.[49]

What the Naval Defence Act failed to do, however, was dissuade other countries from adding to the strengths of their own navies as Hamilton had hoped. Instead of introducing an era of lowered defence spending, therefore, the 1890s saw expenditure on the RN rise to hitherto unheard of levels as Britain was forced to fund further construction programmes in response to the raised building levels of her rivals. This topic will be examined in the next chapter.

Chapter 5

The Pre-dreadnought Fleet 1892–1906

In the 1890s Britain faced a continued challenge to her naval supremacy from her old rivals, France and Russia, and also the emergence of new potential opponents both inside and outside Europe. By 1890 there were also indications that France and Russia were moving towards an alliance. The result was that Britain would have to react with both an unprecedented scale of warship construction and also an unheard of foreign commitment in order to preserve her strategic position.

France had abandoned battleship construction after the *Magenta* of 1883 and, thanks to the influence of the *Jeune École*, had concentrated instead on cruisers and torpedo boats. In 1889, however, she restarted building battleships with the 11,000-ton *Brennus*. This resurgence in French battleship construction marked the beginning of her final attempt to match the RN's battleship strength. Three more battleships (*Charles Martel*, *Carnot* and *Jauréguiberry*) were started in

1891, but as these took some six years to finish they were obsolete by the time they entered service – a further indication of the advantage Britain gained from being able to build battleships quickly. They were followed by the two generally similar *Masséna* and *Bouvet* in 1892–3.[1]

The first true French pre-dreadnoughts (the three *Charlemagne*-class vessels and their near-sister *Iéna*) were started in 1894–8. These vessels were all limited, however, by a lower displacement than contemporary British battleships – even *Suffren* of 1899, the largest French battleship of the decade at 12,527 tons, was over 1,500 tons lighter than the *Royal Sovereign* class of the early 1890s and even more out-weighed by the classes of British battleship that had entered service in the 1890s. It was not until the two-ship *République* class of 1901–02 and the four-ship *Liberté* class begun in 1902–03, all of which displaced *c.* 15,000 tons, that French battleships began to equal their RN

contemporaries in size, but these vessels completed just in time to be totally outclassed by the new *Dreadnought*.[2]

France's battleship building ambitions were stymied by the relative inefficiency of her shipyards compared with Britain's. Her battleships took longer to build (an average of sixty months each, compared with thirty-nine months for Britain) and cost, by the French government's own estimates, 20–25% more. As a result she built fewer battleships than Britain in the period 1889–1906. Many of these ships also completed over-weight, which affected their stability and submerged their armoured belts, but this problem did not occur in Britain following the reforms of the late 1880s. Also, continued tensions with Germany meant that France did not have access to Krupp armour until 1901 – five years after the first British battleship with this armour was laid down.[3]

At the same time Russia was also expanding her navy. Starting in

1882, she had planned to add some twenty battleships to her fleet, and consequently laid down eleven new battleships between 1891 and 1895 to achieve this. Having acquired a lease on Port Arthur from China in 1897, Russia then planned to spend £27,560,000 to build another new fleet of eight battleships, seventeen cruisers and fifty smaller craft in seven years to be based there.[4]

The 1890s also saw the growth of extra-European navies to the point where they could threaten the forces that the RN could afford to station overseas. Aware that she could not match this scale of construction in addition to all the other European challenges, Britain was forced to seek diplomatic solutions. In one case, this saw her taking the unprecedented step of coming to a formal alliance.

Anglo–US relations had been strained during the American Civil War by the building of Confederate commerce raiders in British yards and by incidents such as the *Trent* affair where a Union warship stopped a British mail ship and removed two Confederate representatives who were travelling to Europe. The Treaty of Washington in 1871 and the resulting international tribunal (which ruled that Britain should pay the US $15,000,000 in damages, while the US should pay Canada $5,500,000 for the use of fishing grounds) went a long way to normalising relations. Thereafter, the US entered a period of reconstruction and westward expansion during which the United States Navy (USN) was seen as a low priority.[5]

Post-Civil War, the US's industrial power grew to such an extent that, by 1890, she was producing more pig iron than Britain (9.2 million tons, compared with 7.9 million tons). This led to calls for the USN to be strengthened to a commensurate level. In the 1880s, therefore, the US began to replace Civil War-vintage ships with new cruisers and coastal defence ships, and this trend continued into the 1890s with the construction of a modern fleet essentially from scratch – between 1889 and 1904 she began no fewer than twenty-seven First Class battleships, along with fifteen First Class armoured cruisers and numerous other supporting vessel.[6]

Britain recognised that she could not afford to compete with the USN in addition to France, Russia and others, and instead pursued a conscious policy of attempting to avoid disputes with the US – this can be seen in the explicit British acceptance of the Monroe Doctrine during the border dispute between Venezuela and British Guiana in the mid-1890s, and the desire not to antagonise the US during the Spanish–American War of 1898. This saw Britain issue a call for a peaceful resolution only after she had first cleared any objections with the US. By 1906, the RN had withdrawn all but nominal forces from North America to concentrate on more immediate threats in Europe.[7]

Britain also sought a diplomatic solution to the problem posed by Japanese naval expansion in the Far East. Britain and Japan had developed good relations during the latter half of the nineteenth century

as, following her opening to the world in the 1860s, Japan turned to Britain to modernise her industries and to train and build the Imperial Japanese Navy (IJN).[8] Britain and Japan also shared a similar strategic outlook in that both feared Russian expansion in the Far East, which provided the impetus to reach formal agreement.[9]

The problem of the growth of competing navies was acute for Britain in the Far East. By 1901, the RN planned to maintain a force of four battleships and sixteen cruisers on the China Station, where they would face a combined Franco–Russian force of seven First Class and two Second Class battleships supported by twenty cruisers.[10] This alone provided a challenge the RN would struggle to meet, especially because the growing threat of the German navy was calling for concentration in home waters. The First Lord of the Admiralty in 1901, the Earl of Selbourne, spelt this out in a memorandum to his colleagues:

> For us the odds of nine battleships to four would be too great, and we should have eventually to add to our battleships on the China Station. The effect of this would be twofold. It would leave us with little or nothing more than a bare equality of strength in the Channel and Mediterranean, and a bare equality of strength at the heart of the Empire is a dangerous risk. It would strain our naval system greatly and would add to our expenditure on the manning of the Navy.[11]

If Japan were also to be regarded as a potential enemy, then the addition of the IJN's seven modern First Class battleships and numerous cruisers would render the RN's position untenable.[12] If these ships were to operate in concert with the RN, however, then the Franco–Russian fleet in the Far East would be outnumbered. Britain would not have to commit more ships to the area and could potentially even reduce its naval presence in return for increasing her strength at home – especially if the IJN continued to expand. In 1902, therefore, Britain entered into a formal alliance with Japan, the terms of which stated:

> Great Britain/Japan is resolved so far as possible never to neglect the maintenance of supremacy of its naval forces, which may be apportioned for service in Eastern waters, over the forces of any third power.[13]

This was a suitably vague wording that left the RN free to alter its dispositions as it saw fit. By bringing the IJN onside through alliance, therefore, Britain removed the threat of growing Japanese naval power, countered Franco–Russian strength and enabled the RN to concentrate on a fast-growing threat in home waters. It should be recognised just how radical a move this decision was: the government of the day was potentially committing future administrations to act in support of a foreign country if she were attacked by two or more powers. Nevertheless, the strategic situation for Britain was so grave that such a radical move had to be taken.

One of the main reasons for reaching an agreement in the Far East with Japan in 1902 was the growth of the Germany navy in Europe. Before 1898 this had not really been a concern for Britain, but the appointment of Admiral Alfred Tirpitz as Secretary of State of the Imperial Naval Office in January 1897 changed this. Tirpitz was an enthusiastic advocate of naval expansion, and he oversaw the passage of the 1898 Naval Act that committed Germany over the following seven years to build and subsequently maintain a battlefleet of nineteen battleships, eight coastal-defence ships, six large cruisers and sixteen small cruisers, as well as a Foreign Service Fleet of six large and fourteen small cruisers. A further Naval Act in 1900 increased these ship numbers of thirty-eight battleships, eight large and twenty-four small cruisers in the battlefleet and three large and ten cruisers in the Foreign Service Fleet. The 1900 Act also established a reserve of four battleships, three large and four small cruisers. By 1906 these strengths were all but achieved, with the Imperial German Navy containing thirty-seven of the thirty-eight battleships mandated by the 1900 Act.[14]

What so concerned Britain about the rise of the Imperial German Navy was that it was explicitly designed as a counter to the RN. In so doing, it was the embodiment of Tirpitz's idea of the 'Risk Fleet'; an idea enshrined in the Naval Acts themselves, which stated that the intention was to create a fleet 'so strong that, even for the adversary with the greatest sea power, a war against it would

involve such dangers as to imperil his position in the world'.[15] Tirpitz's hope was that, by creating such a fleet, Britain would not dare risk confrontation with Germany and would instead move to support her. Unfortunately, it achieved the opposite: worried by the explicit German threat, Britain was driven to clarify her relations with the USA, to enter into alliance with Japan and then finally to achieve *rapprochements* with her old rivals France and Russia, who were similarly concerned about German intentions.

Adding to British concerns about her strategic position at the end of the nineteenth century was the fact that the importance of the RN was greater than ever before. Britain had long been worried about threats of invasion, cessation of trade and potential attacks on the Empire, all of which the RN was meant to counter. To these were added a new vulnerability: the British Isles themselves were now at risk of starvation if Britain lost command of the seas. Before the Industrial Revolution Britain had been a net exporter of grain, but by the turn of the twentieth century more than half of all food consumed was imported by sea, and the domestic production of the remainder relied on imported animal food and fertilisers. Britain's domestic industry was also reliant on imports, with 60% of iron ore coming from abroad.[16] An enemy that successfully wrested command of the seas from the RN could therefore threaten to starve the country into submission, and thus compel Britain to capitulate without the need to mount an invasion.

Britain was therefore compelled to continue to build warships, contrary to the hopes expressed in 1889 by Hamilton. Just as the five-year shipbuilding programme of the Naval Defence Act came to an end in 1894, a further five-year programme of seven battleships, twenty cruisers and over one hundred torpedo craft was authorised at a cost of £21,263,000. This was known as the Spencer Programme, after the incumbent First Lord of the Admiralty, and it represented an increase of over 20% in the 1894–5 Naval Estimates compared with the 1893–4 figures, a increase that was expected to rise further in future years. Gladstone resigned, unable to support such increased spending on armaments, and this marked the end of his remarkable political career.[17]

Up until 1897, the government was able to bear the cost of increased naval construction without recourse to borrowing thanks to a period of economic prosperity, which generally increased the amount the government earned from taxation, and an unexpectedly high yield from death duties following the introduction of new graduated rates in 1894–5.[18] After 1897, however, the situation changed for the worse as naval spending continued to rise dramatically while at the same time the government became less able to afford it. Although a similar number of battleships were laid down between 1897 and 1905 compared with the period 1889–97 (twenty-seven and twenty-five respectively), the later vessels were larger and, thanks to the use of Krupp armour,

very much more expensive. As a result, spending on battleships almost doubled from £16.8 million in the first period to £29.6 million in the second.[19]

In addition, the RN was forced to construct greater numbers of armoured cruisers to match those building in France and Russia. As with battleships, these ships were bigger and more expensive than the previous classes of protected cruisers and were constructed in much greater numbers: from 1889 to 1897 nineteen First Class cruisers costing a total of £7.3 million were ordered, but this number ballooned to thirty-five armoured cruisers costing £26.9 million in 1897–1905.[20] By 1905, a modern First Class armoured cruiser cost almost as much as its battleship contemporary. Moreover, these larger cruisers required correspondingly increased crews, which further added to the cost of maintaining the RN, and these extra men required additional barracks and other shore facilities while their larger ships required docks to be enlarged, all of which also had to be paid for. All told, total naval expenditure was £137.3 million in 1889–1897, and £245 million in 1897–1905.[21]

This increased expenditure came at a time when the government could ill afford it. In 1898 the Chancellor of the Exchequer, Sir Michael Hicks-Beach, warned the Prime Minister, Lord Salisbury, that net revenue was likely to fall in the coming year (mainly due to a decrease in the yield from beer and spirit duties) and that this would likely lead to a £4 million budget deficit. What was more, this deficit would only grow in the years

to come.[22] Furthermore, from 1899 to 1902 Britain fought the Second Boer War and the government was compelled to resort to borrowing, rather than risk raising taxes, to pay for this. It was then faced with a decline in tax revenue of over £10 million from 1903 onwards as the economy, which had been geared up to support the war, contracted.[23] Throughout all this warship construction continued as the final ships of Britain's pre-dreadnought fleet were laid down. Dramatic steps would have to be taken, however, to make the RN affordable again, and this requirement led to the appointment of Admiral Sir John Fisher as First Sea Lord and the introduction of the era of the dreadnought.

Renown Second Class Battleship

Considering the design of future First Class battleships in 1891, the Admiralty Board decided that a new 12-inch gun should form their main armament and that no new ships should be started until this gun was available. One year later design work on this new gun had still not been completed, but there was felt to be a pressing need to build something, especially as Pembroke Dockyard needed work once the *Royal Sovereign*-class battleship *Repulse* was finished. It was decided, therefore, to delay two of the 1892 Programme ships to the following year, by which time it was hoped that the 12-inch gun would be ready, and to construct the third as a modified version of *Centurion*, retaining that ship's 10-inch main armament.[24]

This Second Class battleship was named *Renown*. Laid down in 1893, she was completed in 1897 at a cost of £751,206 including armament. She displaced 12,350 tons and was therefore comparable in size and cost to the First Class battleship *Trafalgar* of the mid-1880s, which had been in her day the largest and most expensive warship yet constructed for the RN – illustrating the extent to which battleships had grown in a comparatively short space of time.[25]

Although she could be seen as something of a stop-gap, *Renown* actually pioneered a number of design features that would become standard in subsequent British pre-dreadnought battleships: she was the first British battleship with all-steel armour, the first with a curved protective deck, the first with fully-enclosed gun-houses for her main guns, and the first with her upper deck quick-firing guns in casemates rather than shields.[26]

In previous British battleships the armoured deck was flat and situated on top of the main belt. In *Renown*, however, it was modified to take on the layout found in contemporary cruisers: flat along the ship's centre-line (2 inches thick in *Renown*) and then sloping down at 45° on both sides (3 inches thick) to meet the bottom, rather than the top, of the main belt. Coal bunkers were then placed above and below the slopes to add further protection against splinters and preserve buoyancy if the main belt were to be holed. All told, it was thought that this arrangement in *Renown* was equivalent to 6 inches of vertical armour.[27]

The 12,350-ton Second Class battleship *Renown*. Well-known for being Admiral Sir John Fisher's preferred flagship, *Renown* was derived from the preceding *Centurion*-class battleships and entered service in January 1897. Most of the improvements over the earlier ships were centred on her armour, particularly the increased use of nickel steel and the adoption of a curved armoured deck, but she also mounted a heavier secondary armament (ten 6-inch quick-firers). The layout of her armament, visible in this photograph, would become the standard for subsequent British pre-dreadnoughts: her main guns in two twin fully enclosed gun-houses fore and aft; her 6-inch quick-firers amidships, with four on the upper deck at the corners of the superstructure and the remainder in main-deck casemates; and her 12-pdr anti-torpedo boat guns grouped centrally between the upper-deck 6-inch guns. From this angle it also appears that she had a single funnel but, like many contemporary RN battleships, she actually had two mounted very close together side-by-side. She became a training ship in 1909 and was sold off in 1914. (© The National Archives, United Kingdom, ADM 176/577)

The *Canopus*-class battleship *Glory* under construction at Laird's in Birkenhead. This photograph gives an excellent view of the shape of the main armoured deck of all British battleships from *Renown* onwards: flat across the middle but curved down to meet the bottom edge of the main armoured belt. (© The National Archives, United Kingdom, ADM 176/297)

Renown also dispensed with transverse bulkheads to close the ends of her belt, and instead featured separate strakes of armour (10 inches thick at the level of the main belt and 6 inches at the level of the upper), running from the front and rear of these belts to the outside face of each barbette. In plan, therefore, her vertical armour had the shape of a hexagon rather than a rectangle. The angled strakes removed the need for *Renown*'s belt to be as long as the distance between her two barbettes, and it was consequently reduced to 210 feet in length (compared to 250 feet in *Royal Sovereign*, a ship of the same overall length). As was now standard in British battleships, outside of the belt her ends were protected by a 2–3-inch armoured deck and subdivision.[28]

The remainder of *Renown*'s vertical armour continued the arrangement introduced in *Royal Sovereign*, with a main and an upper belt of 8-inch and 6-inch thickness respectively. For the first time, however, both were made of Harvey steel, which made their protective value greater than their raw thickness might suggest. Definitive comparative figures for different armour types are hard to come by, as different types have different protective properties against different types of projectile, but a plate of Harvey armour was reckoned to be approximately equivalent to a compound armour plate one and a half times as thick. Under this measure,[29] *Renown*'s 8-inch Harvey belt would be equivalent to *Centurion*'s 12-inch compound belt. Indeed, when combined with the extra protection

provided by her curved deck, *Renown* was probably better protected than *Centurion* and perhaps closer to *Royal Sovereign* than a comparison of raw armour thicknesses would suggest.[30]

Renown makes an interesting comparison with the contemporary French First Class battleship *Charles Martel*, which was laid down in 1891 and completed in 1896. The French ship was seemingly far better protected by a 17¾-inch thick main belt and a 4-inch upper belt, but her main belt only extended 20 inches above her waterline and the upper belt only covered an additional 4 feet of the ship's sides. The result was that she was vulnerable to all calibres of gunfire from approximately 5½ feet above her waterline. *Renown* was much more extensively, albeit more thinly, armoured: her main and upper belt protected 9½ feet of her sides above her waterline against small- and medium-calibre shells. It can be remarked again, therefore, that *Renown* was probably more resilient than a simple comparison of armour thicknesses might initially suggest.[31]

Renown's four 10-inch guns were mounted in pairs in two 10-inch armoured circular barbettes (although these did thin to 5 inches in the portions behind the armoured belt). The guns were protected by 6-inch-thick gun-houses, as in *Centurion*, but in *Renown* these were fully enclosed and became standard in all subsequent battleships. She carried the same secondary armament of ten 6-inch quick-firing guns as *Royal Sovereign*, but in *Renown* their layout was reversed with four in 4-inch-

armoured casemates on the upper deck and the remaining six in 6-inch armoured casemates on the main deck. The bulk of her anti-torpedo boat armament (eight 12-pdrs) was concentrated in a battery amidships between the upper-deck casemates (a feature replicated in British battleships for the next decade), with another four 12-pdrs firing through ports in the hull (although these were later moved to the shelter deck). She also carried twelve 3-pdrs.[32]

Renown was designed for 18 kts under forced draught, and an endurance of 8,500 nm at 15 kts. In service she proved to have good sea-keeping characteristics and was accordingly twice chosen to carry royalty from Britain to India. She was a particular favourite of Fisher's who, as Third Naval Lord and Controller of the Navy in 1892–7, played a major part in her genesis and, as Commander-in-Chief of the Mediterranean Fleet in 1899–1902, used her as his flagship in preference to a First Class battleship. She embodied Fisher's ideal of a battleship with 'the lightest big gun and the biggest secondary gun',[33] and he reportedly wanted to construct a class of six.[34]

The Naval Scare of 1893, the Spencer Programme and the *Majestic* First Class Battleships

In 1893 British public opinion again became concerned about the strength of the RN as the delays in development of a new 12-inch gun (remarked on above) meant that only one further battleship, and that a smaller Second Class type, had been laid down by the start of the year. In contrast, France had started work on the final ship of the five *Charles Martel*-class battleships (*Bouvet*) and had recently ordered three *Charlemagne*-class vessels.

The new First Lord of the Admiralty, Lord Spencer, accordingly asked White how many battleships Britain would have to commence over the next five years to maintain superiority over the combined battleship strength of France and Russia, and White responded that as a minimum six new First Class ships would be required. The Board accordingly advised Gladstone's government that such a programme was needed, but

encountered opposition from Gladstone and the Chancellor of the Exchequer, Sir William Harcourt, over the increase in expenditure on armaments that would be required to pay for it. The Naval Lords were so convinced that such a scale of construction was required if the RN were to retain a Two Power Standard, however, that they threatened to resign *en masse* if their recommendation was not acted upon. Unwilling to risk this embarrassment, the government agreed in March 1894 to finance such a programme, although Gladstone was unable to reconcile such expenditure with his principles

and resigned. The resulting naval construction programme (the Spencer Programme) cost £21,263,000 over five years and built seven battleships, twenty cruisers and over one hundred torpedo craft.[35]

The First Class battleship component of the programme was made up of a new class of ships: the *Majestics*.[36] Ultimately the class numbered nine ships, which gave it the distinction of being the most numerous class of battleships ever constructed. All were laid down in 1893–5 and most completed between 1895 and 1897, although three ships (*Caesar*, *Hannibal* and *Illustrious*) were delayed by

The *Majestic*-class battleship *Illustrious*, which was completed in April 1898. From this angle the two funnels mounted side-by-side can clearly be seen, although from other angles they resembled a single funnel. *Illustrious* was one of the later ships of the class, and along

with *Hannibal* and *Caesar* could be distinguished from earlier ships as their bridges were mounted on top of their armoured conning towers, rather than wrapped around the bottom of the foremast. Less visibly, *Illustrious*'s 12-inch guns were

mounted in circular (rather than elliptical) barbettes and could be loaded at any angle of training. *Illustrious* was decommissioned and converted into an ammunition ship in 1916, and was sold off in 1920. (© The National Archives, United Kingdom, ADM 176/351) dockyard strikes and completed in 1898. The level of efficiency now achieved by British ship-builders was shown by the fact that the lead ship of the class, *Majestic*, was built in less than two years by Portsmouth Dockyard. Each of the 15,000-ton vessels cost an average of £954,600, including guns.[37]

Described by Parkes as 'the finest specimens of naval architecture of their day',[38] the *Majestic* class combined the improvements introduced in *Renown* with the 12-inch gun to produce the archetypal British pre-dreadnought First Class battleship.[39] The adoption of the new wire-wound 35-calibre 12-inch gun in place of the *Royal Sovereign*'s 13½-inch gun saved 140 tons, which was used to increase the number of 6-inch quick-firing guns to twelve and to replace the earlier ship's 6-pdrs with eight more 12-pdrs (to make sixteen in total). Only the 3-pdr armament (twelve guns) remained unchanged.[40]

In the first seven ships, the two barbettes for the 12-inch guns were pear-shaped, as in *Royal Sovereign*, and 14-inch thick above the armoured belt thinning to 7 inches below. Also like the main guns in *Royal Sovereign*, these pieces had to be loaded at a fixed angle of training and elevation, although limited provisions for all-round loading were made for eight rounds-per-gun. The final two ships of the class (*Caesar* and *Illustrious*), however, had circular barbettes and could load their guns at any angle of training, although they still had to elevate them to a fixed angle so to do. For the first time in a British

battleship, these mountings also introduced anti-flash measures by breaking the hoist from the magazine to the guns in a loading chamber situated below the turret. This was designed to prevent an explosion in the gun-house from being conducted immediately down to the magazines and so causing a catastrophic explosion. Each barbette in all the *Majestic*-class ships mounted two 12-inch guns, which were further protected by 10-inch-thick fully enclosed gun-houses after the pattern of *Renown*. The 12-inch guns fired an 860-lb projectile capable of piercing 33 inches of iron at 1,000 yards.[41]

The secondary armament of twelve 6-inch quick-firing guns was generally disposed in a similar fashion to *Renown*'s, with four in 6-inch thick casemates on the upper deck situated at the corners of the superstructure and the remaining eight in 6-inch thick main-deck casemates. This layout persisted in many subsequent British battleships, as well as many contemporary foreign vessels, despite the problems encountered with the main-deck casemates flooding in heavy seas. The *Majestic* class also adopted the arrangement, again introduced in *Renown*, of a battery of eight 12-pdrs situated amidships in the superstructure. The remaining four 12-pdrs were mounted singly on the main deck forward and aft of the 6-inch casemates, while the 3-pdrs were carried in the fighting tops.[42]

The *Majestic* class also incorporated *Renown*'s curved armoured deck, thickened to 3 inches on the flat and 4 inches on the slopes, and this, combined with the use of

coal bunkers, provided extra protection to her waterline and so allowed the thickness of her main belt to be somewhat reduced. The weight thus saved was used to armour more of the ship's side against medium-calibre projectiles: *Renown* had moved towards this by having a main and upper belt of similar thickness (8 inches and 6 inches respectively, compared with 18 inches and 4 inches respectively in *Royal Sovereign*), but it was fully realised in *Majestic* with a uniform thickness of 9 inches on both belts. These belts were closed by a 14-inch bulkhead forward and 12 inches aft. This gave *Majestic* a 16-foot deep citadel of Harvey armour (9½ feet of which was above the waterline) covering 220 feet of the length of the hull. Outside of this citadel, as usual, the ends were protected by a 2½-inch armoured deck.[43]

All *Majestic*-class ships were powered by triple expansion engines that made them capable of a maximum speed of 17 kts when using forced draught. In 1905–06 *Mars* was the first large ship to use fuel oil to supplement the burning of coal, although this did make her produce notable quantities of smoke, and all the other *Majestic*– class save *Jupiter* and *Illustrious* were so fitted by 1908. Like all British pre-dreadnoughts, the ships in this class had divided machinery spaces and were unable to perform counter-flooding, and this again put them at risk of capsizing if torpedoed or mined. Indeed, this was the fate that befell *Majestic* when she was torpedoed by *U21* in the Dardanelles in March 1915.[44]

Canopus-class Battleships

While France and Russia had caused concern in 1893, it was the growth of the Imperial Japanese Navy (IJN) that was to prompt the construction of the next class of British battleships. By 1895 Japan had defeated China in the Sino–Japanese War of 1894–5 and had captured a number of Chinese warships, including the battleship *Chen Yuan*, which she was refitting for service in the IJN. In addition, she had also ordered two modern 12,500-ton First Class battleships from Britain (*Fuji* and *Yashima*) to further strengthen her navy.[45]

The resulting class of six British battleships, the *Canopus* class,[46] was begun in 1896–8 and completed between 1899 and 1902. These ships were designed explicitly for service in the Far East and their design was consequently dominated by the need to be able to transit through the Suez Canal. For example, none of the class was sheathed or coppered, despite being designed for overseas service, as this would have added over a foot to their draught. This compromise was accepted, however, as none of the

Vengeance, a *Canopus*-class battleship that entered service in April 1902. The *Canopus*-class ships were designed for overseas service and were the first British battleships to make use of Krupp armour. They could be distinguished from the earlier *Majestic* and the *Royal Sovereign* classes by their funnels being fore-and-aft rather than side-by-side, as can be seen in this photograph. They also introduced the use of sponsons for the end-most main-deck 6-inch casemates, which allowed those guns to be fired at angles closer to the bow and stern. *Vengeance* was the first British battleship to be built, armoured, armed and engined by a single firm (Vickers). While her sisters had the same 12-inch mounts as the later *Majestic* class, which permitted the guns to be loaded at any angle of training, *Vengeance* was also fitted with chain rammers to permit loading at any angle of elevation, and this was said to raise her rate-of-fire from one shell every forty-five seconds to one every thirty-two seconds. She was also unique amongst the class in having her gun-houses made of Krupp steel, and these could be distinguished from those of her sisters by their angled rather than curved sides. *Vengeance* fought in the First World War and was sold off in 1921. (© The National Archives, United Kingdom, ADM 176/745)

Japanese ships were so fitted and the RN had adequate docking facilities in-theatre at Hong Kong where these ships could be cleaned – although currents could make these hard to enter and the RN typically preferred to use the IJN's facilities at Yokohama or Nagasaki instead. The *Canopus*-class vessels were therefore similar in concept to previous Second Class battleships – indeed when their construction was announced the First Lord of the Admiralty referred to them as 'improved *Renowns*'.[47]

Canopus consequently had her displacement lowered from that of *Majestic* to *c*. 13,500 tons. Unlike previous Second Class battleships, however, her armament was not similarly reduced and she carried the same outfit of four 12-inch and twelve 6-inch quick-firing guns as the larger vessel. Instead, weight was saved through the use of water-tube boilers and new Krupp steel for the armoured belt. Harvey armour was an improvement over compound, but it was discovered that its back was not strong enough to resist forged steel projectiles. German manufacturers Krupp therefore developed a procedure for producing steel armour plates with a very hard front and a suitably tough back. This complicated process, involving reheating, cooling, cementing with charcoal and application of pressure with large rollers, resulted in a very strong plate with a deeper hardened face than achieved with the Harvey method, but was also very expensive – as a result, the *Canopus*-class battleships cost an average of £913,500 each, almost the same as a *Majestic* despite their reduced

displacement. The invention of face-hardened armour with an adequately tough back did mean, however, that thick teak backing was finally unnecessary.[48]

The improved protective strength of Krupp armour allowed *Canopus*'s main belt to be reduced in thickness to 6 inches, thus saving weight, whilst still remaining equivalent to approximately 8 inches of Harvey steel. The layout of vertical armour remained unchanged from *Majestic*, however, with the upper belt being the same thickness (6 inches of Krupp steel) as the main belt. These belts were closed by a 6–10-inch bulkhead forward and a 6–12-inch bulkhead aft, giving the *Canopus*-class ships an armoured citadel 14 feet high, with 9 feet above and 5 feet below their waterline. The forward bulkhead was thinner than that at the rear of the citadel because *Canopus* introduced additional protection for the bows in the form of an auxiliary 2-inch belt running from the front of the main and upper belts to the stem. This was designed to protect against light gunfire riddling the bow plating and reducing the ship's speed.[49]

The main change to the armour scheme of the *Canopus* class from that of the *Majestic* class was the layout of their horizontal armour. There were fears, subsequently proven to be unfounded, that the French were planning to mount howitzers on their battleships to attack the decks of British ships with high-angled fire and so avoid their thick vertical armour. *Canopus* was therefore given an additional 1-inch upper armoured deck over her citadel, but to accommodate this the

main armoured deck was reduced in thickness to 2 inches. The ends outside the citadel were protected, as had become standard on British battleships, by a 2-inch deck.[50]

Like the final two *Majestic*-class ships, *Canopus*'s 12-inch guns were mounted in circular barbettes and could be loaded at any angle of training. The barbettes were made of Krupp steel (12 inches thick, thinning to 6 inches behind the belt), although the gun-houses that protected the 12-inch guns were 8-inch non-cemented steel. Early ships in the class had the same ammunition handling arrangements as *Caesar* and *Illustrious*, but in later ships the continuous hoist was reintroduced to reduce loading times.[51]

The 6-inch guns in the *Canopus*-class ships were mounted in Harvey casemates laid out in the same way as in *Majestic*. The end main-deck guns, however, were mounted in sponsons to enable end-on fire. *Canopus*'s 12-pdr guns were reduced in number to ten (compared with *Majestic*) and six were mounted in an upper deck battery amidships with the remainder disposed singly on the main deck. To save weight the class also had no fighting tops on their masts and consequently their 3-pdr armament was reduced to six guns. The use of new Belleville water-tube boilers meant that the *Canopus*-class vessels generated 13,500 hp (versus 10,000 hp in the *Majestic* class) and as a result they were nearly 2 kts faster than previous battleships at over 18 kts.[52]

Although the *Canopus* class was designed to serve in the Far East, the Anglo–Japanese Alliance quickly rendered this unnecessary and as a result they were incorporated into the Home Fleet. They were heavily involved in the First World War: *Canopus* was sent to reinforce Rear Admiral Craddock in 1914, although she arrived too late to fight at the Battle of Coronel, and was present as a guard-ship at Port Stanley when von Spee was bested by the battlecruisers *Invincible* and *Inflexible* at the Battle of the Falklands. All but *Glory* also served in the Dardanelles, where *Goliath* was sunk by torpedoes and *Ocean* was sunk by mines – once again showing the vulnerability of these pre-dreadnoughts to underwater attack.

Formidable and *London* First Class Battleships

By 1897 there had been a number of advances in naval technology, some of which, such as Krupp armour and water-tube boilers, had already been used in the *Canopus* class. In addition there were other developments, including a more powerful 40-calibre 12-inch gun in a mounting that allowed for all-round loading, which could further increase the power of future battleships. White therefore proposed that the three First Class battleships of the 1897 Programme should be built to a modified *Majestic* design incorporating all of these improvements. These ships, which became the *Formidable*-class vessels (*Formidable*, *Irresistible* and *Implacable*), would then serve to counter the French *Iéna* and the two new 15,000-ton Japanese battleships *Shikishima* and *Hatsuse*. White

proposed to used the displacement saved by Krupp armour and water-tube boilers to increase the new class's secondary battery to fourteen 6-inch quick-firing guns to equal that of the Japanese ships, but the Board preferred instead to devote the extra displacement to armour protection. As a result they were given a 9-inch Krupp steel belt (offering better protection than *Majestic*'s 9-inch Harvey belt) and the secondary battery remained unchanged.[53]

The three *Formidable*-class battleships were laid down in 1898 and completed in 1901–2 at an average cost of £1,094,500 each, including guns. The increase in cost over the earlier *Majestic* and *Canopus* classes was mainly due to the more extensive use of Krupp armour: *Canopus*'s armour cost approximately £240,000 (*c.* 25% of her total cost) while that of the *Formidable* cost £330,000 (*c.* 30% of her total cost).[54] Their armour layout largely followed that of *Canopus*, albeit with thicker and more extensive vertical armour: both the main and upper belts were 9-inch Krupp steel and were closed by 9-inch (upper belt) and 10-inch (main belt) bulkheads. The *Formidable*-class ships also incorporated *Canopus*'s thin bow belt, although it was thickened to 3 inches, and introduced a similar supplementary 1½-inch belt running aft from the main belt to the stern. Horizontal protection replicated *Canopus*'s two armoured decks over the citadel (a 1-inch flat deck above a curved 2–3-inch deck), and again the ends outside the citadel were protected by another armoured deck and close subdivision. The forward

armoured deck was 2 inches thick, as in *Canopus*, and the rear was 2½ inches, as in *Majestic*.[55]

The main armament comprised the new 40-calibre 12-inch gun, which fired an 850-lb shell capable of penetrating 12 inches of steel at 4,800 yards (compared with 3,100 yards for the older 35-calibre weapon). All three ships were given mountings that allowed these guns to be reloaded at any angle of training and elevation, and the improved rate-of-fire that this granted allowed the reintroduction of the break in their ammunition hoists that had been abandoned in later ships of the *Canopus* class. The barbettes for the 12-inch guns were circular and 12 inches thick above the belt (thinning to 6 inches behind the belt), while the gun-houses had 10-inch faces and sides and 8-inch rears. The secondary armament of 6-inch quick-firing guns was all mounted in 6-inch thick casemates disposed in the same layout as those of *Majestic*, although the end main-deck casemates were mounted in sponsons like those of *Canopus*.[56]

The use of water-tube boilers gave the *Formidable* class 15,000 hp under normal draught (compared with 12,000 hp for the *Majestic* class) and this raised their maximum speed from 17 kts to 18 kts. Unusually, however, they were given inwards-turning propellers, which allowed for a more compact engine room layout and decreased fuel consumption, but had the downside of reducing low-speed manoeuvrability. All three ships fought in the First World War, where once again the vulnerability of pre-dreadnoughts to underwater attack was exposed: *Formidable* was sunk by *U24* in January 1915 and *Irresistible* was lost to mines in the Dardanelles on the same day as *Ocean* (18 March 1915).[57]

In 1898 the Board became concerned that the three Russian *Peresviet*-class battleships then completing would enjoy a margin of superiority in speed over current British ships. The programme for that year contained provisions for three battleships but, as there was felt to be insufficient time to embark on a new design for these ships in response to the perceived Russian threat, it was decided to make these repeats of *Formidable*. This would allow sufficient time for a new design (which became the *Duncan* class, discussed below) to be drawn up without the risk of losing pace in the developing battleship-building race. As work on the *Duncan* class began while this second batch of *Formidable*-class ships (also known as the *London* class) was being built, certain features of the later ships were worked into the earlier vessels. Two further *London*-class ships, *Queen* and *Prince of Wales*, were laid down under the 1900 Estimates, making a class of five in total.[58]

The *London*-class battleships were very similar in layout to the earlier *Formidable* class. The biggest change, however, lay in the arrangement of their armour, where the layout originally designed for *Duncan* was used in place of that of *Formidable*. This meant that the forward armoured bulkhead, which usually closed the front of the citadel, was entirely replaced by thickened side armour, which

The *Formidable*-class battleship *Implacable*. The *Formidable* class marked the application of a number of the technologies pioneered in the *Canopus* class to the true RN First Class battleship, in particular the use of Krupp armour to provide increased protection without a dramatic increase in displacement. As can be seen from this photograph they could be distinguished from the earlier *Majestic* class by the layout of their funnels and by having their end 6-inch guns on the main deck mounted in sponsons, both features that were inherited from *Canopus*. Less visibly, both their 12-inch and 6-inch guns were of a newer pattern with longer barrels than those on the earlier ships. Of the three ships of the class, only *Implacable* survived the First World War and was sold off in 1921. (© The National Archives, United Kingdom, ADM 176/356)

The *London*-class battleship *Queen*, which entered service in March 1904. The *London*-class ships were developed from the preceding *Formidable* class and most of the changes related to the internal layout of their armour. The only obvious visible difference was the lack of lower-deck scuttles forward in the *London* class vessels, something that is shown to good effect in this photograph. *Queen* and her sister *Prince of Wales* could additionally be distinguished from the preceding class and their earlier sister-ships by their open 12-pdr battery amidships. This is also visible in this photograph, between the two upper-deck 6-inch casemates and beneath the ship's boats. *Queen* fought in the First World War, primarily in the Mediterranean, and was sold off in 1920 and scrapped the following year. (© The National Archives, United Kingdom, ADM 176/557)

stepped down from the 9 inches of the main belt to 7 inches, 5 inches, 3 inches and then 2 inches right forward – an arrangement replicated in all subsequent British pre-dreadnoughts. The *London* class also incorporated *Duncan*'s revised armoured deck layout (introduced for the reasons discussed below) with a flat 2-inch deck over the curved armoured deck, which was correspondingly reduced to 1 inch on the flat portion and 2 inches on the slopes.[59]

All five ships were in service during the First World War and members of the class fought alongside other pre-dreadnoughts in the Dardanelles. Although none were lost to enemy action, *Bulwark* was sunk at Sheerness on 26 November 1914 by the accidental detonation of her magazines.

Duncan First Class Battleships

While the *London*-class battleships were being built, design work progressed on the class of fast battleships thought necessary to counter the Russian *Peresviet*. In order to achieve a top speed of 19 kts, the displacement of the new British ships was reduced to approximately 14,000 tons and they were provided with more powerful machinery and thinner armour than their predecessors. In total six of these *Duncan*-class vessels were constructed, four under the 1898 Supplementary Estimates and two more were provided for under the following year's programme. All were completed between 1903 and 1904. Despite their smaller displacement, their average cost (£1,093,000 each) was almost the same as previous, larger battleships due to their expensive machinery. To have built a battleship capable of 19 kts that was armoured to the same extent as *Formidable* would have been prohibitively expensive.[60]

The *Duncan*-class battleship *Montagu*. The *Duncan*-class ships were designed to counter the perceived threat of foreign fast battleships, and consequently had thinner armour than previous RN pre-dreadnoughts in order to reach higher speeds. Visually, the main distinguishing feature compared with earlier battleships was the lack of ventilator cowls, with wind-sails being fitted instead. Otherwise, they mounted the by-now standard British battleship armament of four 12-inch and twelve 6-inch guns, along with a number of 3-pdrs and 12-pdrs. In 1906, only three years after she was commissioned, *Montagu* ran aground on Lundy Island in thick fog. Attempts to refloat her proved unsuccessful and she was consequently broken up in place. (© The National Archives, United Kingdom, ADM 176/458)

Duncan's armament was unchanged from previous First Class British battleships, and so most of the weight savings were made by reducing the thicknesses and extent of almost all her armour. The barbettes were reduced in diameter by 1 foot compared with *London*, and their armour was thinned to 11-inch front and sides and 10-inch rears on the portions above the armoured belt, and to 7-inch and 4-inch respectively behind the belt. The main and upper armoured belt were similarly reduced in thickness to 7 inches of Krupp steel, continued forward to the bows with thicknesses of 5 inches, 4 inches and 3 inches in place of the forward armoured bulkhead, and aft to the stern by a 1½-inch waterline strake.[61]

The arrangement of horizontal armour was also modified in the *Duncan*-class ships, although the revised arrangement first went to sea in the *London*-class vessels. The single armoured deck of *Majestic* had been replaced with an upper and lower deck in *Canopus* to

An interesting photograph of the *Duncan*-class battleship *Cornwallis* being repainted. While some of her crew are using her torpedo nets and booms to support themselves as they attend to her sides, others are suspended from her funnels by ropes. Like many RN pre-dreadnoughts, *Cornwallis* saw service in the First World War, but she was lost on 9 January 1917 when she was torpedoed by *U32*. (© The National Archives, United Kingdom, ADM 176/160)

defend against the rumoured use of howitzers by the French. Although this threat had proved unfounded, the Board also became very concerned about the threat of deck hits on rolling ships from direct-fire naval weapons. This would expose far more of the ship's machinery and magazine spaces to attack and, as deck armour was usually far thinner than the belt, there was more chance of penetration occurring. It was therefore seen as important to thicken the upper deck as far as possible to resist these shells, and to augment this with a thinner curved lower deck to protect the vitals from splinters.[62]

The higher of the two decks in the *Duncan*-class ships was accordingly thickened to 2 inches, in place of the 1-inch deck in *Canopus*. Because of the need to save weight, however, the curved deck beneath was reduced to a uniform 1-inch thickness. This constituted a major reduction in the protection of the waterline: *Majestic*'s 9-inch Harvey belt could be pierced by French 9.4-inch guns at 3,000 yards, and consequently she relied on the 4-inch slopes of her armoured deck (as well as coal bunkers) to protect her vitals and limit flooding. *Duncan*'s 7-inch Krupp belt was considered equal to 9-inch Harvey steel, but her 1-inch deck did not offer the same reinforcement as *Majestic*'s thicker deck – indeed, it was only just strong enough to resist French 6.3-inch shells. Critics also pointed out that *Duncan*'s 1-inch deck weighed the same as 5 inches of belt armour, and had this been provided instead it could have given sufficient protection on the waterline.

Experience during the Russo–Japanese War also suggested that deck hits were not as common as the Board had feared, while a modern historian has questioned whether the gunnery of the time was capable of reliably scoring hits on heavily rolling targets.[63]

All told, the *Duncan*-class battleships are regarded as the worst of White's designs, thanks to the reduced thickness and poor disposition of their armour. They were hamstrung by the need to achieve 19 kts, but this high speed proved to be unnecessary: the supposedly fast Russian battleships turned out to be capable of no more than 18 kts, and were only armed with 10-inch main guns.

All six ships fought in the First World War except *Montagu*, which was wrecked on Lundy Island in fog on 30 May 1906. Underlining the vulnerability of British pre-dreadnoughts to underwater attack, *Cornwallis* was torpedoed in 1917 (although she remained afloat long enough for all but the fifteen crew killed to be taken off) and *Russell* was mined off Malta in 1916.[64]

Philip Watts and the *King Edward VII* First Class Battleships

By 1900 Britain had thirty-six modern First Class battleships in service or building, as opposed to France's eleven and Russia's thirteen. This margin of superiority meant that, as the twentieth century opened, Britain could afford to reduce the pace of battleship construction compared with the almost frenzied years of the 1890s.

There was a long-standing criticism, however, that British battleships were under-gunned compared with foreign vessels, and this intensified in 1900 when it became clear that Italy (with the *Benedetto Brin*) and the USA (*New Jersey*) had started building battleships similar to the British *Majestic* but with the addition of an intermediate battery of four or eight 8-inch guns in addition to the usual armament of 12-inch and 6-inch weapons.[65]

Fisher's replacement as Third Naval Lord and Controller, Rear Admiral Arthur Wilson, VC, therefore wanted the next class of British battleships to mount a similarly reinforced armament and asked for a series of alternative designs to be drawn up. In 1899 the RN had ordered a trial gun of a new calibre (7.5-inch) from Vickers and it was thought that this might provide the secondary armament for future battleships, replacing the 6-inch gun on a like-for-like basis. Crucially for a secondary gun, like the 6-inch but unlike the larger 8-inch gun, this new weapon could still be loaded by hand. It was soon realised, however, that the casemates required to protect a 7.5-inch gun would have to be larger and heavier than those for a 6-inch weapon (thus reducing the available weight for armour elsewhere) and so thought turned instead to mounting the new gun in turrets on the upper deck, simple shields being seen as insufficient protection.[66]

The favoured design incorporating this 7.5-inch gun was a 17,000-ton 19-kt battleship with eight of the new weapons in pairs on the upper deck, in addition to the usual armament of four 12-inch and twelve 6-inch quick-firing guns. In one of his last actions as DNC, however, White pointed out that replacing the twin 7.5-inch mounts with single 9.2-inch weapons would increase the ship's ability to penetrate the opposition's armour without requiring a change in overall dimensions. The Board agreed to this change, but shortly afterwards White was forced to retire due to ill health. It was his replacement as DNC, Philip Watts, who gave his formal approval to this new design, so although the ship that was to become *King Edward VII* was officially Watts's first battleship for the RN, it was actually White's final British battleship.[67]

Although the initially approved design displaced 17,000 tons and had a maximum speed of 19 kts, the desire soon surfaced to make the ship cheaper. It was consequently decided to limit the new battleships to 18 kts, which in turn allowed the displacement to be reduced to 16,000 tons. As well as being the first British pre-dreadnought to mount an armament composed of three different calibres, the ship was also the first to mount its 6-inch quick-firing guns in a battery instead of the usual casemates. The battery was adopted as there was insufficient space on the upper deck between the 9.2-inch guns to mount the three 6-inch guns on each side in

casemates. A similar arrangement had been adopted in the Japanese *Mikasa*, which lacked the room to mount her ten 6-inch main-deck guns in casemates, and similar configurations were used in contemporary German, Austrian and American ships.[68]

The battery replaced individual armoured casemates with a continuous armoured outside wall and armoured screens between the guns. It required less space than the equivalent number of guns in individual casemates and saved weight, but it did not provide the same level of protection: if a large-calibre shell penetrated the outside armour it would not be stopped from

This photograph of *Commonwealth* provides an extremely clear view of the profile of the *King Edward VII*-class battleships. The photograph is dated 18 August 1905, at which time she had only recently been completed and the distinguishing intermediate armament of 9.2-inch guns in turrets at the corners of her superstructure is particularly visible. Her forward barbette, with the armoured gun-house containing two 12-inch guns on top, is also prominent. *Commonwealth* saw service in the First World War, and was converted into a gunnery training ship in 1919 before being sold off in 1921. (© The National Archives, United Kingdom, ADM 176/149)

The *King Edward VII*-class battleship *New Zealand*. This photograph provides an excellent view of the three main calibres of gun fitted to the class: her forward 12-inch turret is obvious, and her starboard-side 9.2-inch (in single turrets) and 6-inch weapons are trained outboard and thus provide an excellent indication of the difference in size between the two. She was renamed *Zealandia* in 1911 so that her name could be given to the new *Indefatigable*-class battlecruiser that had been paid for by the country of New Zealand, and she served under this name throughout the First World War. She was sold off and scrapped in 1921. (© The National Archives, United Kingdom, ADM 176/477)

ricocheting around inside by the armoured screens, and it could also damage the battery on the other side from behind. The armoured battery wall did, however, add a further belt of armour to the sides of the ship above the upper belt. This protected larger areas of the hull against HE shells compared with casemates, which only protected the guns they mounted and not the spaces in between.[69]

Eight battleships of this new design, known collectively as the *King Edward VII* class,[70] were laid down between 1902 and 1904 and completed between 1905 and 1907. The larger size and complexity of these ships meant that they cost an average of £1,434,800 each, including guns. In total, each mounted four 40-calibre 12-inch, four 9.2-inch, ten 6-inch, fourteen 12-pdr and fourteen 3-pdr guns. Mounting three calibres of main gun (12-inch, 9.2-inch and 6-inch) provoked criticism from within the RN as it was felt that they carried too few guns of too many different types. In some quarters it was questioned why the 6-inch guns were not replaced with four more 9.2-inch guns on each side, while others thought that a uniform 9.2-inch armament would have been preferable as these guns were almost as effective against armour as the larger 12-inch weapons.[71]

Once the ships entered service it was also found that having three different calibres complicated fire control as it was very difficult to distinguish between the different splashes. The mixed-calibre pre-dreadnoughts of the Russian Black Sea Fleet encountered similar

problems when they engaged *Goeben* off Cape Sarych on 18 November 1914.[72] Compounding this problem in the *King Edward VII*-class ships was their short superstructure, which resulted in interference problems between the 9.2-inch and 12-inch guns. Further problems were experienced with the 6-inch battery, which was situated on the main deck and therefore suffered from being too close to the water like earlier ships' main-deck casemates. By 1917, therefore, it had been replaced in five ships of the class by four 6-inch guns on the upper deck. Despite these problems, however, the IJN ordered two more battleships from Britain in 1903 (*Kashima* and *Katori*) whose armament of four 12-inch, four 10-inch and twelve 6-inch guns was obviously inspired by that of *King Edward VII*.[73]

The layout of *King Edward VII*'s armour was generally similar to that of *London*. The main waterline belt was 9 inches thick, with an upper belt of 8 inches, although above this there were the additional 7-inch main-deck battery walls. The main belt was continued forward with 7-inch, 5-inch, 4-inch and 3-inch armour, while the aft belt extension was increased to 3 inches over the 1½ inches of *London*. The aft armoured bulkhead was 10 inches thick at the waterline and 8 inches at the level of the upper belt, while the main-deck battery was closed fore and aft by a 7-inch thick bulkhead running from the end of the battery walls to the main barbettes. The barbettes were reduced in diameter to 34 feet, which saved weight by reducing the amount of armour

required, and were 12 inches thick above side armour and 8–6 inches behind it. The gun-houses had 12-inch faces and 8-inch sides and rears, while the 9.2-inch guns were mounted in 7-inch thick turrets on 4-inch bases, which were also protected by the 7-inch armour of the 6-inch gun main-deck battery.[74]

The horizontal armour was slightly adjusted from that of *London*, with the upper armoured deck raised by one deck to cover the top of the 6-inch gun battery. To preserve stability it consequently had to be reduced to 1 inch in thickness. Otherwise, the remainder of *King Edward VII*'s armour was disposed very similarly to that of the previous class, and within the citadel had a 1-inch deck at the waterline with 2-inch slopes. Protection for the ends outside the citadel was also the same as for *London*.[75]

The *King Edward VII* class was given the nickname of 'The Wobbly Eight' as their hull-form was designed to make them manoeuvrable but this, combined with the use of balanced rudders for the first time since the 1870s, meant they did not straighten out of turns readily. They were also the most stable of any of White's battleships, and although both *King Edward VII* and *Britannia* were lost to underwater attack they stayed upright for much longer than earlier ships. *King Edward VII* stayed afloat for thirteen hours and only sank with a slight list, although this might have been due to a watertight door in the centre line bulkhead of the machinery spaces being left open and allowing both sides to flood evenly. *Britannia* was sunk on 9 November 1918, only two days before the Armistice, but she took 3½ hours to capsize and this gave her time to fire at the periscope of the U-boat that had torpedoed her (the only time a *King Edward VII*-class ship saw action) and allowed her survivors to be taken off.[76]

Swiftsure and *Triumph* Second Class Battleships

These two ships fall somewhat outside the development of British battleships as they were not originally designed for the RN but were instead ordered from Armstrong and Vickers by Chile (as *Constitution* and *Libertad*) in 1901. Their dimensions were dictated by the need to match the Argentine navy's *Garibaldi*-class

cruisers in terms of speed (19 kts) and armament (10-inch and 8-inch guns), whilst still being able to enter the Chilean navy's dock at Talcahuano. To achieve this, their designer, Sir Edward Reed, gave them extreme length (480 feet, or 30 feet more than *Duncan*) combined with a narrow beam (4½ feet less than *Duncan*) for a nominal displacement of approximately 12,000 tons. The RN took them over at the end of 1903 to prevent Russia from acquiring them on the eve of the Russo–Japanese War at a cost of approximately £950,000 each including guns. They were renamed *Swiftsure* and *Triumph* – an appropriate set of names that had last been used, it will be recalled, for a pair of Second Class ironclads of the late 1860s.[77]

Their main armament was four 10-inch guns in two twin turrets, which was supplemented by fourteen 7.5-inch guns, fourteen 14-pdrs, two 12-pdrs and four 6-pdrs. The 7.5-inch guns were new to RN service, although they were subsequently adopted on armoured cruisers from 1905 onwards, and ten of them were mounted in the main-deck battery with the remainder in casemates on the upper deck. The fourteen 14-pdrs constituted a heavier anti-torpedo boat armament than that mounted on any other British battleship, and were mounted on the upper deck (ahead of, astern of and between the upper deck 7.5-inch guns) and in single ports in the bow and stern.[78]

In terms of armour, the whole area of the hull amidships was protected

The Second Class battleship *Triumph*, which, along with her sister *Swiftsure*, was originally laid down for Chile but was purchased for the RN in December 1903. This photograph provides a clear view of the distinctive goose-

necked cranes both ships carried amidships. The long length of the barrels of her 7.5-inch secondary guns, compared with the 6-inch weapons usually carried by RN battleships, is also notable. Both ships of the class took part in

the attack on the Dardanelles in 1915, where *Triumph* was torpedoed by *U21* on 25 May 1915 and subsequently capsized. (© The National Archives, United Kingdom, ADM 176/724)

by 7 inches of Krupp steel: the main and upper belts were both of this thickness, and were topped with the 7-inch thick walls of the 7.5-inch gun battery. By comparison, *Duncan*'s 7-inch armour stopped one deck lower with her upper belt as her secondary guns were mounted in individual casemates rather than a battery. The waterline forward and aft of the main belt was protected by 3-inch strakes of armour, which were therefore thicker than *Duncan*'s 1½-inch aft belt. Their horizontal protection was also better than *Duncan*'s both inside the citadel, with a 1½-inch waterline deck and a 1-inch deck on top of the battery, and also outside, where the forward and after decks at the waterline were both 3 inches. It is worth noting, however, that the citadel sides were only 155 feet long in *Swiftsure* and *Triumph*, compared with 238 feet in *Duncan*, and that their barbettes were of smaller diameter (22¾ feet, rather than 36½ feet) and not as extensively armoured (10 inches, thinning to 3–2-inches at their rear). Also, although 6-inch bulkheads closed both their battery and upper belt, there was nothing similar to close the main belt.[79]

Although *Swiftsure* and *Triumph* were designed for 19 kts both reached 20 kts on trials. They could easily be distinguished from other British pre-dreadnoughts by their large goose-necked cranes amidships and by the scroll-work on their bows (the last British battleships to be so fitted). Both fought in the First World War and like many pre-dreadnoughts they saw service in the Dardanelles.[80]

Lord Nelson and *Agamemnon*

These two ships were the final British pre-dreadnought battleships, and in their design can be seen the move towards an all-12-inch armament that would characterise the beginning of the dreadnought era. Indeed, during their design process it was suggested that their 9.2-inch guns be replaced with 12-inch weapons, but this was felt to be too radical a move. For the first time since the previous *Agamemnon*, however, a British battleship was not given a secondary armament of 6-inch quick-firing guns.[81]

It is notable that this class only included two vessels, a marked difference to the massed ranks of pre-dreadnoughts previously constructed. This was partly due to technological uncertainty, with the revolutionary *Dreadnought* clearly on the horizon, but the strategic situation was also more favourable than in previous years as Britain had concluded the alliance with Japan and entered into an *entente* with France. Both were laid down in 1905 and completed in 1908 and, at approximately 17,000 tons and a cost of over £1,500,000 each, were the largest and most expensive British battleships yet built.[82]

Prior to *Lord Nelson*, Watts had designed a number of classes of armoured cruisers (*Duke of Edinburgh*, *Warrior* and *Minotaur*, described in more detail below), all of which mounted heavy 9.2-inch armaments, and he wanted to carry this over into the new battleships by mounting twelve of these guns in twin turrets amidships on the upper deck. This would rectify one of the

weaknesses of previous British battleships, whose main deck 6-inch guns were often unusable in heavy weather. However, the requirement that the new battleships had to be able to dock in the No. 9 dock at Chatham and the No. 5 dock at Devonport limited their dimensions and made it impossible to mount this armament. Instead, the middle 9.2-inch turret had to be reduced to a single rather than a twin, and the 9.2-inch magazines were placed in-between the coal bunkers along the sides where they would be much more vulnerable to underwater attack than if they could have been placed in the centre of the ship. Unfortunately, the size restriction was unnecessary as, by the time these ships completed, new larger docks were available at all dockyards to meet the needs of the new dreadnought fleet.[83]

Lord Nelson's guns (both 12-inch and 9.2-inch) were five calibres longer than the comparable weapons in *King Edward VII*, which increased their muzzle velocity and hence improved their penetrative power despite firing shells of the same weight. As a result, *Lord Nelson*'s Mk X 12-inch guns could penetrate 12 inches of Krupp steel at 7,600 yards, compared with 12 inches of Krupp steel at 4,800 yards for the 40-calibre weapons of *King Edward VII* and 11½ inches of Krupp steel at 5,000 yards for *Majestic*'s 35-calibre Mk VIII guns. Similarly, *Lord Nelson*'s 45-calibre 9.2-inch guns could penetrate 9.2 inches of Krupp steel at 5,200 yards, compared with 4,550 yards for the 40-calibre weapons of *King Edward VII*.[84]

With the combination of 12-inch and 9.2-inch guns on the upper deck there was the potential for blast interference to cause problems, as had been experienced in *King Edward VII*, and so warning buzzers were fitted in each turret that sounded if they traversed in a direction that endangered another turret. This was so successful that it was fitted to future ships. The only other guns carried by the *Lord*

Nelson class were twenty-four 12-pdrs, the majority of which were carried in a distinctive flying deck over the 9.2-inch turrets.[85]

Although the *Lord Nelson* class were only fitted with 25 tons more armour than *King Edward VII*, it was better concentrated. Their barbettes were again reduced in diameter by a further 5 feet so that they were now only 29 feet across. This meant that their armour

(12 inches, thinning to 3 inches at the rear behind the side armour on both, and to 8 inches on the front of the fore barbette) weighed only 800 tons, compared with 1,210 tons for *Majestic*'s larger pear-shaped barbettes. The main waterline armoured belt was only 190 feet long (35 feet shorter than *King Edward VII*) but was 12 inches thick amidships, and was topped with an 8-inch upper belt and a

The final evolution of the RN pre-dreadnought battleship, *Lord Nelson* (pictured) and *Agamemnon* dispensed entirely with 6-inch guns and increased the number of 9.2-inch guns from the four of the preceding *King Edward VII* class to ten. These extra 9.2-inch guns were mounted in three turrets on either beam, of which the port-side ones are visible in this photograph. The small guns visible on the flying deck above the 9.2-inch turrets were 12-pdr anti-torpedo boat quick-firers. *Lord Nelson* saw a great deal of service in Mediterranean during the First World War alongside *Agamemnon*, participating in the attacks on the Dardanelles and then remaining in the area for most of the remainder of the war to counter any attempt by *Goeben* to sortie into the Eastern Mediterranean. She was sold off in 1920. (© The National Archives, United Kingdom, ADM 176/419)

Although they were both laid down before *Dreadnought*, *Agamemnon* (pictured here) and *Lord Nelson* actually entered service after *Dreadnought* because materials intended for their construction were diverted in order to complete the all-big-gun ship more quickly. *Agamemnon*'s First World War service was largely spent in company with *Lord Nelson* in the Mediterranean, where she had the distinction of successfully shooting down a Zeppelin. After the cessation of hostilities she returned home and was converted into a radio-controlled target vessel in 1923, before being sold off in 1926. (© The National Archives, United Kingdom, ADM 176/9)

further 8-inch belt on the main deck to protect the 9.2-inch turret bases. Their waterlines were protected by a 4-inch strake aft from the main belt and a 9–6-inch strake forward, while one deck above this the upper belt was continued forward to the bows with a thickness of 6–4 inches. The upper belt was also closed to the rear by an 8-inch bulkhead that joined up with aft barbette. Horizontal protection within the citadel was a single 1-inch waterline deck with 2-inch slopes, while outside of the citadel at the waterline there was a curved deck aft (2-inch flat, 3-inch on slopes) and a 1-inch deck forward joined to the forward barbette by a 4-inch slope. Above this was a 1½-inch deck covering the top of the upper belt extension. The 12-inch guns were protected by gun-houses with 12-inch fronts and roofs and 8-inch rears, while the 9.2-inch gun-houses were 7-inch thick.[86]

First Class Protected Cruisers

In the 1890s concerns about the relative numbers of cruisers possessed by Britain and her potential opponents mirrored the concerns about the relative numbers of battleships. It was therefore decided in 1893 to link the number of cruisers in the RN to its battleship strength, so as the latter increased the size of the cruiser fleet would follow suit. The establishment was accordingly set at two cruisers per battleship for fleet work (which equalled fifty-six cruisers) plus eighteen for trade protection. This total of seventy-four vessels was greater than the sixty-three modern cruisers then in service, and as a consequence provisions were made in the Spencer Programme to construct a large number of these vessels to bring the RN up to strength.[87]

Powerful *and* Terrible

In 1890, Russia had laid down the large (*c.* 11,600-ton) armoured cruiser *Rurik*. Reports of this ship's high speed, long endurance and armour protection caused great concern in Britain as it seemed she would prove very difficult for existing British cruisers to catch. Britain's response was delayed until 1893 by the need to first finish the ships of the Naval Defence Act, but once these were complete it was decided to lay down two very large protected cruisers in response.[88]

This photograph shows the First Class cruiser *Powerful* in August 1897 shortly after she had entered service. Enormous ships designed to counter a high-speed Russian threat that never materialised, *Powerful* and *Terrible* were completed (as shown in this photograph) with an armament of two single 9.2-inch guns (one forward and one aft) and twelve 6-inch quick-firers in broadside casemates. For the first time on an RN ship, double-height casemates were used to protect the 6-inch guns at either end. Moved into reserve in the early 1900s, by the end of the First World War *Powerful* was in use as a training ship at Devonport and was sold off in 1929. (© The National Archives, United Kingdom, ADM 176/537)

Little concrete information was available about the Russian ship's performance, so the requirements for the British cruisers were based on White's estimate that *Rurik* would be capable of over 18 kts and have an endurance of 8,500 nm. Accordingly, he designed the British cruisers to be able to sustain 20 kts while carrying a heavier armament and better protection. This required extreme size; not only would they have to be larger than *Rurik*, but they would also have to be larger than any previous British cruiser. The impression made by their size was reinforced by the inclusion of a full-length forecastle, not present on previous British First Class cruisers,

which made them higher by one deck and thus gave them sufficient freeboard to maintain speed in heavy weather.[89]

The two British cruisers, appropriately named *Powerful* and *Terrible*, were laid down in 1894 and completed in 1897–8. They were truly monstrous ships: with a displacement of over 14,000 tons and over 500 feet in length, they were of a similar weight but over 100 feet longer than the contemporary *Majestic*-class battleships. Their dimensions had ultimately been constrained only by the size of the largest available dry-docks. During the design process there had been a suggestion that they be reduced in

length to 450 feet, but White pointed out that this would prevent them from being able to reach the required speed of 20 kts without the use of more powerful machinery, while not actually increasing the number of docks that could accommodate them.[90]

Despite their unprecedented size, a number of innovations had to be introduced in their machinery provisions in order to achieve their demanding speed requirements. Belleville water-tube boilers were fitted for the first time in a large British warship, as older-style cylindrical boilers could not supply the required power within the space and weight available. To ensure that

As well as their enormous cost, another criticism levelled against *Powerful* and *Terrible* was that, for their large size, they seemed to be only slightly more heavily armed than previous First Class cruisers. To rectify this, both ships were refitted between 1902 and 1904, and four extra 6-inch quick-firers were added to

each by making the two middle broadside casemates double-height to match those at either end. This photograph was taken in June 1904 and shows *Terrible* after this refit had been completed, although the lower 6-inch guns in the two middle casemates are not visible here. During the First World War

Terrible was used first as a troop-ship and then an accommodation vessel, before becoming a training ship in 1920. She was sold off in 1932. (© The National Archives, United Kingdom, ADM 176/699)

the ships could steam continuously at their maximum speed, their crews were augmented to contain sufficient stokers to provide 100% natural draught power at all times. This was in contrast with the usual RN cruiser practice of having only enough stokers on watch at any one time to provide 60% power – to raise the remaining 40% required off-watch stokers to be used. In total, therefore, a single *Powerful*-class cruiser required a crew of 894 men – over 300 more than either a *Blake* or an *Edgar*.[91]

As with the *Blake* and *Edgar* classes, *Powerful* and *Terrible* were protected by a curved armoured deck, although in the two large ships this was a uniform thickness of 4 inches. For the first time, however, the ammunition passages ran below the protective deck (instead of above), which obviously improved their protection and also removed the need to store ready-use ammunition in vulnerable gun casemates.[92]

Their armament provoked a good deal of debate, both during their conception and once they had entered service. It was originally suggested that they would have a uniform armament of twenty 6-inch quick-firing guns, with one on the forecastle, one on the quarterdeck, eight in double-height casemates (four to a side, two forward and two aft) and the remaining ten guns in broadside main-deck casemates. Protection against torpedo boats would be provided by ten 25-pdrs on the upper deck. Fisher favoured this arrangement, but it did not find favour with the Director of Naval Ordnance (DNO) who thought that

the single 6-inch guns on the forecastle and poop should be replaced with heavier weapons capable of piercing thicker armour. His preferred weapon was a twin 8-inch mounting, which it was thought was still possible to hand load like a 6-inch gun. If this were to be adopted, it would mark the first time that this calibre had been carried by an RN warship, although a number of cruisers built in Britain for foreign navies had already been so armed (for example, the two Armstrong-built Chilean ships *Blanco Encalada* and *Esmeralda*, launched in 1893 and 1894 respectively).[93]

White felt that if a large gun were thought to be necessary then the 8-inch weapon was insufficient, and that as a minimum the existing 9.2-inch gun should be used. The Board agreed with White, and in July 1893 *Powerful*'s armament was finalised. The single 6-inch guns fore and aft were replaced with single shielded 9.2-inch guns but, because of the increase in weight this represented, the 6-inch guns had to be reduced in number and the 25-pdrs replaced by 12-pdrs. *Powerful* and *Terrible* therefore completed with two 9.2-inch, twelve 6-inch quick-firers, sixteen 12-pdrs and twelve 3-pdrs. This only represented a gain of two 6-inch guns over *Edgar* despite them being twice the earlier ship's displacement, which highlights the premium paid for their exceptional speed and range, and as a consequence they were often criticised as being under-gunned for their size. Possibly in response to this, in 1902–04 both ships were fitted with four additional

6-inch quick-firing guns by turning the two midships casemates on each side into double-deckers to match the forward and rear positions.[94]

The Diadem *class*

Ultimately, *Powerful* and *Terrible* proved to be white elephants. Rumours of the danger posed by *Rurik* proved to be greatly exaggerated: when she completed in 1895 she turned out to be an 18-kt ship, barque-rigged and with a shallow armoured belt. As a response, therefore, *Powerful* and *Terrible* were far more capable than the threat warranted, and as a consequence did not justify their high construction (61% more than *Edgar*) and running costs (their crews were 64% larger than *Edgar's*).[95]

The *Diadems*, the succeeding class of large protected cruisers, was therefore developed from the earlier *Blake* class instead of *Powerful* to reduce their size and cost, although they did incorporate features from the intervening *Edgar* class and *Powerful* as well. Design work began in November 1893, taking as the starting point the idea of a version of *Blake* with water-tube boilers (as in *Powerful*). For the armament, White favoured the layout used in the *Edgar*-class cruiser *Royal Arthur* (with two 6-inch quick-firers forward on a raised forecastle to improve sea-keeping), although he also favoured mounting all the broadside 6-inch guns in armoured casemates and moving the ammunition passages underneath the armoured deck (as in *Powerful*) to improve their protection. *Powerful*'s

The *Diadem*-class cruiser *Andromeda* in the traditional late-Victorian RN colour scheme of black, white and buff. This photograph is interesting as it clearly shows the layout of the two 6-inch guns on the forecastle: unlike in later cruisers these guns were not in a single twin mounting but in two widely spaced single shielded mounts. The two 6-inch guns on the quarterdeck were similarly arranged. The embrasure to permit the forward 6-inch double-height casemate guns to fire forward is also visible. *Andromeda* was converted into a training ship in 1913, but was not sold off and scrapped until 1956. (© The National Archives, United Kingdom, ADM 176/30)

uniform 4-inch protective deck was also chosen as the main form of waterline protection in the new ship.[96]

The extra weight required for the 6-inch casemates and the forecastle meant that *Diadem* had to be larger than *Blake*, although their final displacement (11,000 tons) and length (*c.* 460 feet over-all) still less than that of *Powerful*. Attempts were also made to reduce the manning requirements of the new cruisers: while *Powerful* had increased her complement of stokers to allow for 100% power to be available at all times instead of the usual 60%, in the *Diadem* class this requirement was relaxed to 50%, which allowed the number of stokers to be reduced from 217 to 157. New

technology was also introduced to reduce the crew further (for example electrically powered ammunition hoists replaced an additional forty men). Overall, their crew in service was 677 – 100 more than *Blake* but still a 200-man reduction compared with *Powerful*.[97]

As with *Powerful*, the armament of the *Diadem* class engendered much debate. The DNO again pressed for the adoption of the 8-inch gun in place of the twin-6-inch on *Royal Arthur*'s forecastle, but the Board instead opted for a uniform 6-inch armament (as had initially been proposed for *Powerful*), perhaps because these new cruisers were intended exclusively as trade protection vessels. In such a role their likely

opponents were lightly armoured enemy cruisers, against which the 'hail of fire' from large numbers of 6-inch quick-firing guns was seen as more valuable than the penetrative power of a smaller number of heavier guns. They were accordingly armed with sixteen 6-inch quick-firing guns, with two each on the forecastle and quarterdeck and six on each side in two double-height and two single casemates. Anti-torpedo boat protection was provided by fourteen 12-pdrs and three 3-pdrs.[98]

Eight *Diadem*-class ships were ordered in two groups of four under the 1895–6 and 1896–7 Estimates.[99] Some thought was given to powering the second group with three shafts instead of the usual two, but in the

The *Diadem*-class First Class cruiser *Spartiate*, photographed in March 1903. As a reaction against the high cost of the preceding *Powerful*-class ships, the design of the *Diadem* class was reduced in size. They were consequently slower and less well protected than *Powerful* and *Terrible*, and most notably

replaced the two 9.2-inch guns of the larger ships with four additional 6-inch quick-firers (in addition to maintaining the twelve 6-inch quick-firers in broadside casemates). This photograph shows, however, that they visually maintained a great deal of continuity with the earlier class, most noticeably four funnels and

the use of double-height casemates for some of the broadside 6-inch guns. Like many of her sisters, *Spartiate* had been reduced to harbour service as a training ship by the time that the First World War started, and she was sold off in 1932. (© The National Archives, United Kingdom, ADM 176/658) end the only difference between the two batches was that the later ships were given modified boilers that generated an extra 1,500 hp of power and thus an extra ¼-kt of speed, and that their engine cylinders were reordered to even-out the stress on the crankshaft.[100]

First Class Armoured Cruisers

The RN had abandoned the use of armoured belts on all cruisers (First, Second and Third Class) after the *Orlando* class of 1888 as it was realised that it was impossible to provide sufficiently thick armour to resist modern guns within the weight available on such ships. Instead, White's cruisers were characterised by the use of a waterline armoured

deck, coal bunkers and subdivision to protect their buoyancy and stability. In France, however, the 6,000-ton *Dupuy de Lôme* (laid down in 1888 and completed in 1895) took a different approach by having her entire hull from 4½ feet below her waterline to her upper deck covered in 4-inch steel armour. This protective scheme was replicated in the smaller armoured cruisers of the *Amiral Charner* class and in the single *Pothuau*, albeit with thinner armour. These ships paved the way for the 11,000-ton *Jeanne D'Arc*, laid down in 1896, which was protected by full 3-inch side protection in addition to a 6-inch belt of Harvey steel on the waterline over the machinery. Many regard this ship as the first true armoured

cruiser, and she proved to be the first of eighteen ships of this type built for the French navy before 1906.[101]

Cressy *First Class Armoured Cruisers*

It was appreciated that Krupp armour, first used in Britain in the *Canopus*-class battleships, made possible an effective armoured belt capable of resisting 6-inch shells without adding too much weight and hence displacement and cost. Not only would this allow a British armoured cruiser to face a French armoured cruiser on equal terms, but it would also restore to it the ability, last seen in the belted *Orlando* class, to fight as a fast wing of the battlefleet against French battleships.

The 12,000-ton armoured cruiser *Cressy*, photographed in June 1901 very shortly after she had entered service. The *Cressy* class were the first RN First Class cruisers to benefit from new Krupp armour that provided a viable armoured belt once more, and as such set the style for all subsequent British armoured cruisers. They also saw the reintroduction of the 9.2-inch gun after the wholly 6-inch armed *Diadem* class. At the cutting edge of naval technology when they were laid down, they were obsolete by the time the First World War started less than twenty years later. They are chiefly remembered now for the fate that befell *Aboukir*, *Cressy* and *Hogue*: all three were torpedoed and sunk within two hours of each other by *U9* on 22 September 1914. (© The National Archives, United Kingdom, ADM 176/166)

In April 1897, therefore, work began on the design of a 12,000-ton armoured cruiser with a maximum speed of 21½ kts, which would enter service as the *Cressy*-class. Tellingly, it was to have the same endurance as the battleship *Majestic* and the same armoured belt (6-inch-thick Krupp) as *Canopus*, further indicating its intended role alongside the battlefleet.[102] Indeed, White clearly stated that it was to have 'the capacity for close action as adjuncts to battleships', as well as 'suitability for employment on detached service, if required to be used for the protection of shipping commerce and communication'.[103]

This belt raised the total weight of armour in *Cressy* to 2,500 tons, compared with 1,800 tons for *Diadem*, and accounted for most of the 1,000-ton increase in displacement. Not only was the belt the same material and thickness as that of *Canopus*, but the layout of the remainder of *Cressy*'s armour was also very similar: *Cressy*'s 6-inch belt was 230 feet long and extended from 5 feet below the waterline to 6½ feet above, it was closed fore and aft by 5-inch bulkheads and, as in *Canopus*, extended forward to the

The *Cressy*-class armoured cruiser *Hogue*. Compared with her sister in the previous photograph, *Hogue* is painted grey all over rather than black, white and buff, but this lighter colour provides a better view of the layout of her broadside armament. In particular, it can be seen that the *Cressy* class had the same arrangement as the preceding two classes of First Class cruisers (the *Diadem* and *Powerful* classes), with four 12-pdrs between and above the six 6-inch guns in casemates on each side. (© The National Archives, United Kingdom, ADM 176/337)

bow by a 2-inch thick strake. Horizontal armour also followed that of *Canopus* with two armoured decks covering the belt: the flat main deck was 1 inch, while the lower was 1½ inches and sloped to join the bottom of the belt. Outside of the belt, *Cressy*'s ends were protected by a 1½-inch deck forward and a 2½-inch deck aft (thickening to 3 inches where it covered her steering gear). With comparable armour to a battleship (albeit one with the lightest protection of all contemporary British First Class battleships), the idea of using armoured cruisers alongside the battleship in the 1890s may not have been as dangerous as, with hindsight, the experience of the battlecruisers at Jutland in 1916 might suggest.[104]

As *Cressy* was intended to fight in a general fleet action, the uniform 6-inch armament of *Diadem* was insufficient as these guns could not penetrate the thicker armour of enemy battleships. *Cressy*'s armament was therefore increased to the same level as *Powerful*'s, with a single 9.2-inch gun forward and aft in addition to twelve 6-inch guns in 5-inch-thick casemates. Compared with *Powerful*, however, newer and more powerful marks of guns were mounted, which accounted for much of the remainder of the extra 1,000-ton displacement compared with *Diadem*.[105]

Six *Cressy*-class ships were laid down in 1898–9 and completed between 1901 and 1904.[106] In service they proved to be good sea-boats, although they generated

a lot of spray and the main-deck 6-inch guns were prone to flooding. Unlike previous British cruisers they did not need to be sheathed and coppered, which saved £40,000, 550 tons and ½-kt of speed, thanks to the adoption of effective anti-fouling paint.[107]

Drake *First Class Armoured Cruisers*

While *Cressy* was designed to supplement the strength of the battlefleet as well as fulfilling traditional cruiser roles, the RN also required cruisers to respond directly to the French armoured cruiser programme that had begun with *Jeanne D'Arc*. The requirements for these new cruisers would be very similar to those that had driven the

The 14,150-ton *Drake*-class armoured cruiser *Leviathan*, completed in June 1903. The extra displacement over the preceding *Cressy* class was used to increase their maximum speed (by 2 kts) and to mount four extra 6-inch guns. Their armament of sixteen 6-inch guns was therefore carried in a total of eight double-height casemates, of which the starboard four can clearly be seen in this photograph (although the lower guns in the middle two casemates are not visible). From this photograph it will also be appreciated just how close to the water the lower guns in these casemates were, and consequently how easily they could be rendered unusable. *Leviathan* survived the First World War and was sold off in 1920. (© The National Archives, United Kingdom, ADM 176/410)

design of *Powerful*: as the French ship was thought to be good for 22 kts and have a range of 13,500 nm, the British response would require comparable endurance and higher speed to run her down, and strong armament and protection to defeat her once she was brought to bay. All of this suggested that the British cruiser would have to be a very large ship, although both White and the Board were keen to have a smaller, cheaper ship for reasons of economy.[108]

Design work on the new cruiser, which was to become *Drake*, began in 1897. It is notable that this was only one year after *Jeanne D'Arc* was laid down and five years before she put to sea, and so the Board could not know the true nature of the threat she posed. They were in danger, therefore, of repeating the folly of *Powerful*: over-estimating the enemy's capabilities and consequently designing a response that was more capable and expensive that it needed to be. The Board, though, may have been concerned that a recent round of dockyard strikes, which had delayed the construction of several battleships, was the beginning of further troubles

The First Class cruiser *Drake*, the lead ship of her class, in a photograph taken in December 1902 just as she was entering service. This unusual angle unfortunately obscures many of the details of her appearance, but the view of her ram bow that it provides is quite striking. Just visible are her port-side double-height casemates, whose proximity to the water can be well appreciated. To remedy this shortcoming, in 1916 the lower guns were removed and four replacement 6-inch weapons were mounted on the upper deck. She was torpedoed by *U79* in October 1917 and lost. (© The National Archives, United Kingdom, ADM 176/211)

to come. If this were the case, Britain's prized ability to respond to another power's building programme by quickly building ships of her own would be compromised. They might therefore have decided to act quickly to prevent France from gaining too great a lead in armoured cruiser construction.[109] It is interesting to note that construction of the contemporaneous *Duncan*-class fast battleships was also expedited to counter the reportedly high-speed Russian battleships rather than waiting to see if this threat also materialised.

To achieve 23 kts (2 kts faster than *Cressy*) much more powerful machinery was required than that of the previous cruiser, and this pushed *Drake*'s displacement up to 14,000 tons – 2,000 tons more than *Cressy*. A considerable amount of internal volume had to be given over to this machinery; in previous British First Class cruisers it had been usual for 44% of the ship's length to be given over to her power plant, but in *Drake* (as in *Powerful*) this percentage increased to 50%.[110]

Drake's length and draught were constrained by the need to be able to fit into the available docks and to transit the Suez Canal. This meant that it was not possible to lengthen her hull to achieve her design speed efficiently, and so the only alternative was to reduce her beam. As this obviously affected stability, it became important to reduce top-weight and so it was decided to remove the boat deck and ventilator cowls that had featured on previous cruisers. This also had the advantage of decreasing the ship's silhouette and also reducing the risk of fire, the

latter being something that had recently been highlighted in the Spanish–American War (1898) where fire had been the main cause of Spanish losses. These lessons were also incorporated in the *Cressy* class, where a great deal of wood was removed and special treatments were used on what remained to make it less flammable.[111]

Some consideration was given to arming *Drake* with a uniform 6-inch armament like *Diadem*, and again the DNO championed the virtues of the 8-inch weapon, but it was ultimately decided to carry over *Cressy*'s 9.2-inch and 6-inch guns into the new ship. Perhaps with the criticisms of *Powerful* in mind, however, all her broadside casemates were made double height, and this increased the number of 6-inch guns to sixteen. An anti-torpedo boat armament of fourteen 12-pdrs and three 3-pdrs (making it the same as *Diadem*'s) was also carried.[112]

Drake's armour was generally the same as *Cressy*'s with a 6-inch belt and 5-inch casemates, although it was slightly altered to match contemporary battleship practice. Just as *Cressy*'s armour was modelled on that of *Canopus*, *Drake* included the same changes as the *London* and *Duncan*-class battleships, namely the reversal in thickness of the two armoured decks and the removal of the forward armoured bulkhead in favour of continuing the belt right up to the bow.[113]

Drake's size and Krupp armour made her very expensive – at 14,000 tons and approximately £1,050,000 she was comparable in size and cost to a *London*-class battleship. Indeed,

her large engine-rooms required a correspondingly large crew: her total complement of 900 men was over 150 more than *London* and consequently made her very expensive to run. For this reason, members of the Board of Admiralty thought of the *Drake* class as 'man eating' ships.[114] It was originally planned to build only two *Drake*-class ships, but two more were ordered under the 1898 Supplementary Estimates to make four in total as a counter to additional foreign ships.[115] One ship of the class, *Good Hope*, was Rear Admiral Craddock's flagship at the Battle of Coronel of 1 November 1914, where she was sunk by von Spee's force.

Monmouth *First Class Armoured Cruisers*

Given the political concerns about the cost of the *Drake* class, it seems almost inevitable that the next class would be reduced in size to make them more affordable. Additional cruisers were required to counter a proliferation of smaller foreign commerce-raiding armoured cruisers, such as the French *Kleber* class that was armed with eight 6.84-inch guns, but there was some disagreement as to what form these should take. George Goschen (who became First Lord of the Admiralty in 1895, having been Chancellor of the Exchequer at the time of the 1889 Naval Defence Act) and most of the Board felt that smaller cruisers, which could be built in greater numbers, were required. However, other elements within the RN thought the best solution was to

The *Monmouth*-class armoured cruiser *Donegal*, which entered service in November 1903. Unlike the previous two classes of RN armoured cruisers, the *Monmouth*-class ships were given a uniform armament of fourteen 6-inch quick-firers, sacrificing the penetrative power of the 9.2-inch weapons that such ships normally carried for the additional rate-of-fire offered by 6-inch guns. Ten of these 6-inch guns were carried in broadside casemates, including double-height casemates at either end, but two twin 6-inch turrets of a new design were fitted in place of the single 9.2-inch turrets fore and aft. This photograph of *Donegal* shows her rear 6-inch turret clearly. She saw service in the First World War and was sold off in 1920. (© The National Archives, United Kingdom, ADM 176/206)

build more large cruisers like *Drake*, which would be capable of fighting not only these smaller cruisers but also larger enemy ships.[116]

Ultimately, it was the First Lord of the Admiralty who won out. Work accordingly began on the design of the new cruiser, *Monmouth*, in 1898, based around the requirements for a speed of 23 kts and a displacement of less than 10,000 tons. The reduction in size from *Drake* obviously reduced the price per ship (ten *Monmouth*-class ships could be bought for the same cost as seven *Drake* class), but at the cost of the new cruisers having lower endurance and worse protection. What was more, it was recognised at the time that the more numerous smaller cruisers would actually require 550 more men in total to crew them than the seven larger *Drake*-class ships, which suggests that the move towards smaller ships was not simply a reaction to the running costs of the previous vessels but came about in response to a perceived operational need.[117]

The reduction in displacement obviously had an effect on all facets of *Monmouth*'s design. The combination of limited displacement and the requirement for 23 kts meant that the level of armour protection had to be reduced from that of *Drake*. Consequently, *Monmouth*'s armoured belt was only 4 inches thick, although this was probably sufficient for her intended role of fighting commerce raiders as it could withstand 6-inch HE (but not armour-piercing) and all 4-inch weapons at battle ranges – as was proved at the Falklands in 1914 when *Kent*'s belt proved successful at

stopping *Nurnberg*'s 4.1-inch shells. Otherwise, *Monmouth*'s armour layout was similar to *Drake*'s, if generally thinner: the main belt was continued forward to the bow by 2-inch armour, and it was closed to the rear by a 3-inch bulkhead. She also had two armoured decks within the citadel (the upper one being 1½ inches thick and the lower ¾-inch) and a 2-inch armoured deck ran from the rear armoured bulkhead to the stern.[118]

As *Monmouth*'s role was not to fight large armoured warships, the 9.2-inch guns of *Drake* were not fitted and instead she was given a uniform armament of fourteen 6-inch weapons. Four of these were mounted in two new twin-gun turrets on the forecastle and quarterdeck, with the remainder mounted in two double-height and one single casemates (all 4-inch thick) on each side. The twin 6-inch turret had both guns mounted in a single cradle, which was designed to save weight and allow both to be controlled by one man with a single sight, but because their aim could not be adjusted individually it was often found that there was a large spread of fire between the two guns that could not be rectified.[119]

It was originally planned to order four *Monmouth*-class vessels under the 1898 Supplementary Estimates, but two of these were instead deferred to the following year and were replaced by the two extra *Drake*-class ships. The remaining six ships were ordered as part of the 1900–01 Programme.[120] The name-ship of the class, *Monmouth*, was sunk at the Battle of Coronel alongside Craddock's *Good Hope*.

Devonshire *First Class Armoured Cruisers*

The next class of armoured cruisers, the *Devonshire* class, was conceived as a moderately more powerful version of *Monmouth* capable of acting alongside the battlefleet – a role that all subsequent British armoured cruisers would retain. Displacement was increased by 1,000 tons (to 10,800 tons) and the ship was increased in length by 10 feet and width by 2½ feet to enable her armament and armour to be strengthened. *Monmouth*'s machinery was retained, however, which resulted in *Devonshire*'s maximum speed dropping to approximately 22 kts.[121]

As initially designed, *Devonshire* replaced the twin 6-inch turrets of *Monmouth* with single turreted 7.5-inch weapons – the same guns that had initially been considered for the intermediate armament on the *King Edward VII*-class battleships. The design was further modified before the ships were completed to replace the two forward double-height 6-inch gun casemates with two more single 7.5-inch turrets. Their final armament was therefore four 7.5-inch and six 6-inch guns, supplemented by two 12-pdrs and eighteen 3-pdrs.[122]

Devonshire's 7.5-inch turrets were given 5-inch armour (the same as *Monmouth*'s twin 6-inch turrets) but her belt was restored to the same thickness as *Drake*'s (6 inches) and her casemate armour was increased to 6 inches. Her armoured decks, however, remained the same thickness as in *Monmouth*. Six *Devonshire*-class armoured cruisers

The 10,850-ton First Class cruiser *Carnarvon*, one of six *Devonshire*-class ships that entered RN service in 1905. Unlike the preceding *Monmouth* class the *Devonshire* class had a mixed armament of four 7.5-inch guns in single turrets (one forward, one aft and two in place of the forward 6-inch casemates of previous classes) and six 6-inch guns in two double-height and one single main-deck casemate. This layout can clearly be seen in this photograph. *Carnarvon* fought in the First World War, including at the Battle of the Falklands, and was sold off in 1921. (© The National Archives, United Kingdom, ADM 176/121)

The *Devonshire*-class First Class cruiser *Argyll*, which was completed in December 1905. This photograph is interesting as it shows *Argyll* after her armament had been modified from its original layout. As designed, she had her armament laid out as in her sister-ships like *Carnarvon*. In this photograph, however, the casemates for the 6-inch guns on the main deck (both the single one amidships and the lower of the aft double-height one) have been suppressed and the guns remounted in turrets on the upper deck. Given how easily the original positions could be rendered unworkable in a seaway this repositioning is perhaps unsurprising, and indeed a similar modification was given to the First Class cruiser *Drake* just prior to her loss. *Argyll*'s modifications probably date to a similar period, but like *Drake* she did not remain long in service after they had been finished, as on 28 October 1915 she ran aground on the Bell Rock off the east coast of Scotland and was wrecked. (© The National Archives, United Kingdom, ADM 176/43)

were laid down in 1902 and all were completed in 1905.[123] One ship of the class, *Hampshire*, was mined and lost off the Orkney Islands in June 1916 whilst carrying Lord Kitchener on a visit to Russia. There were only twelve survivors and Kitchener, famed for his victory at Omdurman in the Sudan in 1898, was not amongst them.

Duke of Edinburgh *First Class Armoured Cruisers*

The restrictions that had limited *Devonshire* were relaxed in the subsequent class of armoured cruisers laid down in 1903, and this allowed their designers to give the ships sufficient displacement (*c.* 13,500 tons) to carry a good mixture of speed (23 kts), armament and protection. It was accepted that this would be expensive: the two ships of the class (*Duke of Edinburgh* and *Black Prince*) cost over £1.1 million each, including armament.[124]

The 9.2-inch gun was restored as their main armament of these armoured cruisers, with six of these weapons mounted in single turrets, and these were supplemented by ten 6-inch guns in a main-deck battery in place of the casemates of previous ships. The chosen armament layout owed much to the contemporary *King Edward VII*-class battleships: the 9.2-inch guns were disposed in one turret forward and one aft, with the remaining four mounted at the ends of the 6-inch gun battery to provide end-on fire. A number of problems were experienced with this configuration, however, as it was discovered that the beam 9.2-inch turrets could not be fired within 30° of the centre line without the risk of damage to ship, and that the 6-inch battery was so close to the water that it was rendered unusable in all but perfect weather. The anti-torpedo boat armament of twenty 3-pdrs was also too light to be effective against the large torpedo-boat destroyers then entering service.[125]

The low 6-inch gun battery was the major source of dissatisfaction with these ships. The flaw was identified while the ships were still on the drawing board and some thought was given to replacing the

The *Duke of Edinburgh*-class armoured cruiser *Black Prince* displaced 13,500-tons and entered service in March 1906. Significantly larger than preceding First Class cruisers, the class saw the reintroduction of the 9.2-inch gun (six in total, all in single turrets) after it had been replaced by 7.5-inch weapons and a uniform 6-inch armament in the preceding *Devonshire* and *Monmouth* classes respectively. The *Duke of Edinburgh* class mounted their 6-inch guns in a battery amidships, rather than individual casemates, but like many similar main-deck gun positions this was found to be too close to the water and thus easily rendered unusable. It was therefore suppressed in both vessels in early 1916 and replaced with a smaller number of shielded 6-inch on the upper deck. *Black Prince* was in this modified configuration when she was sunk at the Battle of Jutland shortly afterwards. (© The National Archives, United Kingdom, ADM 176/82)

battery with twin 6-inch turrets on the upper deck. To have completed the necessary design changes, however, would have delayed the ordering of these ships for too long and so it was decided to proceed with the original configuration.[126]

Both ships were armoured with a 6-inch belt on the waterline and 6-inch thick battery walls on the main deck. The ends of the battery were closed by similar 6-inch bulkheads, while the belt was extended with a 4-inch strake to the bow and a 3-inch strake to the stern. The practice of having multiple armoured decks continued, with a 1-inch main deck and a further 1-inch deck over the top of the battery. A lower sloped protective deck was also fitted, which was thinned to ¾-inch in all but a 1½-inch-thick section over the steering gear. The 9.2-inch guns were protected by gun-houses with 7½-inch thick faces (thinning to 5½ inches on the sides and 4½ inches at the rear) and mounted in 6-inch thick barbettes that thinned to 3 inches behind the battery armour.[127]

Warrior *First Class Armoured Cruisers*

The four armoured cruisers built under the 1903–04 Estimates were to have been direct repeats of *Duke of Edinburgh*, but the design was modified in light of the experience in previous ships (including *Cressy* and *Monmouth*) whose main-deck guns were too close to the water.

Warrior was completed in December 1906 and was the lead ship of a class of four 13,500-ton armoured cruisers. Her design was derived from that of the preceding *Duke of Edinburgh*-class cruisers, but with the unsatisfactory main-deck 6-inch battery of the earlier vessels replaced by four 7.5-inch guns in single turrets on the upper deck. *Warrior*'s two port-side 7.5-inch turrets can be clearly seen in this photograph, situated between the 9.2-inch turrets at either end. The class were all originally completed with low funnels, but this photograph shows the appearance of *Warrior* after her forward funnel was raised in 1909 to reduce smoke interference. Indeed, the photograph must date from some time before the end of 1910 as her remaining funnels were all increased in height to match in that year. The same modification was applied to the other three ships of the class shortly afterwards. The improved armament compared with previous armoured cruisers meant that the *Warrior*-class ships were well-liked in service, but they suffered greatly during the First World War: *Warrior* herself was sunk at Jutland in 1916 and *Natal* was lost to an accidental magazine explosion while at anchor in the Cromarty Firth on 31 December 1915. Furthermore, *Cochrane* was wrecked just three days after the Armistice, leaving *Achilles* as the only surviving class member. She was finally sold off in 1921. (© The National Archives, United Kingdom, ADM 176/765)

Accordingly, the main-deck 6-inch battery was replaced by four single 7.5-inch guns in turrets on the upper deck, although the 6-inch thick battery wall was retained to protect the new turrets' bases. Otherwise, these four *Warrior*-class ships (*Achilles*, *Cochrane*, *Natal* and *Warrior*) were essentially identical to *Duke of Edinburgh*, although their average cost increased to almost £1,200,000 each (including guns).[128]

Minotaur *First Class Armoured Cruisers*

These three ships (*Defence*, *Minotaur* and *Shannon*) were built under the 1904–05 Estimates alongside the *Lord Nelson*-class battleships at an average cost of nearly £1,400,000 each. Just as *Lord Nelson* and *Agamemnon* were the last pre-dreadnoughts, so these ships proved to be the last RN armoured cruisers

with mixed medium-calibre armaments. They therefore marked the ultimate development of the type in RN service, but quickly became outclassed by the all-big gun battlecruisers pioneered by *Invincible*.

In the *Minotaur* class, displacement was increased to 14,600 tons to permit a heavier armament of four 9.2-inch guns (in two twin turrets fore and aft) and

The 14,600-ton *Shannon* was a member of the *Minotaur* class and she entered service in March 1908. They mounted a heavier armament than previous classes, with two twin 9.2-inch turrets fore and aft and ten 7.5-inch guns in single turrets (five on either beam). This number of turrets therefore gave them a very

powerful appearance, as can be discerned from this photograph. Like the *Warrior* class, the *Minotaur* class completed with short funnels (as shown here) that were raised in 1909. *Shannon* fought at Jutland in the 2nd Cruiser Squadron alongside her sister *Minotaur*, while *Defence*, the third ship of the class, was also

present (and was lost) as part of the 1st Cruiser Squadron. She then served as a convoy escort until the end of the war, and was used as an accommodation ship from 1920 until she was sold off in 1922. (© The National Archives, United Kingdom, ADM 176/633) ten 7.5-inch guns (in single turrets on the beam). Their anti-torpedo boat armament was also strengthened to sixteen 12-pdrs. Their armour remained very similar to *Warrior*'s, although the main-deck 6-inch armour was removed and the hoists to the 7.5-inch turrets were instead given 7-inch armour (thinning to 2 inches behind the belt).[129]

Despite the introduction of the all-big–gun-ship, the preceding three classes all saw service in the First World War. Four formed Rear Admiral Sir Robert Arbuthnot's 1st Cruiser Squadron at Jutland (*Black Prince, Duke of Edinburgh, Warrior* and *Defence*), but suffered terribly at the hands of the modern

German dreadnoughts: during the Grand Fleet's initial encounter with the High Seas Fleet, Arbuthnot charged into the fray to engage a German light cruiser squadron and exposed his squadron to the concentrated fire of the German battleships and battlecruisers. *Defence*'s magazines exploded (due to fire spreading through her ammunition passages) and she sank immediately with the loss of all hands (including Arbuthnot),[130] while *Warrior* was badly damaged and later foundered whilst being towed home by the seaplane carrier *Engadine*. At the same time, *Black Prince* became separated from the squadron and never rejoined

company. During the night she fell in with the main German battlefleet and was quickly overwhelmed by close-range fire from a number of German dreadnoughts, again being lost with all hands.[131]

Second Class Cruisers

The Second Class cruisers of the period were for the most part direct improvements of previous classes, without the dramatic changes in size (both up and down) evident in First Class cruisers. The first class of ships constructed after the Naval Defence Act were the nine *Eclipse*-class vessels of the Spencer Programme, laid down in 1893–5 and completed

The Second Class cruiser *Eclipse*, photographed in May 1897 shortly after her completion. Developed from the preceding *Astraea* class, the displacement of the *Eclipse* class was increased by over 1,000-tons (to 5,600-tons) in order to incorporate a number of improvements. As can be seen here a forecastle was fitted (to improve sea-

keeping), and her armament was also augmented with three 6-inch quick-firers in place of the some of the earlier ship's 4.7-inch weapons (for a total of five 6-inch and six 4.7-inch quick-firers). One of these extra 6-inch guns was mounted on the quarterdeck aft (alongside the existing 6-inch weapon there), while the other two took the place of the

4.7-inch guns on the broadside between the bridge and fore-funnel. Less obviously, *Astraea*'s 6-pdr anti-torpedo boat guns were replaced with heavier 12-pdrs. *Eclipse* was converted into an accommodation ship in 1916 and sold off in 1921. (© The National Archives, United Kingdom, ADM 176/223)

Isis, an *Eclipse*-class cruiser completed in May 1898. Despite their increased armament compared with the *Astraea* class, the *Eclipse*-class ships were still criticised as being under-armed compared to equivalent foreign vessels. In the early 1900s, therefore, all save *Eclipse* herself had their 6-inch and 4.7-inch guns replaced with eleven 6-inch quick-firers. *Isis* saw service in the First World War and was sold off in 1920. (© The National Archives, United Kingdom, ADM 176/369)

in 1896–8. At 5,600 tons they marked a further increase in displacement from the *Astraea* class of the Naval Defence Act (which were themselves enlarged versions of *Apollo*) and this extra size was used to increase armament and protection. They were armed with five 6-inch and six 4.7-inch guns and their protective deck was 1 inch on the flat and 2–3 inches on the slope. The engine power was increased to give them the same maximum speed of 19½ kts under forced draught as earlier Second Class cruisers.[132]

The next class, the four *Arrogant* ships, were laid down in 1895–6 and completed in 1898–1900. Designated 'Fleet Rams', they marked a departure from previous vessels Second Class cruisers in that their main role was delivering the *coup de grâce* to disabled enemies during fleet actions by ramming. They had a similar displacement and protection to *Eclipse*, but to fulfil their intended purpose they were given improved manoeuvrability by being reduced in length by 30 feet and being fitted with a balanced main rudder and an additional

secondary one. These changes gave them a turning circle of 380 yards, compared with the 650 yards of the similarly sized *Astraea*. Armament was also similar to *Eclipse*, albeit with one fewer 6-inch gun. They cost approximately £300,000 each.[133] It appears that they were never afforded the opportunity to employ their primary weapon, the ram, in the situation for which it had been intended.

The five cruisers of the *Highflyer* and *Challenger* classes that followed marked a return to the traditional RN concept of the

This photograph shows the *Arrogant*-cruiser *Furious*, which was completed in July 1898. From this angle it would normally be possible to see the single 6-inch quick-firer mounted on her quarterdeck, which was the main point of difference from the preceding *Eclipse*-class cruisers that mounted two such weapons in that position. Here, however, a party of Royal Marines are mustering aft, watched by a number of seamen, and so the view of the 6-inch gun is obscured. *Furious* was converted into a hulk attached to *Vernon*, the home of the RN's Torpedo Branch, in 1915 and sold off in 1923. (© The National Archives, United Kingdom, ADM 176/282)

Vindictive, an *Arrogant*-class Second Class cruiser completed in July 1900. The members of this class were designed as ramming vessels rather than for the usual Second Class cruiser roles, and were consequently given a heavy ram bow and increased manoeuvrability. There is only a hint of *Vindictive*'s ram visible in this photograph, although the layout of her conventional gun armament can be seen. This was originally four 6-inch and six 4.7-inch quick-firers, disposed as in the *Eclipse* class (minus one of the rear 6-inch guns), but like the earlier class the *Arrogant* ships were up-gunned to a uniform armament of ten 6-inch quick-firers in 1903-04. *Vindictive* won fame as the assault ship in the St George's Day Raid on Zeebrugge in 1918, and was then sunk as a blockship in the follow-up raid on Ostend on 10 May. (© The National Archives, United Kingdom, ADM 176/757)

Encounter (pictured here) and her sister *Challenger* were derivatives of the three *Highflyer*-class cruisers, with a slight (*c.* 200-ton) increase in displacement. This was used to install slightly more powerful machinery, boosting their speed by 1 kt to 21 kts. Visually, they could be distinguished by their lack of cowls amidships as they relied instead on wind sails to provide the required ventilation. *Encounter* was transferred to the Royal Australian Navy (RAN) in 1912 and in 1923 was converted into a depot ship, taking the name *Penguin* – perhaps as a replacement for the *Osprey*-class sloop of the same name that had also been transferred to the RAN. In this new guise, *Encounter* survived until she was decommissioned and scuttled in 1932. (© The National Archives, United Kingdom, ADM 176/235)

The 5,650-ton Second Class cruiser *Hermes*, completed in 1899. *Hermes* was one of three *Highflyer*-class cruisers, which were developments of the *Eclipse* class but were designed from the outset with a uniform armament of eleven 6-inch quick-firers.

Hermes played an important role in the development of naval aviation in the RN: she was converted into a seaplane carrier for the 1913 Manoeuvres, and the experience thus gained informed the design and construction of the RN's first purpose-built aviation vessel, the seaplane carrier *Ark Royal* of 1914. *Hermes*, however, was an early casualty of the First World War, being torpedoed in the Channel by *U27* in October 1914. (© The National Archives, United Kingdom, ADM 176/330)

Second Class cruiser. Laid down in two batches (three *Highflyer* cruisers in 1897 followed by two *Challenger* class in 1900–01), they were essentially repeats of *Eclipse* fitted with a uniform 6-inch armament.[134]

Third Class and Scout Cruisers

As with Second Class cruisers, the development of Third Class cruisers after 1889 continued essentially linearly from previous designs. The eleven *Pelorus*-class ships laid down in 1895–7 and competed in 1898–1901 were generally similar to the earlier *Pearl* but were slightly smaller (at 2,135 tons) and had a lighter armament of eight 4-inch quick-firing guns. Their beam was also slightly reduced compared with *Pearl*'s, which reduced their stability and made them worse sea-boats. Like the earlier ships, however, they were protected by a curved armoured deck of 1½–2-inch thickness.[135]

The final Third Class cruisers built for the RN were the four *Gem*-class ships of 1902–03. They marked the ultimate evolution of the type, being the largest (at 3,000 tons) and the most heavily armed (twelve 4-inch guns).[136] The construction of medium-sized cruisers (Second and Third Class vessels) ceased at the turn of the century, however, as Fisher initially believed that their trade-protection and scouting roles could better be fulfilled by battlecruisers and by scout cruisers

The 2,135-ton Third Class cruiser *Pactolus*, which was completed in September 1898. She was a member of the *Pelorus* class, which were based on the earlier *Pearl* class but featured an extra knot of speed (for 20 kts) at the expense of a slightly reduced armament (eight 4-inch quick-firers, as opposed to eight 4.7-inch quick-firers). As can be seen in this photograph, however, the two classes were very similar in general appearance and their guns were disposed in exactly the same layout. The *Pelorus* class were constructed at a time when the RN was experimenting with water-tube boilers from a variety of manufacturers, and those fitted to *Pactolus* were supplied by the same company as those of her sister *Pomone*. These boilers proved so problematic, however, that both ships had to be retired before any of the rest of the class. *Pactolus* was converted into a depot ship in 1912, and in this form supported submarines during the First World War. She was sold off and scrapped in 1921. (© The National Archives, United Kingdom, ADM 176/501)

Sapphire, a 3,000-ton Third Class cruiser completed in February 1905. She was one of four *Gem*-class vessels, which were the final Third Class cruisers built for the RN and consequently the largest, fastest and best armed and armoured of the type. Their uniform main armament of twelve 4-inch quick-firers was half as large again as the eight guns of the preceding *Pelorus* class, and their top speed was nearly 2 kts higher (at almost 22 kts). *Sapphire* saw service in the First World War, and was sold off in 1921. (© The National Archives, United Kingdom, ADM 176/615)

The scout cruiser *Adventure*, which entered service in October 1905. *Adventure* was one of a pair of scout cruisers built by Armstrong (the other was *Attentive*), and they could be distinguished from the six similar ships from other builders primarily by having four funnels instead of three. All eight ships had the same original armament of ten 12-pdrs, later increased to twelve, but this was soon felt to be too light and between 1911 and 1912 all had their 12-pdrs replaced by nine 4-inch guns. *Adventure* and *Attentive* must have proved the most successful of the four designs as they went on to provide the starting point for subsequent Admiralty scout cruiser designs. *Adventure* saw service in the First World War, both as a flotilla leader for destroyers and as a patrol vessel, and was sold off in 1920. (© The National Archives, United Kingdom, ADM 176/5)

Cammell Laird's response to the Admiralty's request for scout cruiser designs was the sisters *Pathfinder* (pictured here) and *Patrol*. Unlike the designs from Vickers and Armstrong, *Pathfinder* had a 2-inch armoured belt (in common with the Fairfield-designed ships), although it only protected the engine rooms (and not the entirety of the ship's machinery spaces as in the Fairfield ships). The remainder of the ship was protected by an armoured deck. Like many other scout cruisers, *Pathfinder* was often used to support destroyer flotillas, and it was while she was attached to one such flotilla that she was torpedoed and sunk by *U21* on 5 September 1914 with the loss of 259 of her crew. (© The National Archives, United Kingdom, ADM 176/508)

The Vickers-designed scout cruiser *Sentinel*, which was completed in April 1905. The two Vickers ships could be distinguished from the other three-funnelled scout cruisers by the lower height of their funnels. Like the Armstrong cruisers, *Sentinel* and her sister *Skirmisher* relied on a full-length armoured deck for protection. This photograph provides a good view of the layout of the ten 12-pdr guns, common to all eight cruisers, with three mounted on both the forecastle and quarterdeck and two on each side (one just behind the break of the forecastle and the other further aft). *Sentinel* saw service in the First World War, before becoming a training ship at Chatham. She was sold off in 1923. (© The National Archives, United Kingdom, ADM 176/630)

and large destroyers respectively. It took some time for this to be revealed to be untrue, however, and the construction of *c.* 5,000-ton cruisers did not resume until the *Bristol* class of 1909.[137]

Instead, what small cruiser construction there was after 1903 was concentrated on small 'scout cruisers'. In 1901 Vice-Admiral Fitzgerald argued that there was a need for small, fast cruisers capable of watching enemy ports for a long time in heavy weather (a role analogous to that of Napoleonic-era frigates). When the Admiralty put out a requirement for small cruisers in 1903, however, the stated role was to lead TBD attacks. This meant that less coal stowage was required, which obviously reduced their endurance and made them less suited to scouting duties.[138]

In a similar fashion to early TBD orders of the 1890s (described below), two ships meeting this requirement were ordered from each of four different builders: Armstrong (*Adventure* and *Attentive*), Fairfield (*Forward* and *Foresight*), Cammell Laird (*Pathfinder* and *Patrol*) and Vickers (*Sentinel* and *Skirmisher*). All were generally similar, although they differed in the provision of forecastles, poops and armoured belts, and all made the required speed of 25 kts.[139]

Masted Cruisers

The rise of the effective steam cruiser may have seen gunboats replaced by the Second and Third Class cruisers as the primary means of Imperial defence, but there was still a

Torch, a 960-ton sloop completed in October 1895. *Torch* and her sister *Alert* were steel-hulled, in common with the preceding *Beagle* class, but differed from the earlier vessels in that they had more modern vertical triple-expansion engines and were armed with quick-firing guns. This armament of six 4-inch weapons was, however, disposed in the same manner as the 5-inch breech-loaders of the earlier class, as can be appreciated from this photograph. In terms of size, armament and general appearance, *Torch* and *Alert* were therefore very similar to the final composite-hulled gunboats (the *Redbreasts*) constructed just prior to the Naval Defence Act. In later life, their yards and sails were removed and they relied entirely on steam for propulsion, and *Torch* was sold off in 1920. (© The National Archives, United Kingdom, ADM 176/715)

perceived need for vessels to police Britain's interests abroad outside of war with a major European power. To this end, four final classes of masted cruisers (the *Alert*, *Phoenix*, *Condor* and *Cadmus* classes) totalling sixteen vessels were laid down between 1893 and 1904, when construction of the type finally ceased. Although rated as sloops, these classes marked the final merging of the type with the gunvessel as, with their armament of six 4-inch quick-firers, they were essentially slightly larger (*c.* 1,000 tons) steel-hulled versions of the identically armed composite gunboats of the 1880s. Set against the grim pre-dreadnought battleships and armoured cruisers of the 1890s, these elegant three-masted vessels with their clipper bows and figureheads appear to the modern eye as relics from a bygone age.[140]

Phoenix, a 1,050-ton steel-hulled sloop completed in May 1896. The lead ship of a class of two (the other ship was *Algerine*), *Phoenix* was very similar to the preceding *Alert*-class steel-hulled sloops and mounted the same armament of six 4-inch quick-firers. As in *Alert*, these guns were carried in shielded mounts, with two on the forecastle, two amidships and two on the poop. *Phoenix* was originally rigged as a schooner, as shown in this photograph, but later in her career her yards and sails were removed to leave her entirely steam-propelled. She was lost in Hong Kong harbour on 18 September 1906 when she capsized during a typhoon. (© The National Archives, United Kingdom, ADM 176/523)

Vestal, a 980-ton *Condor*-class steel-hulled sloop launched in February 1900. As with the preceding *Phoenix* class, which the *Condor* class resembled in armament and general appearance, many of the *Condor* class lost their yards and sails in later life. This photograph, however, shows *Vestal* as she originally appeared when she was rigged as a barque. *Vestal* saw service in the First World War, including action off the Belgian coast, and was sold off in 1921. (© The National Archives, United Kingdom, ADM 176/749)

The 1,070-ton steel-hulled *Cadmus*-class sloop *Fantome* as she appeared in May 1902 shortly after she was completed. Despite her designation as a sloop, her armament of six 4-inch quick-firers was identical in both calibre and disposition to the final classes of masted composite-hulled gunboats of the 1880s. Given the advances in steam propulsion during the course of the nineteenth century, it is incredible to think that only four years before *Dreadnought* the RN was still constructing masted warships, although it must be recognised that the *Cadmus* class were the last masted cruisers built for the RN. *Fantome* was almost completely disarmed and converted into a survey ship in 1906 (as was her sister *Merlin*). However, she was rearmed on the outbreak of the First World War and saw service with the Royal Australian Navy as a patrol vessel. She was sold off in 1925. (© The National Archives, United Kingdom, ADM 176/255)

Torpedo Boat Destroyers (TBDs)

For the RN, the Russian War Scare of 1885 had brought to the fore the need for purpose-designed vessels to defend against enemy torpedo craft. The resulting 125-foot torpedo boats, which were designed to mount either extra guns or extra torpedoes, were an attempt to meet this need, as were the larger TGBs described in the previous chapter. Neither class of vessels, however, provided the answer: the large TBs (torpedo boats) were still too small, while the TGBs were thought too slow and expensive. The need for such a ship continued to grow into the early 1890s, however, particularly as France began to construct large high-seas torpedo boats as part of the *Jeune École* response to Britain's battleship fleet.[141]

On becoming Third Naval Lord in 1892, Fisher appointed a committee to investigate the issue of fleet torpedo attack and defence, and this recommended that the solution was to build craft fast enough to catch, and with a powerful enough gun armament to destroy, enemy torpedo boats. This was perhaps an unsurprising outcome: Fisher had published a paper in 1891 while he was still DNO advocating exactly the same thing, and companies like Yarrow and Thornycroft had been suggesting that the Admiralty build larger, more heavily armed torpedo boats for some time.[142]

The order for the RN's first six 'torpedo boat destroyers' (TBDs) was therefore placed in 1892. At approximately 280 tons, these were enlarged torpedo boats that were

Havock, the RN's first torpedo boat destroyer (TBD), photographed in December 1895. Capable of 26 kts and armed with three 18-inch torpedo tubes, one 12-pdr and three 6-pdrs, her turtle-back forecastle and general appearance (e.g. 12-pdr mounted on a 'bandstand' on top of the conning tower) were maintained by all RN TBDs up to the *River*-class vessels of the early 1900s. *Havock* herself was broken up in 1912. (© The National Archives, United Kingdom, ADM 176/321)

Ferret, one of the first 26-knot TBDs built for the RN. This photograph shows her with her original armament of three 18-inch torpedo tubes (one fixed in the bow and two on deck), one 12-pdr and three 6-pdrs, although in later life the two deck-mounted torpedo tubes were removed. The stresses and strains of everyday use meant that by 1907 she was deemed unfit for further service, and so from 1908 she was used as a trial ship for boom-breaking experiments. She was finally expended as a target in 1911. (© The National Archives, United Kingdom, ADM 176/263)

The 27-knot TBD *Boxer*, photographed in December 1895. She was one of an initial order of six such boats, and was initially fitted with a bow torpedo tube (as in the 26-knot boats) when she entered service in June 1895. Experience quickly showed, however, that this generated too much spray, and it is interesting to note that by the time this photograph was taken (only six months later) it had already been removed. The photograph also provides a good profile view of the general appearance of an RN TBD of the time. Visible over her bows is the reconstructed central battery ironclad *Sultan*. *Boxer* was lost in 1918 in a collision with a merchant vessel. (© The National Archives, United Kingdom, ADM 176/94)

The 27-knot TBD *Banshee*, which was completed in July 1895, was one of the first 27-knot boats constructed by Laird. Unlike the initial batch of six 27-knot boats she was completed without a bow torpedo tube. The layout of her gun armament, common to many RN TBDs, can be seen in this photograph: the 12-pdr was carried on the prominent raised platform forward, flanked by two 6-pdrs just behind the forecastle, with two further 6-pdrs further aft near her two 18-inch torpedo tubes and the remaining 6-pdr to the rear. *Banshee* was sold off in 1912. (© The National Archives, United Kingdom, ADM 176/57)

armed with one 12-pdr, three 6-pdrs and three 18-inch torpedo tubes, and proved capable of 26 kts on trial. Each cost approximately £36,000.[143] These 26-knotters are sometimes referred to as the *Havock* class after the first Yarrow vessel; her sister was *Hornet*, while Thornycroft built *Daring* and *Decoy* and Laird built *Ferret* and *Lynx*.[144]

The next TBDs, ordered in 1893–4, were slightly larger (*c*. 300 tons), and this allowed for an increased speed of 27 kts (hence they were known as '27-knotters') and a heavier gun armament (two extra 6-pdrs) at the cost of removing the bow torpedo tube. Although this cut their torpedo armament by a third, it had the added benefit of reducing (but not removing altogether) the amount of spray generated when travelling at speed.

This armament (one 12-pdr, five 6-pdrs and two 18-inch torpedo tubes) became the standard armament for all RN TBDs up to and including the *River* class of the early 1900s.[145]

The first six 27-knot TBDs were ordered from Thornycroft and Yarrow (three each), but the subsequent follow-on order of thirty vessels was spread amongst twelve other manufacturers – a deliberate policy on the part of the Admiralty to give as many firms as possible experience of building such craft. Their larger size was reflected in the higher price of approximately £40,000 per vessel; there was, however, a large degree of variation between different builders, with ships from those firms that did not have as much experience tending to take longer and cost more.[146] To

place the RN's spending on TBDs into perspective, the total cost of these thirty-six 27-kt TBDs was approximately one and a half times that of a single First Class battleship of the *Majestic* class.

The next development was the 30-knotter, which carried the same armament as the 27-knotter on a displacement of *c*. 350–400 tons. The initial order for eight boats under the 1894–5 Programme was placed with two of the firms that had constructed the initial group of six 26-knotters (four from Thornycroft and four from Laird), perhaps because of the considerable delays in completion of the 27-kt boats from inexperienced builders. A further twenty-one boats were ordered in the 1895–6 Programme, mainly from builders who had successfully completed one or more TBDs by

The Doxford-built 27-knot TBD *Haughty* running trials in 1895. This photograph provides some indication of the conditions faced by the crew of a TBD in service: the water appears calm, but even in these conditions there is a plume of spray being thrown up from her bows and the exposed crew (including one stood on the empty 12-pdr bandstand) are wearing waterproof clothing. Like many of the early TBDs, *Haughty* was sold off and broken up in 1912. (© The National Archives, United Kingdom, ADM 176/319)

Desperate was the first of the eight initial 30-kt TBDs ordered in 1894 to be completed (in 1897). Built by Thornycroft, she mounted the standard RN TBD armament of one 12-pdr, five 6-pdrs and two 18-inch torpedo tubes. *Desperate* served in the Mediterranean between 1900 and 1913 and then, like many of her contemporaries, saw service in the First World War as a coastal patrol vessel and was not broken up until 1920. Visible behind her in the photograph are the refitted central-battery ironclad *Audacious*, recognisable by the fighting tops on her fore and main masts, and an *Agamemnon*-class turret battleship. (© The National Archives, United Kingdom, ADM 176/195A)

The 30-knot TBD *Bullfinch*, photographed in June 1901. She was one of the last TBDs to be constructed by the Hull-based firm Earle, which had built a number of such vessels for the RN in the 1890s, as it went bankrupt whilst she was building. This photograph provides an interesting view not only of *Bullfinch* herself but also of an RN dockyard at the turn of the twentieth century. *Bullfinch* served in the First World War and was sold off in 1919. (© The National Archives, United Kingdom, ADM 176/105)

then, and this trusted circle had widened further when sixteen further boats were ordered in 1896–7.[147] The increased size and speed of these boats inevitably resulted in them being more expensive: all 30-knot TBDs cost at least £50,000 each, with some costing nearly £55,000.[148]

Three further extraordinary boats were ordered in 1896 (one each from Thornycroft, Laird and Thomson), and the contracts for these 'Specials' specified a speed of 33 kts. This required larger engines, which in turn required increased displacement (to a total of over 500 tons) and also increased the cost to an average of nearly £70,000 per boat (one third more than a 30-knotter

and almost double that of the original 26-knotters).[149] None of the three actually achieved 33 kts in service, however, and as a result they became in effect large, very expensive 30-knotters and no more were built. They marked a step too far in the use of reciprocating machinery, and improvements in performance over the 30-kt reciprocating-engined boats would have to wait until the introduction of the steam turbine.[150]

With the expensive failure of the 33-kt Specials, TBD orders in subsequent years reverted to the cheaper and more successful 30-kt designs. This was financially more prudent and also made tactical sense: the torpedo boats that France was

building in 1897 were only designed for 26 kts, and were thought unlikely to be able to exceed 28 or 29 kts in service, leaving the 30-kt British boats with an adequate margin of speed. The Admiralty therefore set the minimum speed for the new destroyers at 30 kts, leaving bidding firms to offer higher speeds if they thought they could manage it, but in the event the six TBDs ordered under the 1897–8 Programme were all 30-knotters. Fifteen further 30-knotters were ordered between 1899 and 1901, before the larger River-class boats described below superseded the type.[151]

This period also saw the unusual event (for the time) of a captured enemy ship being put into RN

The 30-knot TBD *Sprightly*, which was completed by her builder Laird along with her sister *Lively* in mid-1902. She was therefore one of the final *Havock*-style TBDs to enter service before the improved *River*-class TBDs were introduced. The projection from her side aft (visible just below the distant sailing ship) is a guard to prevent damage to her propeller blades, a feature common to many TBDs of the time. *Sprightly* was sold off in 1921. (© The National Archives, United Kingdom, ADM 176/664)

service. Four modern German-built Chinese destroyers were captured on 1 June 1900, during the Boxer Rebellion, and one was given to Britain and renamed *Taku*. The RN was keen to examine the ship as it was reported that she was capable of nearly 34 kts under forced draught. In practice, however, this proved to be incorrect: she never reached anything like such speeds and her accommodation was inferior to British 30-knotters.[152]

Even on British-built TBDs, life was testing indeed. At high speed and in anything but moderate weather their bridges would be water-swept, even after the bow torpedo tube was removed in the 27-knotters. Furthermore, the ships were lightly built to achieve high speed, and as a result flexed dramatically, causing rivets to loosen and, in extreme cases (like that of *Seal*) cracks to form in their hulls and decks, both of which would lead to water entering the ship. Their small size also meant that they pitched and rolled greatly. At the same time, creature comforts for the crew were few: their accommodation was not insulated and as a result was cold in winter and hot in summer, and cases of tuberculosis were common.[153]

River-*class TBDs*

As can be seen, a major preoccupation with early TBD design was achieving higher and higher top speeds, something that the Admiralty initially encouraged through the insertion of penalty clauses in the purchase contracts if the required speeds were not met. To

This photograph of the *River*-class TBD *Kennet*, which was completed in January 1905, shows to good advantage the two major improvements introduced in this class compared with earlier destroyers: a raised forecastle and a separate bridge behind the 12-pdr gun. The extra deck forward greatly improved the class's ability to maintain speed in heavy seas and also, combined with the raised bridge, made life more bearable for exposed crewmen. *Kennet* saw service in the Far East and the Mediterranean during the First World War, and was sold off in 1919. (© The National Archives, United Kingdom, ADM 176/384)

This photograph of *Itchen* provides a good view of the overall appearance of the *River* class TBDs. As with the preceding 30-knot TBDs, the *River*-class ships were armed with a single 12-pdr forward, five 6-pdrs (two abaft the forecastle, two amidships and one astern) and two 18-inch torpedo tubes. In the early *River*-class ships the forward 6-pdrs were mounted in sponsons (as visible in this photograph) but, as this position was found to be too exposed, they were moved onto the forecastle alongside the 12-pdr in later ships. Additionally, from 1906 the five 6-pdrs were replaced by three heavier 12-pdrs to improve the class's firepower. Like many of her sisters, *Itchen* was used as a patrol craft during the First World War, and it was while serving in this role that she was torpedoed by *U99* on 6 July 1917. (© The National Archives, United Kingdom, ADM 176/370)

meet these speeds, and avoid the fines, trials were often run in unrealistic conditions (i.e. favourable weather and with the ship lightly loaded) that bore little relation to those that would be experienced in service. Despite being billed as 27- or 30-knotters, therefore, TBDs would be unlikely to reach such speeds under operational conditions. The failure of the 33-knotters further undermined this drive to achieve ever-higher TBD speeds. There was a shift in emphasis, therefore, from faster designed maximum speed to larger, more sturdy TBDs better able to maintain their best speed when loaded and in non-calm seas.[154]

This change was embodied in the *River* class of TBDs. With these, the Admiralty modified its requirements by asking for a designed speed of only 25½ kts (notionally slower than previous TBDs) and a raised forecastle to improve their sea-keeping and allow the 12-pdr to be used in bad weather. The *River*-class vessels were therefore altogether larger than previous TBDs (with a displacement of over 600 tons), even though their armament was identical and the designed speed lower. This extra size and raised forecastle made them far more effective warships than the earlier TBDs, to the extent that they have been described as 'the first true destroyers … simultaneously the true torpedo vessel and the best type of fleet escort'.[155] Ten were ordered under the 1901–02 Estimates, followed by a further eight in 1902–03 and then sixteen in 1903–04.[156] Two further *River*-class TBDs (*Stour* and *Test*) were purchased as replacements for losses after 1906, as were two tubine-engined 30-knotters (*Albacore* and *Bonetta*) in 1908–9. One more *River*-class TBD, built in Italy, was purchased for the RN during First World War and named *Arno*.[157]

Somewhat surprisingly, the arrival of the TBD did not immediately spell the end of the First Class torpedo boat. Ten 140-foot TBs were added to the RN in 1892–5 at the same time as the first TBDs were coming into service, and at the same time seven 130-foot TBs originally ordered by the India Office in 1887 were also taken over by the RN. What is more, at the same time as the *River*-class vessels were entering service in the early 1900s, the RN also bought thirteen 160-foot TBs, which were slower (25 kts) and less heavily armed (three 3-pdrs, in addition to three 18-inch torpedo tubes) than contemporary TBDs. These were the last TBs ordered by the RN, however.[158]

An interesting photograph of the 140-foot *Torpedo Boat No. 95*, being repaired in dry-dock following a collision. One of her sisters, which has also suffered damage, is visible behind her. *TB 95* served in the Mediterranean during the First World War, and was scrapped in 1919. (© The National Archives, United Kingdom, ADM 176/734)

Torpedo Boat No. 91 was one of the class of 140-foot torpedo boats built for the RN alongside the first TBDs of the 1890s. Her three 18-inch torpedo tubes (one in the bow and two on deck) are visible, but her usual gun armament of three 3-pdrs is not. Like the early TBDs, the 140-foot boats had the turtleback forecastle pioneered in *Torpedo Boat No. 80* to improve their sea-keeping over that of earlier boats. *TB 91* was based at Gibraltar for much of the First World War and was not broken up until 1919–20. (© The National Archives, United Kingdom, ADM 176/732)

The Introduction of the Steam Turbine

The stresses on the reciprocating engines required to drive TBDs at high speed were great, and the resulting vibration was a problem not only for the crew (in addition to all the other discomforts) but also for the machinery itself. A few TBDs experienced dramatic mechanical failures, such as *Foam* (where a break in an engine cylinder led to the connecting rod going through the bottom of her hull) and *Bat* (a broken connecting rod allowed a piston to be ejected out of its cylinder and up through her upper deck).

Such accidents could easily have fatal consequences: when *Bullfinch* suffered a broken connecting rod whilst travelling at 30 kts, she cracked a cylinder and the resultant steam escape killed eleven crewmen. Similarly, in 1904 *Chamois* lost a propeller blade while underway and the resulting damage to her hull caused her to sink.[159]

It was not just small ships that suffered problems caused by reciprocating engines when travelling at speed, however, as illustrated by the experience of the 2nd Cruiser Squadron (*Drake*, *Essex*, *Bedford*, *Cumberland*, *Cornwall* and *Berwick*) during and after their high-speed voyage from New York to Gibraltar in November 1906. Three ships (*Drake*, *Berwick* and *Cumberland*) completed the voyage in a less than seven and a half days, at an average speed of 22½ kts, but the remaining three took much longer as they suffered severe mechanical failures. Furthermore, all were found to need major repair work on both their engines and hulls, where a large number of rivets had been loosened by vibration.[160]

The steam turbine appeared to offer the solution to the vibration problems of high-speed reciprocating machinery, and raised the possibility of reaching much higher speeds than could hitherto have been achieved. Although the adoption of the turbine in large ships falls just outside the period covered by this book, it was proved first in small vessels including TBDs. Charles Parson's *Turbinia* (built in 1894) had graphically demonstrated the benefits of turbines when she upstaged the Diamond Jubilee Review at Spithead in 1897

by steaming around the anchored fleet faster than the RN vessels sent to catch her. This event was not the shock to the late-Victorian naval establishment that has sometimes been claimed; White and the Engineer-in-Chief, Sir John Durston, had attended *Turbinia*'s trials in the previous year (where she reached 34½ kts) and it has been suggested that the gate-crashing of the review was a publicity stunt encouraged by Durston himself.[161]

Shortly after *Turbinia*'s dramatic public display, the RN ordered its first turbine-engined destroyer. Named *Viper*, she was ordered in March 1898 and completed in 1900. At 210 feet in length and approximately 370 tons in displacement, she was of a similar size to the contemporary 30-knotters, but thanks to her turbine engines she reached over 33 kts on trials. On one run, specially lightened, she even reportedly

This photograph was taken in May 1901 and shows *Viper*, the RN's first turbine-engined TBD, shortly before her loss in August of that year. Externally, there is little to differentiate her from the 30-knot reciprocating-engined TBDs of the day, and she mounted the same armament of two 18-inch torpedo tubes and one 12-pdr and five 6-pdr guns. (© The National Archives, United Kingdom, ADM 176/760)

steamed at 36½ kts for an hour. In service, the lack of vibration at speed was remarked upon, as was her coal consumption at low speeds (which was approximately twice that of reciprocating-engined boats). Eager to gain more experience with this novel propulsive machinery, in 1900 the RN purchased a second turbine-engined destroyer being built speculatively by Armstrong and named her *Cobra*.[162]

The RN's experiments were interrupted, however, when both *Viper* and *Cobra* were lost during 1901: *Viper* ran aground off Alderney in August, and *Cobra* broke in half and sank on her delivery voyage in September. *Cobra*'s loss prompted fears about the structural strength of all TBDs, and not just turbine-engined ones, for which an official inquiry was convened to investigate. The RN was therefore forced to acquire a third turbine-engined TBD from Parson's company to continue evaluation of

The *Gem*-class Third Class cruiser *Amethyst*, which was constructed with turbine engines so that her performance could be directly compared with that of her reciprocating-engined sisters. This made *Amethyst* notable as the first RN warship larger than a TBD to be powered by turbine engines. She was completed in March 1905, some seven months before *Dreadnought* was laid down but well after the design work on the turbine-engined battleship had begun, suggesting that the decision to power *Dreadnought* with turbines was taken before the outcome of the comparison between *Amethyst* and the other *Gem*-class ships was known. *Amethyst* herself served with the Grand Fleet and in the Dardanelles during the First World War, and was sold off in 1920. (© The National Archives, United Kingdom, ADM 176/23)

The ship that marked the end of the era begun by *Warrior*: the turbine-engined, all-big-gun battleship *Dreadnought*. Captured on camera in January 1907, comparing this photograph to those of battleships built over the preceding decade gives some clue as to the impact *Dreadnought* must have had on contemporary observers. In place of the standard mix of four 12-inch and numerous 6-inch guns, she mounted ten 12-inch guns in five separate turrets, and was thus a far more powerful warship than her predecessors. What cannot be seen from this static photograph is that her turbines were capable of driving her at 21 kts, which made her approximately 2–3 kts faster than a standard RN pre-dreadnought. Older battleships therefore could not run away from her, and were distinctly inferior once caught. There were a number of compromises to get her finished quickly and without a dramatic increase in displacement that became clear as her career progressed – the location of the fire control platform on the foremast relative to the forward funnel being one of the most visible, as well as the lack of the upper armoured belt that had been fitted to British pre-dreadnoughts. But the profound effect she had on contemporary naval opinion can be judged from the fact that she gave her name to a whole generation of battleships. (© The National Archives, United Kingdom, ADM 176/212)

such craft. This boat was originally to have been named *Python* but, given what had happened to the previous two turbine TBDs, the RN had come to regard snake names as unlucky and she was re-christened *Velox*, the Latin word meaning 'quick' or 'rapid'. In an attempt to overcome the problems of low-speed fuel efficiency experienced in *Viper*, she featured turbines for high speeds and reciprocating engines for low-speed cruising, but this was not a success and in 1906 the reciprocating engines were replaced by special low-speed turbines.[163]

Also in 1901, the *River*-class TBD *Eden* was fitted with turbines to enable direct comparison with her reciprocating-engined sisters. The RN went on to gain experience of using such machinery in larger ships with the *Gem*-class Third Class cruiser *Amethyst* (laid down in 1903). Turbines were then employed in a capital ship for the first time with *Dreadnought* of 1906. With hindsight, this choice of machinery might seem a natural choice, given the obvious benefits over reciprocating machinery, but it should be born in mind that the decision to fit *Dreadnought* with turbines was taken before *Amethyst* put to sea. The choice must have been made, therefore, on the basis of the success of such engines in the small TBDs and also in merchant craft such as the *King Edward* of 1901 and the liners *Carmania* (1901) and *Virginia* (1902).[164]

Conclusion

Faced at the turn of the Twentieth Century with spiralling Naval Estimates, Admiral Sir John Fisher was appointed First Sea Lord in 1904 to implement a programme designed to cut wastage by scrapping many old ships and making better use of available manpower through a system of 'nucleus crews'. Fisher's radical overhaul also saw the introduction of two new ship-types in the all-big-gun *Dreadnought* and *Invincible*. By making the RN pioneer such vessels he hoped to steal a march on rival nations (who were also considering such types) and allow Britain to build a lead that her rivals would be hard-pressed to claw back. This was a conscious abandonment of the traditional policy of allowing other nations to make the first move, and recognised how much Britain's place in the world had changed since 1860.

In light of the all-big-gun battleship, the capital ships of the 1890s came to be referred to retrospectively as pre-dreadnoughts.

Lumping so many battleships together under this term does, however, hide the technological developments that occurred prior to 1906, and these were developments that led to the obsolescence of older warships even before large numbers of dreadnoughts had entered service. In the RN's War Plans of 1907, the eight *Royal Sovereign*-class ships (including *Hood*), along with *Renown*, *Centurion*, *Barfleur* and the turret ships *Nile* and *Trafalgar* were the oldest capital units still considered fit for some form of service. Even then, while the more modern pre-dreadnoughts formed the main battlefleet alongside *Dreadnought* herself, the older ships were given the potentially much more dangerous in-shore tasks of covering the operations to close the Elbe with blockships and to seize the island of Borkum in Plan B, and in addition for attacks on German coastal fortifications in the Baltic under Plan C. The War Plans were explicit that the choice of the older ships for such tasks was based on their reduced value as battlefleet combatants:

> These vessels are no longer fit for first line duties in war, but they do provide a magnificent force for bombarding purposes, equipped with ideal weapons, and capable of standing considerable punishment at long ranges.[1]

These ships were not especially old in absolute terms, however. By 1908, the oldest (*Trafalgar*) had been in service for eighteen years, while the most modern (*Renown*) was only ten years old, having been completed in 1898. By comparison, some RN battleships that saw service in the Second World War were much older: *Barham*, *Valiant* and *Warspite*, for example, fought at Jutland in 1916 and again at Matapan in 1941, a span of twenty-five years. The ships relegated from the battlefleet in the 1907 War Plans were chosen not because dreadnoughts were now the only battleships that counted, but because subsequent pre-dreadnoughts had outclassed them.

The time would come, however, when dreadnoughts would outnumber pre-dreadnoughts in RN service, although for most of the 1900s the RN's battlefleet was made up of combination of both types of ship. Indeed, on the outbreak of war in 1914, the *King Edward VII*-class battleships of the 3rd Battle Squadron (3BS) were still part of the Grand Fleet, but this practice ended in May 1916 when 3BS was detached to the Thames. Accompanying them was *Dreadnought* herself, which was now also considered inferior to the latest ship types.

Notes

Chapter 1

1. Quoted in Kenneth Bourne, *The Foreign Policy of Victorian England 1830–1902* (Oxford: Clarendon Press, 1970), p. 44.
2. Paul Kennedy, *The Rise and Fall of British Naval Mastery*, 3rd Edition (London: Fontana Press, 1991) p. 131.
3. Quoted in C.J. Bartlett, *Great Britain and Sea Power 1815–53* (Oxford: Clarendon Press, 1963), p. 57.
4. Andrew Lambert, *The Last Sailing Battlefleet – Maintaining Naval Mastery 1815–1859* (London: Conway Maritime Press Ltd, 1991), p. 5.
5. Bartlett, *Great Britain*, p. 23.
6. Lambert, *Sailing Battlefleet*, p. 19.
7. Bartlett, *Great Britain*, p. 23.
8. Lambert, *Sailing Battlefleet*, p. 24.
9. Bartlett, *Great Britain*, p. 52.
10. Bartlett, *Great Britain*, p. 27.
11. Lambert, *Sailing Battlefleet*, p. IX.
12. Quoted in D.K. Brown, *Before the Ironclad – Development of Ship Design, Propulsion and Armament in the Royal Navy, 1815–60* (London: Conway Maritime Press Ltd, 1990), p. 1.
13. D.K. Brown, 'Wood, Sail, and Cannonballs to Steel, Steam and Shells, 1815–1895', in *The Oxford Illustrated History of the Royal Navy*, pp. 202–3; Brown, *Before the Ironclad*, pp. 47–51, p. 53.
14. Brown, *Before the Ironclad*, p. 62, pp. 64–70; Brown, 'Wood, Sail, and Cannonballs', p. 203.
15. Brown, *Before the Ironclad*, p. 119.
16. Brown, *Before the Ironclad*, p. 102; Brown, 'Wood, Sail, and Cannonballs', pp. 205–6.
17. Brown, 'Wood, Sail, and Cannonballs', p. 207; Brown, *Before the Ironclad*, pp. 122–3.
18. Brown, *Before the Ironclad*, p. 131, p. 137; Brown, 'Wood, Sail, and Cannonballs', p. 209.
19. Brown, *Before the Ironclad*, p. 75, p. 204.
20. Brown, *Before the Ironclad*, pp. 73–8, p. 80; Andrew Lambert, 'The Shield of Empire, 1815–1895' in *The Oxford Illustrated History of the Royal Navy*, ed. J.R. Hill (Oxford: Oxford University Press, 1995) p. 180.
21. Brown, *Before the Ironclad*, pp. 82–4; Richard Holmes, *Redcoat – The British Soldier in the Age of Horse and Musket* (London: HarperCollins Publishers, 2002), p. 349.
22. Brown, *Before the Ironclad*, p. 85–6.
23. Brown. *Before the Ironclad*, pp. 74–5, p. 202.
24. Brown, *Before the Ironclad*, p. 91. Brown, 'Wood, Sail, and Cannonballs', p. 205.
25. Basil Greenhill and Ann Giffard, *The British Assault on Finland 1854–55 – A Forgotten Naval War* (Naval Institute Press, 1988), p. 35.
26. Greenhill and Giffard, *British Assault*, p. 336; Andrew Lambert, *The Crimean War – British Grand Strategy 1853–56* (Manchester: Manchester University Press, 1990), p. 287.
27. Brown, *Before the Ironclad*, pp. 156–7.
28. Brown, *Before the Ironclad*, p. 158.
29. Lambert, *Crimean War*, p. 287; Greenhill and Giffard, *British Assault*, p. 45; William C. Fuller, Jr, *Strategy and Power in Russia 1600–1914* (New York: The Free Press, 1992), p. 274.
30. C.I. Hamilton, *Anglo-French Naval Rivalry 1840–1870* (Oxford: Clarendon Press, 1993), p. 64; Brown, *Before the Ironclad*, p. 145.
31. Brown, *Before the Ironclad*, p. 154.
32. Lambert, *Crimean War*, p. 316.
33. Brown, *Before the Ironclad*, p. 208.
34. Charles Stephenson, '"To the Imperial Mind": The Secret War Plan of Lord Dundonald; Kronstadt

and Sevastopol', in Nicholas Tracy (ed.), *The Age of Sail – The International Annual of the Historic Sailing Ship*, (London: Conway Maritime Press, 2002), Volume 1 (2002–2003), pp. 69–84.
35. Greenhill and Giffard, *British Assault*, p. 339.
36. Lambert, *Crimean War*, p. xvii.
37. Greenhill and Giffard, *British Assault*, p. 313.
38. David M. Goldfrank, *The Origins of the Crimean War* (London: Longman, 1994), p. 22.
39. Olive Anderson, *A Liberal State at War – English Politics and Economics During the Crimean War* (London: Macmillan, 1967), p. 271–2.
40. Anderson, *Liberal State*, p. 270.
41. Paul Kennedy, *The Rise and Fall of the Great Powers – Economic Change And Military Conflict From 1500 to 2000* (London: Fontana Press, 1989), p. 224.
42. Brown, *Before the Ironclad*, p. 158.
43. Brown, 'Wood, Sail, and Cannonballs', p. 210, p. 162.
44. Brown, *Before the Ironclad*, pp. 164–5.

Chapter 2
1. Lawrence Sondhaus, *Navies of Europe 1815–2002* (London: Pearson Education Limited, 2002), p. 51.
2. Andrew Lambert, 'Iron Hulls and Armour Plate', in Robert Gardiner and Andrew Lambert (eds.), *Steam, Steel and Shellfire: The Steam Warship 1815–1905* (London: Conway Maritime Press, 1992), p. 53.
3. Pascal Barras, 'The Royal Navy and the Role of Seapower In Global Politics, 1856–1871', in Antony Preston (ed.), *Warship 2001–2002* (London: Conway Maritime Press, 2001), pp. 19–32.
4. Brown, *Before the Ironclad*, p. 174.
5. Brown, *Before the Ironclad*, p. 186.
6. Brown, *Before the Ironclad*, p. 177; Oscar Parkes, *British Battleships: 'Warrior' to 'Vanguard'*

1860–1950: A History of Design, Construction and Armament, (London: Seeley Service & Co. Ltd, 1957), pp. 17–8.
7. *Conway's All the World's Fighting Ships 1860–1905* (London: Conway Maritime Press, 1979); p. 7, Parkes, *British Battleships*, p. 3.
8. Sondhaus, *Navies of Europe*, pp. 51–2.
9. Sondhaus, *Navies of Europe*, p. 53.
10. Sondhaus, *Navies of Europe*, p.53.
11. *Conway's*, p. 9; Parkes, *British Battleships*, pp. 30–32.
12. Parkes, *British Battleships*, p. 25; D.K. Brown, *Warrior to Dreadnought: Warship Development 1860–1905* (London: Chatham Publishing, 1997), p. 15.
13. Parkes, *British Battleships*, p. 30.
14. Brown, *Warrior to Dreadnought*, p. 15.
15. *Conway's*, p. 9.
16. Parkes, *British Battleships*, p. 42.
17. Parkes, *British Battleships*, pp. 39–44.
18. Parkes, *British Battleships*, p. 34.
19. Parkes, *British Battleships*, pp. 34–6.
20. *Conway's*, pp. 7–9.
21. Andrew Lambert, 'Iron Hulls and Armour Plate', in Robert Gardiner and Andrew Lambert (eds.), *Steam, Steel and Shellfire: The Steam Warship 1815–1905* (London: Conway Maritime Press, 1992), p. 59.
22. *Conway's*, p. 10.
23. Parkes, *British Battleships*, pp. 59–64
24. *Conway's*, p. 10; Parkes, *British Battleships*, pp. 64–7.
25. Brown, *Warrior to Dreadnought*, p. 16; Parkes, *British Battleships*, pp. 63–6.
26. *Conway's*, p. 10.
27. Parkes, *British Battleships*, p. 67.
28. Parkes, *British Battleships*, p. 50.
29. *Conway's*, pp. 10–11.
30. Parkes, *British Battleships*, p. 53.
31. Parkes, *British Battleships*, pp. 50–58.
32. John Beeler, *Birth of the Battleship: British Capital Ship Design*

1870–1881 (London: Chatham Publishing, 2001), p. 31.
33. Lawrence Sondhaus, *Navies in Modern World History* (London: Reaktion Books, 2004), p. 56.
34. *Conway's*, p. 7, p. 286.
35. *Conway's*, pp. 286–7.
36. It will be recalled, however, that in June 1914, just prior to the outbreak of the First World War, a squadron of British dreadnoughts visited Kiel for the regatta and received a visit from Kaiser Wilhelm II himself (wearing his uniform of a British admiral). See Robert K. Massie, *Dreadnought: Britain, Germany and the Coming of the Great War* (London: Pimlico, 1993), pp. 849–52.
37. Colin Jones, 'Entente Cordiale, 1865', in David McLean and Antony Preston (eds.), *Warship 1996* (London: Conway Maritime Press, 1996), pp. 31–40.
38. Sondhaus, *Navies of Europe*, p. 55.
39. Brown, 'Wood, Sail, and Cannonballs', p. 212.
40. Brown, *Warrior to Dreadnought*, p. 29; Parkes, *British Battleships*, p. 103.
41. *Conway's*, p. 13; Parkes, *British Battleships*, pp. 94–7.
42. *Repulse* was to be the last wooden battleship laid down for the RN.
43. *Conway's*, p. 13; Parkes, *British Battleships*, pp. 108–111.
44. Parkes, *British Battleships*, p. 111.
45. Parkes, *British Battleships*, pp. 112–3.
46. *Conway's*, p. 17; Parkes, *British Battleships*, pp. 121–4.
47. Parkes, *British Battleships*, p. 123.
48. D.K. Brown, 'The Era of Uncertainty, 1863–1878', in Robert Gardiner and Andrew Lambert (eds.), *Steam, Steel and Shellfire: The Steam Warship 1815–1905* (London: Conway Maritime Press, 1992), p. 80.
49. Vice-Admiral Symonds told a committee in 1871 that the 10-inch guns could not be fired through the

fore or aft ports, while Captain Lambert of *Vanguard* commented on the risk of blast damage and the dangers of moving guns whilst at sea. See Brown, *Warrior to Dreadnought*, pp. 35–7.

50. Barras, *Seapower*, pp. 21–3.
51. *Conway's*, p. 302; Barras, *Seapower*, p. 23.
52. Brown, *Warrior to Dreadnought*, p. 37. *Fatikh* was actually sold to Germany, where she was named *König Wilhelm*.
53. *Conway's*, pp. 15–6, p. 302.
54. *Conway's*, p. 16.
55. Parkes, *British Battleships*, pp. 157–8.
56. Barras, *Seapower*, p. 23; *Conway's* p 16; Parkes, *British Battleships*, p. 154.
57. Parkes, *British Battleships*, p. 150.
58. Parkes, *British Battleships*, p. 150.
59. Barras, *Seapower*, p. 23.
60. *Conway's*, p. 16; Parkes, *British Battleships*, pp. 162–5.
61. Sondhaus, *Modern World History*, p. 57.
62. Sondhaus, *Navies of Europe*, p. 58.
63. Sondhaus, *Modern World History*, p. 57.
64. This was the RN's senior decision-making body. It was presided over the by the First Lord of the Admiralty (a civilian appointee with a position in the Cabinet) and composed of a mixture of admirals (the Naval, later Sea, Lords) and civilians (the Civil Lords).
65. Brown, *Warrior to Dreadnought*, pp. 41–5.
66. *Conway's*, p. 19; Parkes, *British Battleships*, pp. 73–4.
67. *Conway's*, p. 19; Parkes, *British Battleships*, pp. 70–71.
68. *Conway's*, p. 19; Brown, *Warrior to Dreadnought*, p. 43.
69. Jones, 'Entente Cordiale', p. 34.
70. *Conway's*, p. 20, Parkes, *British Battleships*, p. 78.
71. Parkes, *British Battleships*, pp. 188–9.
72. Brown, *Warrior to Dreadnought*, p. 46; *Conway's*, p. 20.

73. Parkes, *British Battleships*, p. 128.
74. *Conway's*, p. 21; Brown, *Warrior to Dreadnought*, p. 48; Parkes, *British Battleships*, pp. 137–9.
75. Brown, *Warrior to Dreadnought*, p. 50.
76. Parkes, *British Battleships*, p. 143.
77. Antony Preston and John Major, *Send a Gunboat! A Study of the Gunboat and its Role in British Policy, 1854–1904* (London: Longman, Green and Co. Ltd, 1967), p. 61.
78. Brown, *Warrior to Dreadnought*, pp. 47–51; *Conway's*, p. 21.
79. Beeler, *Birth of the Battleship*, pp. 89–90.
80. Beeler, *Birth of the Battleship*, p. 93.
81. Beeler, *Birth of the Battleship*, p. 93.
82. Brown, *Warrior to Dreadnought*, pp. 57–8; Andrew Lambert, 'The Royal Navy, 1856–1914: Deterrence and the Strategy of World Power', in Keith Neilson and Elizabeth Jane Errington (eds.), *Navies and Global Defence: Theories and Strategy* (Westport, CT: Praeger Publishers, 1995), p. 78.
83. Brown, *Warrior to Dreadnought*, p. 56.
84. *Conway's*, p. 23.
85. Parkes, *British Battleships*, p. 196.
86. *Conway's*, p. 23; Brown, 'Era of Uncertainty', p. 82.
87. *Conway's*, p. 23.
88. Brown, *Warrior to Dreadnought*, p. 63; *Conway's*, p. 24.
89. Beeler, *Birth of the Battleship*, p. 53, p. 95.
90. Their obsolescence is commented on in *Conway's* p. 17, Parkes, *British Battleships*, p. 218 and Brown, *Warrior to Dreadnought*, p. 68.
91. *Conway's*, p. 17; Parkes, *British Battleships*, p. 218.
92. Brown, *Warrior to Dreadnought*, p. 68.
93. *Conway's*, p. 17; Parkes, *British Battleships*, p. 221.
94. Brown, *Warrior to Dreadnought*, pp. 66–7.

95. Parkes, *British Battleships*, p. 226, quoting Admiral G.A. Ballard. Ballard came to be regarded as one of the RN's premier strategic thinkers – in the early 1900s he was in charge of producing the service's first considered plans for what do in the event of war with Germany, including the establishment of a distant rather than a close blockade. His memoirs appeared in the *Mariner's Mirror* 1975–77.
96. *Conway's*, p. 18; Parkes, *British Battleships*, pp. 222–6.
97. Colin Jones, 'Ruling the Waves', in David McClean and Antony Preston (eds.), *Warship 1997–1998* (London: Conway Maritime Press, 1997), pp. 9–15. This not only describes the journey of the 1869 Flying Squadron, but also details the questions as to its strategic value – one critic was Admiral Ballard, who served as a junior officer in the 1880–82 cruise.
98. Brown, *Warrior to Dreadnought*, p. 18.
99. Sondhaus, *Navies of Europe*, p. 59; *Conway's*, p. 124.
100. *Conway's*, p. 47, p. 124.
101. *Conway's*, p. 47; Brown, *Warrior to Dreadnought*, p. 19.
102. Sondhaus, *Navies of Europe*, p. 59.
103. Brown, 'Era of Uncertainty', p. 89.
104. *Conway's*, p. 52.
105. *Conway's*, p. 41, 51, 54–7.
106. Preston and Major, *Send a Gunboat!*, p. 94; *Conway's*, pp. 55–7.
107. Preston and Major, *Send a Gunboat!*, pp. 88–9; *Conway's*, p. 107.
108. *Conway's*. pp. 107–109; Preston and Major, *Send a Gunboat!*, pp. 207–15
109. Preston and Major, *Send a Gunboat!*, p. 86.
110. *Conway's*, p. 111.
111. Preston and Major, *Send a Gunboat!*, p. 93.
112. *Conway's*, p. 111.

113. Preston and Major, *Send a Gunboat!*, pp. 95–6; *Conway's*, p. 108.
114. Bryan Perrett, *Gunboat! Small Ships at War* (London: Cassell & Co., 2001), pp. 37–49.
115. Perrett, *Gunboat!*, pp. 50–62, pp. 87–91.

Chapter 3

1. See for example Parkes, *British Battleships*, p. 264.
2. Parkes, *British Battleships*, p. 230.
3. Figures from Beeler, *Birth of the Battleship*, p. 157.
4. Figures from Beeler, *Birth of the Battleship*, p. 157.
5. Parkes, *British Battleships*, p. 264.
6. See for example Beeler, *Birth of the Battleship*, and Lambert, 'Shield of Empire'.
7. Jon Tetsuro Sumida, *In Defence of Naval Supremacy: Finance, Technology and British Naval Policy, 1889–1914* (London: Routledge, 1993), p. 11, Appendix Table 1.
8. Beeler, *Birth of the Battleship*, p. 22.
9. John Roberts, 'Warships of Steel, 1879–1889', in Robert Gardiner and Andrew Lambert (eds.), *Steam, Steel And Shellfire: The Steam Warship 1815–1905* (London: Conway Maritime Press, 1992), p. 97.
10. Beeler, *Birth of the Battleship*, pp. 38–40.
11. Sondhaus, *Navies of Europe*, p. 76.
12. Brown, *Warrior to Dreadnought*, p. 75.
13. *Conway's*, p. 74; Brown, *Warrior to Dreadnought*, p. 75, pp. 109–110.
14. Roberts, 'Warships of Steel', p. 98.
15. Parkes, *British Battleships*, p. 287.
16. Roberts, 'Warships of Steel', p. 98.
17. Sumida, *Naval Supremacy*, pp. 39–40.
18. David Lyon, 'Underwater Warfare and the Torpedo Boat', in Robert Gardiner and Andrew Lambert (eds.), *Steam, Steel and Shellfire: The Steam Warship 1815–1905* (London: Conway Maritime Press, 1992), p. 135.
19. Beeler, *Birth of the Battleship*, p. 66.
20. Alan Cowpe, 'The Royal Navy and the Whitehead Torpedo', in Bryan Ranft (ed.), *Technical Change and British Naval Policy 1860–1939* (Sevenoaks: Hodder & Stoughton Ltd, 1977), p. 23.
21. France did not start trials until 1873, while the Germans constructed their own version, which they called the Schwartzkopff – clearly a reference to the original inventor. See Lyon, 'Underwater Warfare', p. 137.
22. Beeler, *Birth of the Battleship*, p. 66; Lyon, 'Underwater Warfare', p. 137.
23. Cowpe, 'Royal Navy', pp. 24–5; *Conway's*, p. 86.
24. *Conway's*, p. 88.
25. Lyon, 'Underwater Warfare', p. 118.
26. *Conway's*, p. 88.
27. Brown, *Warrior to Dreadnought*, pp. 84–5; Beeler, *Birth of the Battleship*, p. 151; *Conway's*, p. 88.
28. Lyon, 'Underwater Warfare', p. 139. The first dedicated small torpedo boat was the Norwegian *Rap*, built by Thornycroft in 1872.
29. *Conway's*, p. 86; Brown, *Warrior to Dreadnought*, p. 86.
30. *Conway's*, pp. 101–102. The builders of the seven additional *Lightning* ships of the late 1870s were Maudslay (*TB 13*); Yarrow (*TB14*, *TB 17-18*); Hanna, Donald & Wilson (*TB 15*); White (*TB 19*) and Rennie (*TB 20*).
31. Sondhaus, *Navies of Europe*, pp. 89–92.
32. David Lyon, *The First Destroyers* (London: Caxton Editions, 2001), p. 13.
33. *Conway's*, pp. 102–103. The builders were Thornycroft (*TB 25–29, TB 41–60*); Yarrow (*TB 30–33, TB 61–78*); White (*TB 34–38*) and Yarrow (*TB 79*).
34. *Conway's*, pp. 103–104.
35. Brown, *Warrior to Dreadnought*, p. 117.
36. Lyon, 'Underwater Warfare', p. 137, p. 141.
37. Brown, *Warrior to Dreadnought*, p. 117; *Conway's*, p. 105.
38. Sondhaus, *Navies Of Europe*, p. 88.
39. *Conway's*, p. 106.
40. *Conway's*, p. 80; Brown, *Warrior to Dreadnought*, p. 115.
41. *Conway's*, p. 81; Brown, *Warrior to Dreadnought*, p. 115.
42. *Conway's*, p. 88; Brown, *Warrior to Dreadnought*, p. 115.
43. *Conway's*, p. 89; Lyon, *First Destroyers*, p. 13.
44. *Conway's*, pp. 87–90; Lyon, *First Destroyers*, p. 13.
45. Parkes, *British Battleships*, pp. 244–5.
46. Parkes, *British Battleships*, p. 235.
47. Parkes, *British Battleships*, pp. 235–7; Brown, *Warrior to Dreadnought*, p. 69; *Conway's*, p. 63.
48. *Conway's*, p. 64.
49. Parkes, *British Battleships*, p. 252; *Conway's*, p. 26; Brown, *Warrior to Dreadnought*, p. 64.
50. Brown, *Warrior to Dreadnought*, p. 64; Parkes, *British Battleships*, p. 254; *Conway's*, p. 26.
51. Brown, 'Era of Uncertainty', p. 86; Brown, *Warrior to Dreadnought*, p. 66
52. Beeler, *Birth of the Battleship*, p. 113; Parkes, *British Battleships*, p. 291.
53. Pictures of the replica *Ting Yuan* can be found at http://www.beiyang.org/dingyuan/bd.htm (accessed 14 April 2008). Note that this page is image-heavy and the text is in Chinese.
54. Beeler, *Birth of the Battleship*, pp. 114–15.
55. *Conway's*, p. 26.
56. Parkes, *British Battleships*, p. 262; *Conway's*, p. 26.

57. Parkes, *British Battleships*, pp. 262–5; *Conway's*, p. 27. It is not clear whether or not their turret armour was a wood/metal sandwich, as in *Inflexible*, or a single thickness of metal. *Conway's* suggests it was a sandwich, but Parkes and Roberts favour the latter.
58. Brown, 'Era of Uncertainty', p. 86.
59. Bourne, *Foreign Policy*, pp. 126–8.
60. Bourne, *Foreign Policy*, pp. 130–35; Sondhaus, *Navies of Europe*, p. 89.
61. Parkes, *British Battleships*, pp. 277–80; *Conway's*, p. 25.
62. Parkes, *British Battleships*, pp. 273–5; *Conway's*, p. 18.
63. *Conway's*, p. 18; Parkes, *British Battleships*, p. 268.
64. Bourne, *Foreign Policy*, p. 134.
65. Sumida, *Naval Supremacy*, p. 11.
66. Parkes, *British Battleships*, p. 324.
67. Beeler, *Birth of the Battleship*, p. 52, p. 203.
68. Brown, *Warrior to Dreadnought*, p. 79; *Conway's*, p. 27; Parkes, *British Battleships*, p. 288.
69. Roberts, 'Warships of Steel', pp. 98–9.
70. Beeler, *Birth of the Battleship*, p. 160.
71. Beeler, *Birth of the Battleship*, pp. 161–5; Roberts, 'Warships of Steel', p. 101.
72. See Beeler for a full discussion of this debate and the various designs proposed.
73. Parkes, *British Battleships*, p. 300; Beeler, *Birth of the Battleship*, p. 166.
74. *Conway's*, p. 29; Parkes, *British Battleships*, p. 302; Brown, *Warrior to Dreadnought*, pp. 92–3.
75. Brown, *Warrior to Dreadnought*, pp. 91–2 provides a comparison of the relative merits of the French and British ships. *Conway's* p. 291 provides details of the *Amiral Baudin* and *Formidable*.
76. Beeler, *Birth of the Battleship*, pp. 167–8.

77. Brown, *Warrior to Dreadnought*, p. 95. Brown suggests that if the sub-10,000-ton displacement restriction had been relaxed it would have been possible to provide *Collingwood* and the subsequent *Admiral* class with a forecastle that would have dramatically improved their sea-keeping.
78. Parkes, *British Battleships*, p. 356.
79. Beeler, *Birth of the Battleship*, p. 167.
80. Beeler, *Birth of the Battleship*, p. 168, p. 180.
81. Beeler, *Birth of the Battleship*, p. 170.
82. Beeler, *Birth of the Battleship*, p. 181.
83. Brown, *Warrior to Dreadnought*, p. 95.
84. *Conway's*, p. 29; Parkes, *British Battleships*, p. 318.
85. Parkes, *British Battleships*, pp. 317–8; Brown, *Warrior to Dreadnought*, p. 95; *Conway's*, p. 29.
86. *Conway's*, p. 30; Parkes, *British Battleships*, pp. 320–21.
87. Bourne, *Foreign Policy*, p. 140.
88. Sumida, *Naval Supremacy*, p. 11.
89. See for example Lambert, 'Shield of Empire', p. 194.
90. Parkes, *British Battleships*, p. 328.
91. Parkes, *British Battleships*, pp. 305–306, p. 330.
92. Parkes, *British Battleships*, pp. 331–3.
93. Roberts, 'Warships of Steel', p. 103.
94. Parkes, *British Battleships*, p. 330; Brown, *Warrior to Dreadnought*, p. 99; *Conway's*, p. 30.
95. Parkes, *British Battleships*, pp. 334–5; Roberts, 'Warships Of Steel', p. 101.
96. Brown, *Warrior to Dreadnought*, pp. 99–100.
97. Lambert, 'Shield of Empire', p. 197.
98. Andrew Gordon, *The Rules of the Game: Jutland and British Naval Command* (London: John Murray (Publishers) Ltd, 1996), p. 190. This is a fascinating book, containing not only a reinterpretation of Jutland but also a thorough examination of the system of command built up by the RN in the preceding decades that explains many of the events of 1916.
99. Gordon, *Rules of the Game*, pp. 199–201.
100. Brown, *Warrior to Dreadnought*, p. 100; Parkes, *British Battleships*, p. 336–8. Reportedly, Tryon's last words were 'It was all my fault'.
101. Lambert, 'Shield Of Empire', p. 197.
102. Nicholas Blanford and Alan Hamilton, 'Navy gets sinking feeling as shipwreck resurfaces', from *The Times* of 2 September 2004. A copy of this article was accessed on-line at http://www.timesonline.co.uk/tol/news/uk/article477374.ece on 10 April 2008. For a fuller account of the discovery, see 'HMS Victoria's Secret – Lebanon' on-line at http://diving-industry.com/news/2006/03/31/hms-victorias-secret-lebanon/ (also accessed 10 April 2008). Only one other shipwreck, located in the Philippines, has ever been recorded in such an orientation, and has since collapsed – a fate that will presumably eventually befall *Victoria*.
103. Parkes, *British Battleships*, p. 347.
104. Brown, *Warrior to Dreadnought*, p. 103.
105. Brown, *Warrior to Dreadnought*, p. 103.
106. *Conway's*, p. 31; Parkes, *British Battleships*, p. 342–6.
107. *Conway's*, p. 31; Roberts, 'Warships Of Steel', p. 104; Keith McBride, '*Nile* And *Trafalgar*; The Last British Ironclads', in Antony Preston (ed.) *Warship 2000–2001* (London: Conway Maritime Press, 2000), p. 70.

108. Parkes, *British Battleships*, pp. 343–4; McBride, 'Nile and Trafalgar', p. 71.
109. Parkes, *British Battleships*, p. 342.
110. Beeler, *Birth of the Battleship*, p. 183.
111. *Conway's*, p. 186; Beeler, *Birth of the Battleship*, p. 184.
112. *Conway's*, p. 52; Brown, *Warrior to Dreadnought*, pp. 109–110.
113. *Conway's*, p. 53.
114. Roberts, 'Warships Of Steel', p. 106; *Conway's*, pp. 57–8. One *Doterel*-class sloop, *Gannet*, is now preserved as a museum ship at the Chatham Historic Dockyard.
115. *Conway's*, pp. 57–8.
116. *Conway's*, p. 59
117. *Conway's*, p. 76. The *Medea*-class ships were initially rated as Second Class cruisers but were re-rated in 1889.
118. *Conway's*, pp. 81–2.
119. Beeler, *Birth of the Battleship*, p. 197.
120. Robert, 'Warships Of Steel', p. 103; Beeler, *Birth of the Battleship*, p. 199.
121. *Conway's*, p. 65.
122. Parkes, *British Battleships*, p. 311.
123. *Conway's*, p. 75; Brown, *Warrior to Dreadnought*, p. 111; Roberts, 'Warships of Steel', p. 107.
124. *Conway's*, p. 75; Brown, *Warrior to Dreadnought*, p. 111.
125. Sondhaus, *Navies of Europe*, p. 93; Roberts, 'Warships of Steel', p. 109.
126. Brown, *Warrior to Dreadnought*, p. 113.
127. Quoted in David Topliss and Chris Ware, 'First Class Cruisers: Part One', in Antony Preston (ed.) *Warship 2000–2001* (London: Conway Maritime Press, 2000), p. 10.
128. Topliss and Ware, 'First Class Cruisers 1', pp. 10–11; *Conway's*, p. 65.
129. Brown, *Warrior to Dreadnought*, p. 135; *Conway's*, p. 66.
130. Brown, *Warrior to Dreadnought*, p. 135; *Conway's*, p. 66.

131. Beeler, *Birth of the Battleship*, p. 203.
132. Preston and Major, *Send a Gunboat!*, pp. 145–6; *Conway's*, p. 108.
133. *Conway's*, p. 107.
134. *Conway's*, p. 110.
135. *Conway's*, p. 108.
136. *Conway's*, p. 107.
137. *Conway's*, p. 108.

Chapter 4
1. Brown, *Warrior to Dreadnought*, p. 123; Sumida, *Naval Supremacy*, p. 11.
2. Brown, *Warrior to Dreadnought*, pp. 123–4; Beeler, *Birth of the Battleship*, pp. 78–9.
3. Sumida, *Naval Supremacy*, p. 12. Budget figures are from Tables 1 and 2 in the Appendix of the same work.
4. Parkes, *British Battleships*, p. 351; Brown, *Warrior to Dreadnought*, p. 125; Sumida, *Naval Supremacy*, p. 13.
5. Gordon, *Rules of the Game*, pp. 193–4; Parkes, *British Battleships*, p. 352; Brown, *Warrior to Dreadnought*, p. 125.
6. Sumida, *Naval Supremacy*, pp. 13–15; Brown, *Warrior to Dreadnought*, p. 125.
7. Sumida, *Naval Supremacy*, pp. 13–14; Brown, *Warrior to Dreadnought*, p. 125.
8. Sumida, *Naval Supremacy*, p. 14; Brown, *Warrior to Dreadnought*, p. 126.
9. Sumida, *Naval Supremacy*, p. 14.
10. Quoted in Sumida, *Naval Supremacy*, p. 14.
11. Nicholas A. Lambert, *Sir John Fisher's Naval Revolution* (Columbia, SC: University of South Carolina Press, 1999), pp. 18–19.
12. Quoted in Sumida, *Naval Supremacy*, p. 15.
13. John Roberts, 'The Pre-Dreadnought Age, 1890–1905', in Robert Gardiner and Andrew Lambert (eds.), *Steam, Steel and Shellfire: The Steam Warship*

1815–1905 (London: Conway Maritime Press, 1992); Brown, *Warrior to Dreadnought*, p. 127; Parkes, *British Battleships*, p. 354; *Conway's*, p. 32.
14. Sumida, *Naval Supremacy*, p. 12.
15. Brown, *Warrior to Dreadnought*, p. 150; Roberts, "Pre-Dreadnought Age", p. 113;
16. Brown, *Warrior to Dreadnought*, p. 127; Parkes, *British Battleships*, p. 355; Roberts, 'Pre-Dreadnought Age', p. 116.
17. *Empress of India, Ramillies, Repulse, Resolution, Revenge, Royal Oak* and *Royal Sovereign*.
18. Parkes, *British Battleships*, p. 355.
19. Brown, *Warrior to Dreadnought*, p. 128; Parkes, *British Battleships*, p. 359; *Conway's*, p. 32.
20. Roberts, 'Pre-Dreadnought Age', p. 116; Parkes, *British Battleships*, p. 359.
21. Brown, *Warrior to Dreadnought*, pp. 128–9.
22. In effect, therefore, this was not very different from the loading arrangements in *Inflexible*, whose MLRs had to be lined up with ports in an armoured glacis to be reloaded.
23. *Conway's*, p. 32; Roberts, 'Pre-Dreadnought Age', p. 116; Brown, *Warrior to Dreadnought*, p. 128; Parkes, *British Battleships*, p. 358.
24. Roberts, 'Pre-Dreadnought Age', p. 113; Parkes, *British Battleships*, pp. 358–9; *Conway's*, p. 32.
25. Parkes, *British Battleships*, pp. 355–6.
26. See, for example: Brown, *Warrior to Dreadnought*, p. 131; *Conway's* p. 32; Roberts, 'Pre-Dreadnought Age', p. 116; Parkes, *British Battleships*, pp. 361–2;
27. Parkes, *British Battleships*, p. 356.
28. Parkes, *British Battleships*, pp. 412–4.
29. Brown, *Warrior to Dreadnought*, p. 129.
30. Parkes, *British Battleships*, p. 364; Brown, *Warrior to Dreadnought*, p. 130; *Conway's* p. 33.

31. Brown, *Warrior to Dreadnought*, p. 131; Parkes, *British Battleships*, pp. 366–7; *Conway's*, p. 33;
32. Parkes, *British Battleships*, p. 368; *Conway's*, p. 33;
33. Parkes, *British Battleships*, pp. 368–9; *Conway's*, p. 33;
34. Although *Blake* and *Blenheim* proved to be only capable of similar endurance, their design had been for a radius of action of 15,000 nm at 10 kts.
35. *Conway's*, p. 66; Topliss and Ware, 'First Class Cruisers 1', pp. 11–12;
36. *Conway's*, p. 66; Topliss and Ware, 'First Class Cruisers 1', pp. 12–14;
37. *Conway's*, p. 66; Topliss and Ware, 'First Class Cruisers 1', p. 12;
38. *Conway's*, p. 66; Brown, *Warrior to Dreadnought*, pp. 135–6;
39. *Conway's*, p. 76; Brown, *Warrior to Dreadnought*, p. 163;
40. Both *Intrepid* and *Iphigenia* were successfully sunk in the canal at Zeebrugge, although *Thetis* was disabled before reaching her blocking position. Due to navigational difficulties, however, *Brilliant* and *Sirius* ran aground a mile to the east of Ostend and were scuttled. For more details, see Roy Humphreys, *The Dover Patrol 1914–18* (Stroud: Sutton Publishing Limited, 1998), pp. 133–73.
41. Brown, *Warrior to Dreadnought*, p. 155;
42. Brown, *Warrior to Dreadnought*, p. 163; *Conway's*, p. 77;
43. *Conway's*, p. 82;
44. I realise that this only gives a total of sixteen TGBs, rather than the eighteen usually quoted. It seems that eighteen TGBs were originally planned but only sixteen completed due to dissatisfaction with their performance and the introduction of the destroyer by 1892. I found listed for sale a letter of 20 October 1909 from Watts to the journalist Archibald Hurd in which Watts questions Hurd's summary of the Naval Defence Act. Although in agreement on the numbers of battleships and First Class cruisers, Watts felt that the figures for smaller ships required correction – in particular, the '18 Torpedo gunboats of the Sharpshooter class'. Watts noted that 'the actual Programmes included certain ships which were never built; whereas the figures given [by Watts to Hurd] include ships only which were actually built'. Unfortunately, I did not purchase the letter and am only able to quote from the seller's summary.
45. See, for example, *Brassey's Naval Annual 1892* pp. 348–9 and *Brassey's Naval Annual 1894* p. 8.
46. *Conway's*, pp. 89–90.
47. Brown, *Warrior to Dreadnought*, p. 116.
48. Sumida, *Naval Supremacy*, p. 15.
49. Sumida, *Naval Supremacy*, p. 16.

Chapter 5

1. Roberts, 'Pre-Dreadnought Age', p. 100, pp. 118–19; *Conway's*, pp. 292–6;
2. Roberts, 'Pre-Dreadnought Age', pp. 119–20; *Conway's*, pp. 296–7;
3. Brown, *Warrior to Dreadnought*, p. 150; Sondhaus, *Navies of Europe*, pp. 118–19.
4. Sondhaus, *Navies of Europe*, p. 114; N. Lambert, *Naval Revolution*, p. 23;
5. Bourne, *Foreign Policy*, pp. 95–6;
6. *Conway's*, pp. 137–49; Roberts, 'Pre-Dreadnought Age', pp. 121–3;
7. Bourne, *Foreign Policy*, pp. 169–75;
8. Ian H. Nish, *The Anglo-Japanese Alliance – The Diplomacy of Two Island Empires 1894–1907* (London: The Athlone Press, 1966), p. 7.
9. C.J. Lowe and M.L. Dockrill, *The Mirage Of Power, Vol. 2: British Foreign Policy 1914–22* (London: Routledge and Kegan Paul, 1972), p. 275.
10. Kennedy, *Naval Mastery*, p. 252.
11. Selbourne Memorandum, 'Balance of Naval Power in the Far East', 4 September 1901, in Kennedy, *Naval Mastery*, pp. 252–3.
12. Kennedy, *Naval Mastery*, p. 253.
13. Nish, *Anglo–Japanese Alliance*, p. 214.
14. Sondhaus, *Navies Of Europe*, pp. 119–21.
15. Naval Act quoted in Parkes, *British Battleships*, p. 435.
16. Avner Offer, *The First World War: An Agrarian Interpretation* (Oxford: Clarendon Press, 1991), p. 81
17. Sumida, *Naval Supremacy*, p. 16; Parkes, *British Battleships*, p. 381. Sources disagree on the cost of the Spencer Programme and the exact numbers of cruisers and torpedo-craft that it paid for. I have followed the costs and general construction figures given in Sumida, *Naval Supremacy*, p. 16. Brown *Warrior to Dreadnought*, p. 15 has the cost as £23,225,000, while Parkes, *British Battleships*, p. 381 and Roberts, 'Pre-Dreadnought Age', p. 116 puts the cost at £31,000,000.
18. Sumida, *Naval Supremacy*, pp. 17–18; Parkes, *British Battleships*, p. 381;
19. Sumida, *Naval Supremacy*, p. 20.
20. Sumida, *Naval Supremacy*, pp. 20–21.
21. Sumida, *Naval Supremacy*, p. 22.
22. N. Lambert, *Naval Revolution*, p. 30.
23. Sumida, *Naval Supremacy*, p. 23.
24. Parkes, *British Battleships*, p. 370; Brown, *Warrior to Dreadnought*, p. 142;
25. Parkes, *British Battleships*, p. 371; Roberts, 'Pre-Dreadnought Age', p. 116;
26. John Roberts, 'Pre-Dreadnought Age', p. 116; Parkes, *British Battleships*, p. 371; Brown, *Warrior to Dreadnought*, p. 142;
27. Parkes, *British Battleships*, p. 373; Brown, *Warrior to Dreadnought*, p. 143; Roberts, 'Pre-Dreadnought Age', p. 116;
28. Parkes, *British Battleships*, pp. 371–4; Brown, *Warrior to Dreadnought*, p. 142;
29. Parkes, *British Battleships*, p. 356, has 1 inch of Harvey equalling 1.6 inches of compound; Brown,

Warrior To Dreadnought, p. 150, is generally similar with 7½ inches of Harvey said to be equivalent to 12 inches of compound, but against uncapped projectiles only.

30. Parkes, *British Battleships*, pp. 372–4; Brown, *Warrior to Dreadnought*, p. 142;

31. Parkes, *British Battleships*, p. 354;

32. *Conway's*, p. 34;

33. Quoted in Brown, *Warrior to Dreadnought*, p. 142.

34. Parkes, *British Battleships*, p. 370–71; *Conway's*, p. 34;

35. Sumida, *Naval Supremacy*, p. 16; Parkes, *British Battleships*, pp. 380–81; Roberts, 'Pre-Dreadnought Age', p. 116.

36. *Caesar, Hannibal, Illustrious, Jupiter, Magnificent, Majestic, Mars, Prince George* and *Victorious*.

37. Parkes, *British Battleships*, p. 381, p. 387; Roberts, SSS, p. 117;

38. Parkes, *British Battleships*, p. 382.

39. Parkes, *British Battleships*, p. 383; Brown, *Warrior to Dreadnought*, p. 143; Roberts, 'Pre-Dreadnought Age', p. 117;

40. Parkes, *British Battleships*, p. 384; *Conway's*, p. 34.

41. Parkes, *British Battleships*, p. 384; Roberts, 'Pre-Dreadnought Age', p. 117; Brown, *Warrior to Dreadnought*, p. 153.

42. Parkes, *British Battleships*, pp. 384–5.

43. Parkes, *British Battleships*, p. 381, p. 385; Roberts, 'Pre-Dreadnought Age', p. 117; Brown, *Warrior to Dreadnought*, p. 143.

44. Parkes, *British Battleships*, pp. 385–6; *Conway's*, p. 34.

45. Parkes, *British Battleships*, p. 392; Brown, *Warrior to Dreadnought*, p. 144.

46. *Canopus, Glory, Albion, Goliath, Ocean* and *Vengeance*.

47. Beeler, *Birth of the Battleship*, p. 33; Parkes, *British Battleships*, pp. 392–4.

48. Parkes, *British Battleships*, pp. 393–4; Brown, *Warrior to Dreadnought*, p. 143, p. 152;

49. Parkes, *British Battleships*, p. 396; Brown, *Warrior to Dreadnought*, p. 144.

50. Parkes, *British Battleships*, pp. 394–7; Brown, *Warrior to Dreadnought*, p. 144; *Conway's*, p. 35.

51. Parkes, *British Battleships*, pp. 393–4, 396, 399; Brown, *Warrior to Dreadnought*, p. 153; *Conway's*, p. 35.

52. Parkes, *British Battleships*, pp. 393–7; *Conway's*, p. 35; Brown, *Warrior to Dreadnought*, p. 144.

53. Parkes, *British Battleships*, p. 403; Brown, *Warrior to Dreadnought*, pp. 145–6; Roberts, 'Pre-Dreadnought Age', p. 117.

54. Parkes, *British Battleships*, p. 403; Brown, *Warrior to Dreadnought*, p. 146;

55. Parkes, *British Battleships*, pp. 405–06; Brown, *Warrior to Dreadnought*, p. 145; *Conway's*, p. 36.

56. Parkes, *British Battleships*, pp. 404–05; Brown, *Warrior to Dreadnought*, p. 153; *Conway's*, p. 36;

57. Parkes, *British Battleships*, pp. 406–07; Brown, *Warrior to Dreadnought*, p. 146; *Conway's*, p. 36.

58. Parkes, *British Battleships*, p. 408; Brown, *Warrior to Dreadnought*, p. 146. The five *London*-class battleships were *Bulwark, London, Prince of Wales, Queen* and *Venerable*.

59. Parkes, *British Battleships*, p. 409; Brown, *Warrior to Dreadnought*, p. 146, p. 152; *Conway's*, p. 37.

60. The six *Duncan*-class ships were *Albermarle, Cornwallis, Duncan, Exmouth, Montagu* and *Russell*. Parkes, *British Battleships*, pp. 415–6, p. 419; Brown, *Warrior to Dreadnought*, p. 146.

61. Parkes, *British Battleships*, pp. 416–7; Brown, *Warrior to Dreadnought*, p. 146; *Conway's*, p. 37.

62. Parkes, *British Battleships*, p. 418; Brown, *Warrior to Dreadnought*, p. 152.

63. Parkes, *British Battleships*, p. 418, p. 420; Brown, *Warrior to Dreadnought*, p. 152 expresses doubts about the quality of contemporary gunnery.

64. *Conway's*, p. 37, p. 182; Parkes, *British Battleships*, p. 420.

65. Roberts, 'Pre-Dreadnought Age', p. 117; Keith McBride, '"The Wobbly Eight": The *King Edward VII* Class Battleships, 1897–1922', in Antony Preston (ed.) *Warship 2001–2002* (London: Conway Maritime Press, 2001), p. 63. It should be noted, however, that *Benedetto Brin*'s four 8-inch guns, mounted at the corners of the central upper deck battery like *Majestic*'s 6-inch QFs, were later replaced with 6-inch guns.

66. Parkes, *British Battleships*, p. 423; McBride, 'Wobbly Eight', pp. 63–4.

67. Parkes, *British Battleships*, p. 423; Brown, *Warrior to Dreadnought*, p. 147. Watts served as DNC until 1912 and so was responsible for the design of many of the ships of the British *Dreadnought*-era fleet: twenty-nine battleships and battlecruisers of the Grand Fleet at Jutland in 1916, as well as many of the cruisers and destroyers, were built during his tenure – see Parkes, *British Battleships*, p. 440.

68. Parkes, *British Battleships*, p. 423; Roberts, 'Pre-Dreadnought Age', pp. 117–18.

69. Parkes, *British Battleships*, p. 423; Brown, *Warrior to Dreadnought*, p. 147.

70. *Africa, Britannia, Commonwealth, Dominion, Hibernia, Hindustan, King Edward VII* and *New Zealand* (later renamed *Zealandia* when the battlecruiser of that name entered service).

71. Parkes, *British Battleships*, pp. 426–9

72. For a thorough discussion of this First World War action, see Stephen McLaughlin, 'Predreadnoughts vs A

Dreadnought: The Action Off Cape Sarych 18 November 1914', in Antony Preston (ed.) *Warship 2001–2002* (London: Conway Maritime Press, 2001), pp. 117–40.

73. Parkes, *British Battleships*, p. 428; McBride, 'Wobbly Eight', p. 67.

74. Parkes, *British Battleships*, p. 425, p. 428; *Conway's*, p. 38.

75. Parkes, *British Battleships*, p. 428; *Conway's*, p. 38.

76. McBride, 'Wobbly Eight', pp. 67–8; Parkes, *British Battleships*, p. 423; *Conway's*, p. 38.

77. Parkes, *British Battleships*, pp. 436–7; Sondhaus, *Navies of Europe*, p. 125.

78. Parkes, *British Battleships*, p. 436–8; *Conway's*, p. 39.

79. Parkes, *British Battleships*, p. 436, p. 439.

80. Parkes, *British Battleships*, p. 439.

81. Parkes, *British Battleships*, p. 451.

82. Parkes, *British Battleships*, p. 451; Sondhaus, *Navies of Europe*, p. 125.

83. Brown, *Warrior to Dreadnought*, p. 147; Parkes, *British Battleships*, pp. 452–3.

84. Parkes, *British Battleships*, 454; Brown, *Warrior to Dreadnought*, p. 153.

85. Parkes, *British Battleships*, p. 454.

86. Parkes, *British Battleships*, pp. 451–2, p. 454; Brown, *Warrior to Dreadnought*, p. 147.

87. Brown, *Warrior to Dreadnought*, p. 156.

88. *Conway's*, p. 189; Topliss and Ware, 'First Class Cruisers 1', p. 15; Brown, *Warrior to Dreadnought*, p. 136.

89. Topliss and Ware, 'First Class Cruisers 1', p 16; Roberts, 'Pre-Dreadnought Age', p. 130.

90. Topliss and Ware, 'First Class Cruisers 1', p16; *Conway's*, p. 67.

91. Topliss and Ware, 'First Class Cruisers 1', p. 16; Brown, *Warrior to Dreadnought*, p. 136; *Conway's*, p. 67.

92. Topliss and Ware, 'First Class Cruisers 1', p. 16; Brown, *Warrior to Dreadnought*, p. 136.

93. Topliss and Ware, 'First Class Cruisers 1', p. 17; *Conway's*, p. 412 gives details of the Chilean ships.

94. Topliss and Ware, 'First Class Cruisers 1', p. 17; Brown, *Warrior to Dreadnought*, p. 136; *Conway's*, p. 67.

95. Topliss and Ware, 'First Class Cruisers 1', p. 17; Brown, *Warrior to Dreadnought*, p. 136; *Conway's*, pp. 67–8; Roberts, 'Pre-Dreadnought Age', p. 130.

96. David Topliss and Chris Ware, 'First Class Cruisers: Part Two', in Antony Preston (ed.) *Warship 2001–2002* (London: Conway Maritime Press, 2001), pp. 9–10.

97. Topliss and Ware, 'First Class Cruisers 2', p. 10; *Conway's*, p. 68.

98. Topliss and Ware, 'First Class Cruisers 2' p. 10; Brown, *Warrior To Dreadnought*, p. 136; *Conway's*, p. 68; Roberts, 'Pre-Dreadnought Age', p. 130.

99. First group: *Andromeda*, *Diadem*, *Europa* and *Niobe*. Second group: *Amphitrite*, *Argonaut*, *Ariadne* and *Spartiate*.

100. Topliss and Ware, 'First Class Cruisers 2', p. 9, p. 11.

101. Parkes, *British Battleships*, p. 441; Roberts, 'Pre-Dreadnought Age', p. 128.

102. Topliss and Ware, 'First Class Cruisers 2', p. 12; Brown, WTD, p. 157.

103. Quoted in Topliss and Ware, 'First Class Cruisers 2', p. 12.

104. Topliss and Ware, 'First Class Cruisers 2', pp. 12–13; Brown, *Warrior to Dreadnought*, p. 158; *Conway's*, p. 68.

105. Topliss and Ware, 'First Class Cruisers 2', p. 13; Brown, *Warrior to Dreadnought*, p. 158.

106. They were named *Aboukir*, *Bacchante*, *Cressy*, *Euryalus*, *Hogue* and *Sutlej*.

107. Brown, *Warrior to Dreadnought*, p. 158

108. Topliss and Ware, 'First Class Cruisers 2', p. 14; Brown, *Warrior to Dreadnought*, p. 158.

109. Topliss and Ware, 'First Class Cruisers 2', p. 14

110. Topliss and Ware, 'First Class Cruisers 2', p. 14.

111. Brown, *Warrior to Dreadnought*, p. 168; Topliss and Ware, 'First Class Cruisers 2', p. 14; *Conway's*, p. 69.

112. Topliss and Ware, 'First Class Cruisers 2', p. 15; Brown, *Warrior to Dreadnought*, p. 158; *Conway's*, p. 69.

113. Topliss and Ware, 'First Class Cruisers 2', pp. 15–16; Brown, *Warrior to Dreadnought*, p. 158.

114. Lambert, *Naval Revolution*, p. 23.

115. The four ships were named *Drake*, *Good Hope*, *King Alfred* and *Leviathan*.

116. Topliss and Ware, 'First Class Cruisers 2', p. 17.

117. Brown, *Warrior to Dreadnought*, p. 159.

118. Topliss and Ware, 'First Class Cruisers 2', p. 17; Brown, *Warrior to Dreadnought*, p. 159.

119. Topliss and Ware, 'First Class Cruisers 2', p. 17; Brown, *Warrior to Dreadnought*, p. 159; *Conway's*, p. 70.

120. *Conway's*, p. 70. The ten ships were named *Bedford*, *Berwick*, *Cornwall*, *Cumberland*, *Donegal*, *Essex*, *Kent*, *Lancaster*, *Monmouth* and *Suffolk*.

121. Topliss and Ware, 'First Class Cruisers 2', p. 18; Brown, *Warrior to Dreadnought*, p. 159.

122. Brown, *Warrior to Dreadnought*, p. 160; *Conway's*, p. 71.

123. *Conway's*, p. 71. The six ships were named *Antrim*, *Argyll*, *Carnarvon*, *Devonshire*, *Hampshire* and *Roxburgh*.

124. Parkes, *British Battleships*, p. 442.

125. Parkes, *British Battleships*, p. 443; *Conway's*, p. 72.

126. Brown, *Warrior to Dreadnought*, pp. 161–2; Parkes, *British Battleships*, p. 443.

127. Parkes, *British Battleships*, pp. 442–4; Brown, *Warrior to Dreadnought*, p. 161.
128. Brown, *Warrior to Dreadnought*, p. 162; Parkes, *British Battleships*, pp. 444–5; *Conway's*, p. 72.
129. Parkes, *British Battleships*, p. 448; Brown, *Warrior to Dreadnought*, p. 162.
130. Brown, *Warrior to Dreadnought*, p. 162.
131. Gordon, *Rule of the Game*, pp. 443–5.
132. Brown, *Warrior to Dreadnought*, p. 163; *Conway's*, p. 78.
133. Brown, *Warrior to Dreadnought*, p. 163; Roberts, 'Pre-Dreadnought Age', p. 129; *Conway's*, p. 78.
134. Brown, *Warrior to Dreadnought*, p. 163; Roberts, 'Pre-Dreadnought Age', p. 129.
135. *Conway's*, p. 83.
136. *Conway's*, p. 84.
137. *Conway's*, p. 51.
138. Brown, *Warrior to Dreadnought*, p. 163.
139. Brown, *Warrior to Dreadnought*, p. 164.
140. Preston and Major, *Send a Gunboat!*, p. 164; *Conway's*, pp. 59–60.
141. Lyon, *First Destroyers*, pp. 13–14; Brown, WTD, p. 137.
142. Lyon, *First Destroyers*, p. 17.
143. The costs were £72,648 for the two Yarrow TBDs, £73,680 for the two Thornycroft craft and £72,631 for the two Laird's craft. See Lyon, *First Destroyers*, p. 40, p. 53 and p. 59.
144. *Conway's*, pp. 90–91; Brown, *Warrior to Dreadnought*, p. 137.
145. Brown, *Warrior to Dreadnought*, pp. 138–40; *Conway's*, p. 91; Lyon, *First Destroyers*, p. 19.
146. Lyon, *First Destroyers*, pp. 19–21.
147. The possible builders for the 1896–7 boats were Thornycroft, Yarrow, Laird, Thomson, Palmer's, Naval Construction & Armament (Barrow) (later Vickers), Fairfield and Earle's, while those for 1896–7 also included Doxford and Hawthorn Leslie. See Lyon, *First Destroyers*, p. 23.
148. Lyon, *First Destroyers*, p. 21; Brown, *Warrior to Dreadnought*, p. 138.
149. Lyon, *First Destroyers*, pp. 27–8.
150. Lyon, *First Destroyers*, p. 29; Brown, *Warrior to Dreadnought*, p. 141.
151. Lyon, *First Destroyers*, pp. 24–5; *Conway's*, p. 97.
152. Lyon, *First Destroyers*, p. 119; *Conway's*, p. 99.
153. Brown, *Warrior To Dreadnought*, pp. 140–01; Lyon, *First Destroyers*, pp. 110–03.
154. Lyon, *First Destroyers*, p. 16.
155. Quote from Lyon, *First Destroyers*, p. 16.
156. *Conway's*, pp. 99–100.
157. Lyon, *First Destroyers*, p. 37; *Conway's*, p. 100.
158. *Conway's*, p. 104.
159. Brown, *Warrior to Dreadnought*, p. 141.
160. Brown, *Warrior to Dreadnought*, p. 166.
161. Brown, *Warrior to Dreadnought*, p. 183.
162. Lyon, *First Destroyers*, p. 31; *Conway's*, p. 98; Brown, *Warrior to Dreadnought*, p. 183.
163. Lyon, *First Destroyers*, pp. 30–33, p. 183; *Conway's*, p. 98.
164. Brown, *Warrior to Dreadnought*, p. 184.

Conclusion

1. Quotation from the *Introductory Remarks to the 1907 War Plans*, reproduced in Lt Cdr P.K. Kemp, *The Papers of Admiral Sir John Fisher*, Volume II (London: The Naval Records Society, 1964), p. 364.

Bibliography

Olive Anderson, *A Liberal State at War – English Politics and Economics During the Crimean War* (London: Macmillan, 1967)

Pascal Barras, 'The Royal Navy and the Role of Seapower in Global Politics, 1856–1871', in Antony Preston (ed.), *Warship 2001–2002* (London: Conway Maritime Press, 2001)

C.J. Bartlett, *Great Britain and Sea Power 1815–53* (Oxford: Clarendon Press, 1963)

John Beeler, *Birth of the Battleship: British Capital Ship Design 1870–1881* (London: Chatham Publishing, 2001)

Kenneth Bourne, *The Foreign Policy of Victorian England 1830–1902* (Oxford: Clarendon Press, 1970)

D.K. Brown, *Before the Ironclad – Development of Ship Design, Propulsion and Armament in the Royal Navy, 1815–60* (London: Conway Maritime Press Ltd, 1990)

D.K. Brown, 'The Era of Uncertainty, 1863–1878', in Robert Gardiner and Andrew Lambert (eds.), *Steam, Steel and Shellfire: The Steam Warship 1815–1905* (London: Conway Maritime Press, 1992)

D.K. Brown, 'Wood, Sail and Cannonballs to Steel, Steam and Shells, 1815–1895', in *The Oxford Illustrated History of the Royal Navy*, J.R. Hill (ed.) (Oxford: Oxford University Press, 1995)

D.K. Brown, *Warrior to Dreadnought: Warship Development 1860–1905* (London: Chatham Publishing, 1997)

P.J. Cain and A.G. Hopkins, *British Imperialism: Innovation and Expansion 1688–1914* (London: Longman Group UK Limited, 1993)

Conway's All the World's Fighting Ships 1860–1905 (London: Conway Maritime Press, 1979)

Conway's All the World's Fighting Ships 1906–1921 (London: Conway Maritime Press, 1985)

Alan Cowpe, 'The Royal Navy and the Whitehead Torpedo', in *Technical Change and British Naval Policy 1860–1939* Bryan Ranft (ed.) (Sevenoaks: Hodder & Stoughton Ltd, 1977)

William C. Fuller, Jr, *Strategy and Power in Russia 1600–1914* (New York: The Free Press, 1992)

David M. Goldfrank, *The Origins of the Crimean War* (London: Longman, 1994)

Andrew Gordon, *The Rules of the Game: Jutland and British Naval Command* (London: John Murray (Publishers) Ltd, 1996)

Gerald S. Graham, *The Politics of Naval Supremacy – Studies in British Maritime Ascendancy* (Cambridge: Cambridge University Press, 1965)

Basil Greenhill and Ann Giffard, *The British Assault on Finland 1854–55 – A Forgotten Naval War* (Naval Institute Press, 1988)

C.I. Hamilton, *Anglo–French Naval Rivalry 1840–1870* (Oxford: Clarendon Press, 1993)

Richard Hill, *War at Sea in the Ironclad Age* (London: Cassell, 2000)

Richard Holmes, *Redcoat – The British Soldier in the Age of Horse and Musket* (London: HarperCollins Publishers, 2002)

Roy Humphreys, *The Dover Patrol 1914–18* (Stroud: Sutton Publishing Limited, 1998)

Rear Admiral William Jameson KBE CB, *The Fleet That Jack Built: Nine Men Who Made a Modern Navy* (London: Rupert Hart-Davis, 1962)

Colin Jones, 'Entente Cordiale, 1865', in David McLean and Antony Preston (eds.), *Warship 1996* (London: Conway Maritime Press, 1996)

Colin Jones, 'Ruling The Waves', in *Warship 1997–1998* David McClean and Antony Preston (eds.) (London: Conway Maritime Press, 1997)

Lt Cdr P.K. Kemp, *The Papers of Admiral Sir John Fisher*, Volume II (London: The Naval Records Society, 1964),

Paul Kennedy, *The Rise and Fall of the Great Powers – Economic Change and Military Conflict From 1500 to 2000* (London: Fontana Press, 1989)

Paul Kennedy, *The Rise and Fall of British Naval Mastery*, 3rd Edition (London: Fontana Press, 1991)

Andrew Lambert, *The Crimean War – British Grand Strategy, 1853–56* (Manchester: Manchester University Press, 1990)

Andrew Lambert, *The Last Sailing Battlefleet – Maintaining Naval Mastery 1815–1859* (London: Conway Maritime Press Ltd, 1991)

Andrew Lambert, 'Iron Hulls And Armour Plate', in *Steam, Steel And Shellfire: The Steam Warship 1815–1905* Robert Gardiner and Andrew Lambert (eds.) (London: Conway Maritime Press, 1992)

Andrew Lambert, 'The Shield of Empire, 1815–1895' in *The Oxford Illustrated History of the Royal Navy*, J.R. Hill (ed.) (Oxford: Oxford University Press, 1995)

Andrew Lambert, 'The Royal Navy, 1856–1914: Deterrence and the Strategy of World Power', in *Navies and Global Defence: Theories and Strategy* Keith Neilson and Elizabeth Jane Errington (eds.) (Westport CT: Praeger Publishers, 1995)

Nicholas A. Lambert, *Sir John Fisher's Naval Revolution* (Columbia, SC: University of South Carolina Press, 1999)

C.J. Lowe and M.L. Dockrill, *The Mirage Of Power, Vol. 2: British Foreign Policy 1914–22* (London: Routledge and Kegan Paul, 1972)

R.D. Layman, *Naval Aviation in the First World War: Its Impact and Influence* (London: Chatham Publishing 1996)

Commander Geoffrey L. Lowis AFC RN, *Fabulous Admirals and Some Naval Fragments: Being a Brief Account of Some of the Froth on Those Characters Who Enlivened the Royal Navy a Generation or Two Ago* (London: Putnam, 1957)

David Lyon, 'Underwater Warfare and the Torpedo Boat', in *Steam, Steel and Shellfire: The Steam Warship 1815–1905* Robert Gardiner and Andrew Lambert (eds.) (London: Conway Maritime Press, 1992)

David Lyon, *The First Destroyers* (London: Caxton Editions, 2001)

Robert K. Massie, *Dreadnought: Britain, Germany and the Coming of the Great War* (London: Pimlico, 1993)

Keith McBride, '*Nile* and *Trafalgar*; The Last British Ironclads', in Antony Preston (ed.) *Warship 2000–2001* (London: Conway Maritime Press, 2000)

Keith McBride, ' "The Wobbly Eight": The *King Edward VII* Class Battleships, 1897–1922', in Antony Preston (ed.) *Warship 2001–2002* (London: Conway Maritime Press, 2001)

Stephen McLaughlin, 'Predreadnoughts vs A Dreadnought: The Action Off Cape Sarych 18 November 1914', in *Warship 2001–2002* Antony Preston (ed.) (London: Conway Maritime Press, 2001)

Ian H. Nish, *The Anglo–Japanese Alliance – The Diplomacy Of Two Island Empires 1894–1907* (London: The Athlone Press, 1966)

Avner Offer, *The First World War: An Agrarian Interpretation* (Oxford: Clarendon Press, 1991)

Peter Padfield, *The Battleship Era* (London: Rupert Hart-Davis, 1972)

Peter Padfield, *Rule Britannia: The Victorian and Edwardian Navy* (London: Routledge & Kegan Paul, 1981)

Oscar Parkes, *British Battleships: 'Warrior' To 'Vanguard' 1860–1950: A History of Design, Construction And Armament* (London: Seeley Service & Co. Ltd, 1957)

Bryan Perrett, *Gunboat! Small Ships at War* (London: Cassell & Co., 2001)

Antony Preston and John Major, *Send a Gunboat! A Study of the Gunboat and its Role in British Policy, 1854–1904* (London: Longman, Green and Co. Ltd, 1967)

John Roberts, 'Warships of Steel, 1879–1889', in *Steam, Steel and Shellfire: The Steam Warship 1815–1905* Robert Gardiner and Andrew Lambert (eds.) (London: Conway Maritime Press, 1992)

John Roberts, 'The Pre-Dreadnought Age, 1890–1905', in *Steam, Steel and Shellfire: The Steam Warship 1815–1905* Robert Gardiner and Andrew Lambert (eds.) (London: Conway Maritime Press, 1992)

Lawrence Sondhaus, *Navies of Europe, 1815–2002* (London: Pearson Education Limited, 2002)

Lawrence Sondhaus, *Navies in Modern World History* (London: Reaktion Books, 2004)

Charles Stephenson, ' "To the Imperial Mind": The Secret War Plan of Lord Dundonald; Kronstadt and Sevastopol', in *The Age of Sail – The International Annual Of The Historic Sailing Ship*, Volume 1 (2002–2003), Nicholas Tracy (ed.) (London: Conway Maritime Press, 2002)

Jon Tetsuro Sumida, *In Defence of Naval Supremacy: Finance, Technology and British Naval Policy, 1889–1914* (London: Routledge, 1993)

David Topliss and Chris Ware, 'First Class Cruisers: Part One', in *Warship 2000–2001* Antony Preston (ed.) (London: Conway Maritime Press, 2000)

David Topliss and Chris Ware, 'First Class Cruisers: Part Two', in *Warship 2001–2002* Antony Preston (ed.) (London: Conway Maritime Press, 2001)

Wilfrid Pym Trotter, *The Royal Navy in Old Photographs* (London: J.M. Dent & Sons Ltd, 1975)

Index of British Ships